川大史学系列精品教材

外国史学要籍选读

WAIGUO SHIXUE YAOJI XUANDU

原祖杰 王禹／主编

四川大学出版社

项目策划：李思莹　于　俊
责任编辑：张　晶
责任校对：于　俊
封面设计：墨创文化
责任印制：王　炜

图书在版编目（CIP）数据

外国史学要籍选读 / 原祖杰，王禹主编． — 成都：四川大学出版社，2020.8（2024.1重印）
ISBN 978-7-5690-3299-4

Ⅰ．①外… Ⅱ．①原… ②王… Ⅲ．①史学－著作－介绍－世界 Ⅳ．①K0

中国版本图书馆CIP数据核字（2019）第292760号

书　名	外国史学要籍选读
主　编	原祖杰　王　禹
出　版	四川大学出版社
地　址	成都市一环路南一段24号（610065）
发　行	四川大学出版社
书　号	ISBN 978-7-5690-3299-4
印前制作	四川胜翔数码印务设计有限公司
印　刷	四川五洲彩印有限责任公司
成品尺寸	185 mm×260 mm
印　张	13.5
字　数	427千字
版　次	2020年8月第1版
印　次	2024年1月第3次印刷
定　价	68.00元

◆ 版权所有　◆ 侵权必究

◆ 读者邮购本书，请与本社发行科联系。
　 电话：(028)85408408/(028)85401670/
　 (028)86408023　邮政编码：610065
◆ 本社图书如有印装质量问题，请寄回出版社调换。
◆ 网址：http://press.scu.edu.cn

四川大学出版社
微信公众号

前　言

本教材应四川大学历史文化学院专业必修课"外国史学要籍选读"的需求而编订，内容主要来自各位任课老师在教学中所使用的材料。老师们在每篇选读材料之前的"导读"中阐述了所选文献的史学价值和历史影响，并对选文中一些疑难之处进行了注释，汇成一册，供历史学专业师生在开展本课程或者其他类似课程教学时参考使用。

一、本课程及教材的界定

"外国史学要籍选读"是四川大学历史学专业的必修课程，也可以作为文科通识课。这门课程主要面向历史学专业的本科生，但不一定局限于世界史专业或世界史方向的学生。课程受众的这一设定，决定了本课程及其教材在遴选教学文献时要尽可能覆盖外国历史的各个断代和区域，同时文献难度不宜过大。

"外国历史文献"是一个涵盖面很广的概念，暗含文献的多国家、多时代、多语种性质，并且意味着教材中的文献也应具备上述性质。然而，由于课程主要面向本科生，其中包括很多中国史方向的学生，"外国史学要籍选读"只能将文献语言限定为所有学生共同修习的一门外语——英语，这意味着文献在构成上会尽量偏重近现代时期的欧美史学。

本课程由四川大学历史文化学院开设，教材由世界史系教师团队集体编撰，因此教材内容与该团队的研究领域有明显联系。比如，文艺复兴研究是四川大学世界史系的传统强项，在国内高校中也具有一定优势，因此本教材特辟出一章"早期现代史"。同时，世界近现代史、史学理论与史学史是四川大学的传统学科方向，因此在教材内容中，这两个方向所占比重也较大。

二、文献阅读训练的重要性

历史学研究的核心环节就在于对史料的处理，可以说史料就是历史学研究的生命。现代中国史学的奠基人之一梁启超说："史料为史之组织细胞，史料不具或不确，则无复史之可言。"[1] 另一位奠基人傅斯年也曾指出"近代历史学只是史料学"，并留下一句名言："上穷碧落下黄泉，动手动脚找东西。"[2] 英国著名历史学家埃尔顿（G. R. Elton）认为，"合理的历史知识必须建立在对一切相关材料的公正无私的批判之上"，甚至极

---

[1] 梁启超：《中国历史研究法》，上海：上海古籍出版社，1998年，第40页。
[2] 傅斯年：《历史语言研究所工作之旨趣》，载于傅斯年：《中国古代思想与学术十论》，桂林：广西师范大学出版社，2006年，第187页。

端地认为,"原则上而言,学者考虑的材料,应当不少于与他的探究可能相关的所有历史材料"。[1] 法国史学家安托万·普罗斯特(Antoine Prost)则认为,如果"没有资料",历史学家提出的将是"天真幼稚的问题"。[2] 国内当代著名世界史学者李剑鸣在谈历史学家的修养与技艺时也曾指出:搜集、考订、解读和运用史料是历史学家的优势能力,是历史学家的"看家本领";"没有史料,就无从谈及治史"。[3]

何谓史料?梁启超的说法是:"过去人类思想行事所留之痕迹,有证据传留至今日者也。"[4] 他又将史料分为两种:一种是"在文字记录之外者",一种是"在文字记录者"。文字记录之外的史料多指历史遗存,如古迹、文物。后现代理论关于"文本"外延的扩展,更丰富了史料的内涵。但应该说,即便非文字类史料的种类已经十分丰富,历史学研究中最常见,也最重要的史料仍是文字史料,即"在文字记录者",通常指所谓文献。

关于文献,历史学家有一系列的工作要做,相应地也需要具备一系列的能力。比如文献的搜集、整理、分类、辨别,都需要长期的训练。但其最重要的能力,仍是对文献的解读,以及进一步阐释的能力。无疑,要想高水平、高质量地解读和阐释文献,最根本的是培养文献阅读的能力。相比其他社会科学,历史学更加强调建立在扎实的文献功底基础上的经验研究,对文献加以甄别、阅读和阐释,可以说这就是历史学最重要的研究方法,运用这种方法的能力也是历史学研究者的基本功。

就文献种类来说,本科生在学年论文和毕业论文的写作中一般会接触到两大类型的文献,即原始文献(一手文献)和研究性文献(二手文献)。一般来讲,本科生在必修课、选修课上,会在相关教师的指导下接触一定量的研究性文献,因此本课程主要涉及原始文献。国外大学历史教材多辅以文献选编,有的通史教材本身即包含一定数量的原始文献。相比之下,国内的历史教学对原始文献的阅读训练重视不够,很多学校并没有将外国文献阅读纳入历史学专业本科的教学计划,这是创建世界一流历史学科需要弥补的。

三、世界史文献阅读的特点和方法

中国史学,乃至整个中国古代学术,都非常重视对阅读方法意识的培养。西方近代史学也非常重视史学理论和方法论的训练。可以说,古今中外,前人留下了非常丰富的读书心得和方法论。这些方法,有的强调对阅读内容去芜存菁,有的强调阅读过程中要敏捷多思,有的则介绍了一些专门领域的阅读心得。但总体来说,无论是中国历史学传统还是西方传统,在读书方面与其说强调方法论,不如说重视培养一种刻苦笃实的心性,强调"板凳要坐十年冷,文章不著一字空",强调"读书百遍,其义自见"。

尽管如此,具体到世界史文献的阅读上,方法论仍是一种非常重要的修养。相比中国史研究,世界史研究有一些特点和难度。其中最难之处便在于世界史研究是用外语进

---

[1] G. R. 埃尔顿:《历史学的实践》,刘耀辉译,北京:北京大学出版社,2008年,第55-56页。
[2] 普罗斯特:《历史学十二讲》,王春华译,北京:北京大学出版社,2012年,第67-68页。
[3] 李剑鸣:《历史学家的修养和技艺》,上海:上海三联书店,2007年,第149、248页。
[4] 梁启超:《中国历史研究法》,上海:上海古籍出版社,1998年,第40页。

前 言

行的,一些初学者(比如本科生)甚至是凭着相当生疏的外语知识在展开研究。历史文献种类繁多,有的甚至古奥难辨,而历史学的阅读和阐释要求研究者读出文字背后的意义与联系,这也正是世界史学习与研究的困难所在。

因此,对于世界史的初学者而言,除了熟悉历史文献阅读的一般方法,还要有一些特殊的方法论储备。

首先要掌握并充分地使用工具书。初涉世界史的研究者可能会立刻接触到各种繁杂的、生僻的语言,接触到大量人名、地名和其他专有名词,接触到一些难以辨别的俗语、习惯用语、谚语和典故。很多关键字词一旦曲解便可能使文意谬以千里,这使得外语本身成了世界史研究者面临的首要难题。这些问题,即便是那些外语考试成绩优异的初学者也不可避免,因此配备一些必要的工具书是必须的。值得一提的是,今天的学生过多地依赖网络或电子词典,而这类词典的专业性是值得怀疑的,有必要熟悉并学会使用一些权威的工具书,如 *Oxford English Dictionary, Webster's New World Dictionary*, 以及陆谷孙先生编的《英汉大词典》及《英汉大词典补编》。[1] 电子词典则要使用"专业版",同时不能过于信任它,要与纸质版词典参照使用。有了工具书,还要培养勤查工具书的意识,在囫囵吞枣式的阅读中,初学者对文意的理解很可能不犯大错,却难以捕捉到文字背后的幽微涵义,而后者对历史研究是非常关键的。

其次要详做笔记。中国史研究非常强调笔记或札记功夫。对于刘知几的史家三才之一的"史学",梁启超解读出来的第一条便是"勤于抄录"。[2] 外语文献不同于母语文献,初学者极易遗忘且不易查找,因此阅读的同时记笔记是至关重要的。甚至一些成熟的学者,也宁愿在初次阅读时将核心文献全文译出;否则,等日后想要核对一个知识点的正误,再去查找外文原文,便如同大海捞针。因此,初学者要勤于做笔记。不仅如此,在文本电子化已非常普及的今天,初学者更要学会系统地管理自己的笔记。

除了在阅读中扩大词汇量,还要积累一些能够帮助我们理解史料的知识,有学者将这些知识归纳为年代学(chronology)、古书学(paleography)、语言学(philology)和校勘学(textual criticism)四大学科。[3] 以英语为例,英语词汇本身也是有历史的,历史文献中很多词汇含义和今天已经不太一致,这就是普通工具书的局限之处。这就要求阅读者在阅读训练中积累经验,了解文字演变的历史脉络,最好借助一些词源学、语义学的知识来达到这一目的。这样做一是能更加准确地理解文字的语境含义,少犯时代错置的错误;二是有助于领会文字的隐含意思,激发有益的联想,解读出历史文献的深意。总之,世界史初学者应该在吸收历史学研究一般方法论的同时,意识到用外语做研究的特殊难处,逐渐丰富自己的知识储备,熟悉各种文献所含内容的历史语境。

最后要养成一种对理解历史现象、历史事实有重要帮助的理论修养,这一点当然不局限于世界史学习。历史学在现代学科体系中相对偏向经验主义,理论上的建树往往为人所诟病,一些初学者甚至将"理论修养"与"史学理论"混为一谈。但实际上,国

---

[1] 参见思果:《翻译研究》,桂林:广西师范大学出版社,2018年。
[2] 梁启超:《中国历史研究法》,上海:上海古籍出版社,1998年,第161页。
[3] 李隆国:《史学概论》,北京:北京大学出版社,2009年,第85-114页。

内外的历史学名家通常非常重视对理论素养的培育,比如法国年鉴学派非常强调社会科学理论,或是20世纪下半叶的"文化史转向"。提高理论修养,首先需要广泛涉猎历史学以外的其他人文社会学科知识和研究路径;其次,要关注各学科、各知识领域最前沿的动态,20世纪史学经历了若干次"新"史学转向,其实每一次转向背后的动力都来自其他知识领域的创新;最后,还有必要涉猎一些对文科学者来说较难掌握的学科或领域,比如人口统计学、计量学、经济学等。[1]

四、教材内容及各篇作者

综合上述世界史研究的方法论特性,本教材在文献选取上力求类别丰富、难度适中,符合本科生训练和培养的要求。所选文献主要来自历史典籍、历史性文献、政府法律及档案、历史人物文集、日记、书信、演说词、外交档案、史学名著等。

各篇文献由相关领域教师遴选。鉴于本科生系世界史初学者,教师除了选择文献外,还对每一篇文献进行了扼要的导读,从宏观和微观上提点学生,帮助其有效地阅读文献。

本教材各章编写分工如下(括号中的数字为每部分的序号):

第一章　世界上古史:庞霄骁

第二章　世界中古史:邹薇

第三章　早期现代史:刘耀春(一、二),刘君(三)

第四章　世界近现代史:王磊(一、二),石芳(三、四),李若愚(五、六),原祖杰(七),王禹(八)

第五章　国际关系及外交史:刘祥(一、二),王蕾(三)

第六章　史学理论与史学史:徐波(一、二),张骏(三、四、五),吕和应(六)

第七章　跨学科与新范式:辛旭(一),邹薇(二),王禹(三)

本教材为四川大学历史文化学院所编的首部世界史教材,主要是为了满足本科生阅读外国史籍的专业需求。由于需求迫切,时间紧迫,编撰过程中虽已尽量集思广益,教材中仍不免预料不到的舛讹或缺憾。但可以期待的是,每隔一定年限,本教材还将在吸收学生反馈意见的基础上推出新的、更合理的版本。

原祖杰　王禹
2020年1月

---

[1] 参见李隆国:《史学概论》,北京:北京大学出版社,2009年,第115-142页;J. 勒高夫、P. 诺拉、R. 夏蒂埃等:《新史学》,姚蒙编译,上海:上海译文出版社,1989年。

目　录

第一章　世界上古史 …………………………………………………… 001

　　一、希罗多德论希波战争爆发的原因 ………………………………… 001

　　二、埃涅阿斯之盾 ……………………………………………………… 005

第二章　世界中古史 …………………………………………………… 011

　　一、尼基塔斯·侯尼亚迪斯《记事》节选 …………………………… 011

　　二、1215年英国《大宪章》 …………………………………………… 021

第三章　早期现代史 …………………………………………………… 033

　　一、洛伦佐·瓦拉《论拉丁语的优雅》 ……………………………… 033

　　二、弗朗切斯科·圭恰尔迪尼《意大利史》 ………………………… 036

　　三、乔尔乔·瓦萨里《意大利艺苑名人传》序言 …………………… 039

第四章　世界近现代史 ………………………………………………… 049

　　一、1688年英国《权利法案》 ………………………………………… 049

　　二、《北爱尔兰和平协议》导言 ……………………………………… 058

　　三、阿瑟·扬《1787、1788、1789年法国游记》节选 ……………… 074

　　四、一封被篡改的伏尔泰致达朗贝尔的信 …………………………… 089

　　五、新渡户稻造笔下的"武士道" …………………………………… 094

　　六、冈仓天心《茶之书》节选 ………………………………………… 096

七、康涅狄格殖民地首部宪法 ·· 098

八、布赖恩《金十字架》演说 ·· 103

第五章 国际关系及外交史 ·· 110

一、美西战争与美国外交大辩论 ·· 110

二、凯南"长电报" ·· 118

三、NSC 13/2 号文件 ·· 127

第六章 史学理论与史学史 ·· 133

一、弗兰西斯·培根的史学思想 ·· 133

二、博林布鲁克论历史 ·· 142

三、布洛赫《历史学家的技艺》节选 ·· 149

四、克罗齐《历史作为自由的故事》 ·· 154

五、比尔德《书写历史作为一种信仰行为》 ·· 157

六、特勒尔奇《历史主义及其问题》节选 ·· 167

第七章 跨学科与新范式 ·· 174

一、儿童史专题：洛克论儿童教育 ·· 174

二、医疗史专题：《约翰二世·科穆宁皇帝为君士坦丁堡救世主基督修道院所立的规章》节选 ·· 185

三、环境史专题：约翰·缪尔笔下的美国国家公园 ·· 198

第一章　世界上古史

一、希罗多德论希波战争爆发的原因

导读

说起希罗多德（Herodotus）的《历史》（The Histories，又称为《希波战争史》），也许同学们并不陌生。这部以公元前5世纪希腊—波斯战争为背景的历史作品，一直被认为是西方历史上第一部叙事体历史著作。

下面选读的内容是学界较为关注的《历史》第一卷前五节。在这篇近1000词的小短文中，希罗多德对希波战争爆发的原因和他自己写作《历史》的目的进行了阐述。他称自己写作《历史》的目的是保存希腊人与非希腊人的功业，让它们不至于因岁月而失去光彩；希波战争的爆发源于东西方之间因相互抢夺妇女而引发的矛盾；最后，希罗多德希望以自己的写作来告诫世人，幸福不会长久地留在同一个地方。

近代以来，学界以此为基础，围绕希罗多德的写作目的，《历史》反映的史学思想及其历史渊源，《历史》是否是一种新的文体，它与早期史诗之间是否存在传承关系等问题进行过长时间的讨论。

在众多的问题中，《历史》内容的真伪一直是学界关注的热点，也是希罗多德研究中最早和最常见的研究路径。早在古典时代，史学家修昔底德就曾将希罗多德归为"史话家"（logographos）范畴，认为他的叙述不追求事实真相，只以娱乐大众为主要目的。希腊化时期的史学家马涅托（Manetho）、西西里的狄奥多罗斯（Diodorus Siculus）、普鲁塔克（Plutarchus）等人也各自撰写过相关著作，对希罗多德叙述中的错误进行了指正。即使是将希罗多德歌颂为"史学之父"的西塞罗也在一些文章中将希罗多德与塞奥旁浦斯（Theopompus）一起称为"说谎者"。不过，从总体上看，在20世纪中期之前，对希罗多德的评价还是以正面为主，无论是古希腊罗马时期哈利卡那索斯的迪奥尼西乌斯（Dionysius of Halicarnassus）、琉善（Lucian）等人，还是近代文艺复兴和启蒙运动时期的各大学者，抑或是意大利学者莫米尼亚诺（Arnaldo Momigliano），他们无一不认为希罗多德是真正的历史学家，他的叙述大致正确，即使存在错误也是史料来源的问题，而非希罗多德的本意。

20世纪80年代后，随着历史学的发展，对希罗多德的质疑再次出现。如波尔德克尔（D. Boedeker）的《论希罗多德与历史的发明》、戴特福·费赫林（Detlve Fehling）的《希罗多德与他的"史料"》、弗朗索瓦·阿尔托格

(François Hartog)的《希罗多德之镜》、雷德菲尔德的《旅行家希罗多德》等,他们从希罗多德游历的城市、引用的铭文入手,指出希罗多德记载的不合理之处。不过,更多的学者则将目光从苛责希罗多德的叙述错误,转向分析这些错误出现的原因。如德国学者迈耶尔(Christian Meier)的《史学的起源》、唐纳德·拉特内尔(Donald Lateiner)的《希罗多德的历史方法》、罗德斯的《为希腊史学家辩护》,他们在肯定希罗多德历史学家身份的同时,认为希罗多德的不足主要还是历史的局限所致,他的材料和叙述的混乱,正好是史学发展初期人们逻辑和思维水平较低的一种体现。

第二个问题主要针对希罗多德《历史》的写作风格。这是20世纪末到现今较受关注的领域。早在1913年,历史学家菲利克斯·雅可比(Felix Jacoby)在为《保利-韦索瓦百科全书》(*Realencyclopdie der Classischen Altertumswissenschaft*,通称 *Pauly-Wissowa*)编写有关希罗多德的词条时,就曾经对希罗多德的相关问题,包括《历史》的写作风格、语言、材料、结构、内容、书写传统和对后人的影响等进行了汇总。最后他提出:"希罗多德的《历史》并不是完全由希罗多德独立创造的,希罗多德肯定从其前辈赫卡泰厄斯的作品中获益良多。"

这一观点后来得到了奥斯文·穆瑞(Oswyn Murray)、约翰·马琳科拉(John Marincola)等人的支持。穆瑞在其作品《早期希腊》中指出:在早期伊奥尼亚哲学的理性思想的影响下,学者们开始通过自己的调查取证来认识和解释世界,其中就包括米利都的赫卡泰厄斯(Hecataeus of Miletus),他的作品《大地环游记》(仅剩大量的残篇)关注的是自己看到和听到的地理情况,而"historia"一词也最早出现在早期伊奥尼亚自然哲学家的笔下,这种研究思潮和哲学思想很可能影响了希罗多德,很有可能"希罗多德正在试图创造一个适合英雄的故事,因为这是一场新的特洛伊战争"。

哈佛大学希腊研究中心前主任格里高利·纳吉(Gregory Nagy)通过对《荷马史诗》、古风时代抒情诗以及希罗多德《历史》对比,进一步指出,三者之间存在很大的相似性:同样重视传颂美名(kleos)、保存功业,同样拥有环状史诗架构等。它们的区别仅在于诗人一般使用固定韵律的词语,而"史话家"则不限文体。

以传颂美名为例:荷马史诗中常常出现"kleos"这个词,它指的是英雄因丰功伟绩而流芳百世的美名。在英雄死后仍然留存,是对死亡的一种补偿。而史诗诗人最主要的目的就是要让英雄们名垂千古,让他们的美名不朽。在《奥德赛》中,奥德修斯之子特勒马科斯用欣羡的口吻如此赞美为父报仇的俄瑞斯特斯:"阿凯亚人将广传他的美名,给后人留下诗曲一篇。"同样,阿伽门农的鬼魂向来到冥府的奥德修斯赞美后者的妻子:"她的美德赢获的美名将永不消逝,不朽的神明会为她给凡人送来动听的诗篇。"这就正好对应了希罗多德《历史》的开篇第一段话:"在这里发表的,乃是哈利卡那索斯人希罗多德的研究成果,他之所以要把这些研究成果发表出来,是为了保存人类的功业，使之不至由于年深日久而被人们遗忘，为了使希腊人和异邦人的那些值得赞叹的丰功伟绩不致失去它们的光彩，特别是为了把他们发生纷争的原因记下来。"在这里，希罗多德就明确地提出他写这部书的目的就是通过公开展示他的"探究"，使得人类的伟业不至被遗忘，使希腊人和异邦人的那些值得赞叹的丰功伟绩不致失去它们的光彩。这就很明显保留了荷马史诗传诵美名的基本传统。

1. What Herodotus the Halicarnassian (哈利卡那索斯人) has learnt by inquiry is here set forth: in order that so the memory of the past may not be blotted out from among men by time, and that great and marvellous deeds done by Greeks and foreigners and especially the reason why they warred against each other may not lack renown.

The Persian learned men say that the Phoenicians (腓尼基人) were the cause of the feud. These (they say) came to our seas from the sea which is called Red[1], and having settled in the country which they still occupy, at once began to make long voyages. Among other places to which they carried Egyptian and Assyrian (亚述) merchandise, they came to Argos (阿戈斯，希腊城邦之一), which was about that time preeminent in every way among the people of what is now called Hellas. The Phoenicians then came, as I say, to Argos, and set out their cargo. On the fifth or sixth day from their coming, their wares being now well-nigh all sold, there came to the sea shore among many other women the king's daughter, whose name (according to Persians and Greeks alike) was Io (伊娥), the daughter of Inachus. They stood about the stern of the ship: and while they bargained for such wares as they fancied, the Phoenicians heartened each other to the deed, and rushed to take them. Most of the women escaped: Io with others was carried off; the men cast her into the ship and made sail away for Egypt.

2. This, say the Persians (but not the Greeks), was how Io came to Egypt, and this, according to them, was the first wrong that was done. Next, according to their tale, certain Greeks (they cannot tell who) landed at Tyre in Phoenice and carried off the king's daughter Europe. These Greeks must, I suppose, have been Cretans. So far, then, the account between them stood balanced. But after this (say they) it was the Greeks who were guilty of the second wrong. They sailed in a long ship to Aea of the Colchians (科尔基斯) and the river Phasis[2]: and when they had done the rest of the business for which they came, they carried off the king's daughter Medea. When the Colchian king sent a herald to demand reparation for the robbery, and restitution of his daughter, the Greeks replied that as they had been refused reparation for the abduction of the Argive Io, neither would they make any to the Colchians.

3. Then (so the story runs) in the second generation after this Alexandrus (特洛伊王子帕里斯) son of Priam (特洛伊国王普里阿摩斯), having heard this tale, was minded to win

---

1　Not the modern Red Sea, but the Persian Gulf and adjacent waters. 本书选读材料中的英文注释皆为原著作者所加。
2　This is the legendary cruise of the Argonauts.

himself a wife out of Hellas by ravishment; for he was well persuaded that, as the Greeks had made no reparation, so neither would he. So he carried off Helen. The Greeks first resolved to send messengers demanding that Helen should be restored and atonement made for the rape; but when this proposal was made, the Trojans pleaded the rape of Medea, and reminded the Greeks that they asked reparation of others, yet had made none themselves, nor given up the plunder at request.

4. Thus far it was a matter of mere robbery on both sides. But after this (the Persians say) the Greeks were greatly to blame; for they invaded Asia before the Persians attacked Europe. "We think," say they, "that it is wrong to carry women off: but to be zealous to avenge the rape is foolish: wise men take no account of such things: for plainly the women would never have been carried away, had not they themselves wished it. We of Asia regarded the rape of our women not at all; but the Greeks, all for the sake of a Lacedaemonian woman, mustered a great host, came to Asia, and destroyed the power of Priam. Ever since then we have regarded Greeks as our enemies." The Persians claim Asia for their own, and the foreign nations that dwell in it; Europe and the Greek race they hold to be separate from them.

5. Such is the Persian account of the matter: in their opinion, it was the taking of Troy which began their feud with the Greeks. But the Phoenicians do not tell the same story about Io as the Persians. They say that they did not carry her off to Egypt by force: she had intercourse in Argos with the captain of the ship: then, perceiving herself to be with child, she was ashamed that her parents should know it, and so, lest they should discover her condition, she sailed away with the Phoenicians of her own accord.

These are the stories of the Persians and the Phoenicians. For my own part, I will not say that this or that story is true, but I will name him whom I myself know to have done unprovoked wrong to the Greeks, and so go forward with my history, and speak of small and great cities alike. For many states that were once great have now become small: and those that were great in my time were small formerly. Knowing therefore that human prosperity never continues in one stay, I will make mention alike of both kinds.

选自 Herodotus. *The Histories*, 1. 1-5, translated by A. D. Godley, *The Loeb Classical Library*, Cambridge, Mass.: Harvard University Press, 1995-1999.

推荐阅读

从版本上讲，目前国内学者使用的《历史》英译本主要是高德利的希腊文、英文对照本（Herodotus. *The Histories*, in Four Volumes, translated by A. D. Godley, *The Loeb Classical Library*, Cambridge, Mass.: Harvard University Press, 1995-1999），其次是罗林森的英译本（Herodotus, *History of the Greek and Persian War*, translated by George Rawlinson, edited and abridged with an introduction by W. G. Forrest, New York：Washington Square Press, 1963），译本中最权威的当属豪乌和威尔斯的注释本（W. W.

How, J. Wells, *A Commentary on HERODOTUS*, in Two Volumes, Oxford: Oxford University Press, 1979)。

除此之外，还有一些导读类的书籍不能被忽视，分别是巴克等人主编的《布瑞尔希罗多德指南》［Egbert J. Bakker, Irene J. F. de Jong, Hans van Wees (eds.), *Brill's Companion to Herodotus*, Leiden: Brill, 2002］、杰西卡·普雷斯特里和瓦西里卡·扎里的《布瑞尔古代及之后对希罗多德接受史研究指南》(Jessica Priestley, Vasiliki Zali, *Brill's Companion to the Reception of Herodotus in Antiquity and Beyond*, Leiden: Brill, 2016)，以及卡洛琳·德瓦尔德和约翰·马琳科拉主编的《剑桥希罗多德指南》［Carolyn Dewald, John Marincola (eds.), *The Cambridge Companion to Herodotus*, Cambridge: Cambridge University Press, 2006］。

中文译本中，国内最常见的是王以铸的全文译本（希罗多德：《历史》，王以铸译，北京：商务印书馆，1959年）。虽然这本书是1959年出版的，但内容翻译自《牛津古典文献》中修德（C. Hude）的编订版，而且是直接从古希腊文翻译成中文的，其译文非常可靠。不过，正如作者所说，这部书的缺陷主要在于它仅供普及之用，凡涉及考证和带有研究性质的注释一概不收，学术性略有不足。目前较新的译本是徐松岩的译本（希罗多德：《历史》，徐松岩译，上海：上海三联书店，2008年）。这个译本译文简洁流畅，附有大量的注释、详尽的索引，还有若干地图，有较强的学术性。

其次是王敦书的选译本（希罗多德：《历史》（节选本），王敦书译，北京：商务印书馆，2002年）。这本书精选了《历史》第7卷和第8卷的部分内容，有一定的注释，而且译文非常生动、流畅，值得一读。

此外，国内的相关研究亦可见：

黄洋：《希罗多德：历史学的开创与异域文明的话语》，《世界历史》，2008年第4期；

李尚君：《希罗多德与西方历史学的起源》，《历史教学》（高校版），2009年第1期；

杨俊明、付静：《评希罗多德〈历史〉的结尾——兼论希罗多德的写作目的》，《湖南师范大学社会科学学报》，2003年第1期；

张巍：《希罗多德的"探究"——〈历史〉序言的思想史释读》，《世界历史》，2011年第5期。

二、埃涅阿斯之盾

导读

维吉尔的史诗《埃涅阿斯纪》一直被认为是"罗马人的《荷马史诗》"。这部史诗以公元前6世纪希腊抒情诗人创作的《埃涅阿斯海上漂流记》为蓝本，描述了特洛伊陷落后，王子埃涅阿斯率领残余的特洛伊人在地中海上漂泊，最后到达意大利建立罗马的故事。

从情节上看,《埃涅阿斯纪》与《荷马史诗》有非常多的相似之处:同样有海上漂流,同样有英雄游地府,同样有神灵打造武器,同样有英雄决斗,甚至是吟诵时的格律与节拍都用"六音步扬抑格"(又称为"六音步英雄格")。这无疑是罗马人继承希腊文化的一种表现。然而,与《荷马史诗》不同,由于《埃涅阿斯纪》的作者维吉尔深受奥古斯都的优遇,诗中花了一定的篇幅对恺撒、奥古斯都的伟业进行了歌颂;《埃涅阿斯纪》中的英雄们展现的也是敬神、爱国、为民族利益克制自己个人感情等罗马民族传统,而非希腊史诗中英雄个人对荣耀的追求。

由于《埃涅阿斯纪》文笔优美,主角埃涅阿斯服从命运、克制隐忍的态度非常符合罗马帝国,甚至是后中世纪基督教会的英雄标准,这部史诗成为罗马学校、中世纪教会学校的必读教材,诗歌创立的典范影响了后世文学和史学作品的写作风格。维吉尔本人也成了"桂冠诗人",成为但丁、歌德、席勒等文学巨擘争相效仿的偶像。

下面选读的内容是《埃涅阿斯纪》第 8 卷 626—729 行,讲的是埃涅阿斯与图尔努斯决斗之前,其母女神维纳斯将火神伏尔甘打造的盾牌交给埃涅阿斯的故事。诗人花费大量的篇幅对这面盾牌的图案进行了细致的描绘,这与《荷马史诗》中阿喀琉斯的母亲将火神赫淮斯托斯打造的新盾牌交给阿喀琉斯的情节十分相似。但是,与"阿喀琉斯之盾"不同,埃涅阿斯之盾的图案展示的是罗马历史上的一些重要事件,包括母狼喂养罗慕洛斯兄弟的故事,罗马人和周围部落第一次建立联盟的故事,驱逐最后一位国王后建立共和制的故事,抗击高卢人入侵的故事等,而盾牌中央最突出的部位雕刻的则是亚克兴海战的场面,这场海战最后以屋大维凯旋罗马,万邦来朝而结束。可以说,《埃涅阿斯纪》是罗马人对希腊史诗模仿和改写的典型范例。

目前,作为学界探讨维吉尔对奥古斯都和罗马帝国的态度、维吉尔诗歌与荷马史诗的关系等问题的重要依据之一,对"埃涅阿斯之盾"一节的研究已经形成若干值得注意的观点。

第一种观点源于 4 世纪罗马文学家霍诺拉图斯 (Maurus Servius Honoratus),他在校注《埃涅阿斯纪》的过程中,通过对比《荷马史诗》提出,维吉尔试图效仿荷马,借祖先的事迹来颂扬奥古斯都。这一观点后来逐渐被古典学家们所接受,以英国学者哈里森 (T. W. Harrison)、德国学者博施 (V. Pöschl)、阿德勒 (E. Adler) 等为代表的学者都认为,《埃涅阿斯纪》中的埃涅阿斯有着与基督教徒相同的使命感,盾牌上关于罗马历史的描绘实际上是在宣扬罗马国祚的绵长和统治的合法性,他所描绘的帝国实际上是荷马式、柏拉图式以及西塞罗式的帝国观的集中体现。

另一种观点以美国学者克劳森、布鲁克斯等人为代表,他们认为《埃涅阿斯纪》中虽有对罗马帝国的歌颂,但维吉尔本人对罗马帝国的看法是非常消极的。因为整个《埃涅阿斯纪》充满了悲剧色彩,无论是埃涅阿斯和克列乌莎、狄多的爱情悲剧,还是最后图尔努斯在决斗中被埃涅阿斯所杀,都暗示了全诗的悲剧性基调。哈迪（P. Hardie）就指出，《埃涅阿斯纪》带有明显的史诗悲剧的性质，也有抒情诗中挽歌对句的影子。因此，不少学者认为，这些消极的情绪很可能表明，维吉尔本人实际上对罗马帝国怀着深深的隐忧，他是借着对罗马历史的歌颂来警醒世人。

除此之外，亦有相当一部分学者抛开政治史的窠臼，从文学史的角度来探讨《埃涅阿斯纪》与《荷马史诗》，甚至与早期希腊神话的关联性。法贝尔（Riemer Faber）就曾经专门撰文分析过托名赫西奥德的"赫拉克勒斯之盾"与"埃涅阿斯之盾"的关系，指出两篇诗歌在结构、故事情节和修辞手法上的相似性。如法瑞尔（Joseph Farrell）和普登那（Michael C. J. Putnam）联合编著的《维吉尔〈埃涅阿斯纪〉及其传统指南》对《埃涅阿斯纪》和《荷马史诗》的关系、《埃涅阿斯纪》的版本沿革、近代以来的研究现状都有细致的分析，在此不再赘述。

626 There the story of Italy and the triumphs of Rome had the Lord of Fire fashioned, not unversed in prophecy, or unknowing of the age to come; there, every generation of the stock to spring from Ascanius（埃涅阿斯之子）, and the wars they fought one by one. He had fashioned, too, the mother-wolf outstretched in the green cave of Mars; around her teats the twin boys hung playing, and mouthed their dam without fear; she, with shapely neck bent back, fondled them by turns, and molded their limbs with her tongue. Not far from this he had set Rome and the Sabines（萨宾人，罗马周边部落，后被罗马征服）, lawlessly carried off, what time the great Circus-games were held, from the theatre's seated throng; then the sudden uprising of a fresh war between the sons of Romulus and aged Tatius（萨宾人领袖）and his stern Cures. Next, the self-same kings, their strife laid at rest, stood armed before Jove's（众神之王朱庇特的另一种写法）altar, cup in hand, and each with each made covenant o'er sacrifice of swine. Not far thence, four-horse cars, driven apart, had torn Mettus（阿尔巴人领袖，因背叛罗马人而被杀）asunder [but thou, O Alban（拉丁语呼格，阿尔巴人）, should have stood by thy words!], and Tullus（图鲁斯）dragged through the woods the liar's limbs, and the brambles dripped with dew of blood. There, too, was Porsenna, bidding them admit the banished Tarquin（塔克文）, and hemming the city with mighty siege: the sons of Aeneas rushed on the sword for freedom's sake. Him thou mightiest have seen like one in wrath, like one who threats, for that Cocles（罗马英雄）dared to tear down the bridge, and Cloelia（罗马女英雄）broke her bonds and swam the river.

652 At the top, Manlius（罗马将军）, warder of the Tarpeian fort, stood before the temple, and held the lofty Capitol; the palace was rough, fresh with the thatch of Romulus. [1] And here the silver goose, fluttering through gilded colonnades, cried that the Gauls were on the threshold.

1　In 390 B. C., when the Gauls attacked the Capitol, they were driven back by Manlius, who had been roused from sleep by cackling geese.

The Gauls were near amid the thickets, laying hold of the fort, shielded by darkness, and the boon of shadowy night. Golden are their locks and golden their raiment; they glitter in striped cloaks, and their milk-white necks are entwined with gold; two Alpine spikes (阿尔卑斯矛) each brandish in hand, and long shields guard their limbs. Here he had wrought the dancing Salii (萨利祭司,信奉战神马尔斯,以祭祀舞蹈闻名) and naked Luperci (卢佩里奇祭司,信奉森林之神,祭祀时披狼皮), the crests bound with wool, and the shields that fell from heaven; and in cushioned cars chaste matrons moved through the city in solemn progress.[1] Away from these he adds also the abodes of Hell, the high gates of Dis, the penalties of sin, and thee, Catiline (古罗马阴谋家), hanging on a frowning cliff, and trembling at the faces of the Furies; far apart, the good, and Cato (立法家) giving them laws. Amidst these scenes flowed wide the likeness of the swelling sea, all gold, but the blue water foamed with white billows, and round about dolphins, shining in silver, swept the seas with their tails in circles, and cleft the tide. In the centre could be seen brazen ships with Actium's battle; one might see all Leucate aglow with War's array, and the waves ablaze with gold. Here Augustus Caesar, leading Italians to strife, with peers and people, and the great gods of the Penates, stands on the lofty stern; his joyous brows pour forth a double flame, and on his head dawns his father's star. Elsewhere Agrippa (古罗马政治家,屋大维女婿) with favouring winds and gods, high-towering, leads his column; his brows gleam with the beaks of the naval crown, proud device of war. Here Antonius with barbaric might and varied arms, victor from the nations of the dawn and from the ruddy sea[2], brings with him Egypt and the strength of the East and utmost Bactra; and there follows him (O shame!) his Egyptian wife. All rush on at once, and the whole sea foams, uptorn by the sweeping oars, and triple-pointed beaks. To the deep they speed; thou wouldst deem the Cyclades (爱琴海南部的基克拉底群岛), uprooted, were floating on the main, or that mountains high clashed with mountains: in such mighty ships the seamen assail the towered sterns.[3] Flaming tow and shafts of winged steel are showered from their hands; Neptune's fields redden with strange slaughter. In the midst the queen calls upon her hosts with their native cymbal, nor as yet casts back a glance at the twin snakes behind. Monstrous gods of every form and barking Anubis (死神阿努比斯) wield weapons against Neptune and Venus and against Minerva. In the midst of the fray storms Mars, embossed in steel, with the fell Furies (复仇女神) from on high; and in rent robe Discord strides exultant, while Bellona follows her with bloody scourge. Actian (阿克提乌姆的) Apollo saw the sight, and from above was bending his bow; at that terror all Egypt and India, all Arabians, all Sabaeans, turned to flee. The queen herself was

---

1 Roman matrons were allowed to ride at sacred processions in pilenta, because of their self-sacrifice after the capture of Veii, 395 B. C.
2 This is the mare Erythraeum, or Indian Ocean, not the Red Sea, as we know it.
3 Conington takes mole in the sense of molimine, "with giant effort." Benoist refers tanta mole to the huge ships of Antony, while the turritae puppes are the ships of Octavius, which Agrippa, as Servius tells us, armed with towers. This seems the most plausible solution of a much debated passage.

seen to woo the winds, spread sail, and now, even now, fling loose the slackened sheets. Her, amid the carnage, the Lord of Fire had fashioned pale at the coming of death, borne on by waves and the wind of Iapyx(西北风); while over against her was the mourning Nile, of mighty frame, opening wide his folds and with all his raiment welcoming the vanquished to his azure lap and sheltering streams.[1] But Caesar(实指奥古斯都), entering the walls of Rome in triple triumph[2], was dedicating to Italy's gods his immortal votive gift—three hundred mighty fanes throughout the city. The streets rang with gladness and games and shouting; in all the temples was a band of matrons, in all were altars, and before the altars slain steers strewed the ground. Himself, seated at the snowy threshold of shining Phoebus, reviews the gifts of nations and hangs them on the proud portals. The conquered peoples move in long array, as diverse in fashion of dress and arms as in tongues. Here had portrayed the Nomad race and the ungirt Africans, here the Leleges(勒勒吉人) and Carians(卡利亚人) and quivered Gelonians(格隆尼亚人). Euphrates moved now with humbler waves, and the Morini(莫里尼人) were there, furthest of mankind and the Rhine of double horn,[3] the untamed Dahae(达海人), and Araxes chafing at his bridge[4].

729 Such sights he admires on the shield of Vulcan, his mother's gift, and, though he knows not the deeds, he rejoices in their portraiture, uplifting on his shoulder the fame and fortunes of his children's children.

选自 Virgil, *Aeneid*, 8. 626 – 729, translated by H. Rushton Fairclough, *The Loeb Classical Library*, Cambridge, Mass.: Harvard University Press, 1942.

推荐阅读

从版本上讲，国内比较常见的《埃涅阿斯纪》是由菲尔克劳的英译本（Virgil, *Aeneid*, translated by H. Rushton Fairclough, *The Loeb Classical Library*, Cambridge, Mass.: Harvard University Press, 1942）翻译过来的版本。相对可靠的版本是近年来尼古拉斯·霍尔斯福出版的一系列注释本（Nicholas Horsfall, Virgil, *Aeneid*, *A Commentary*, Leiden: Brill, 2009-2017）。目前，国内比较常见的中译本是杨周翰的译本（维吉尔：《埃涅阿斯纪》，杨周翰译，南京：译林出版社，1999年）。

导读类书籍有约翰·马林科拉的《希腊罗马历史作品指南》（John Marincola, *A Companion to Greek and Roman Historiography*, Hoboken: Wiley-Blackwell, 2010），法瑞尔和普登那联合编著的《维吉尔〈埃涅阿斯纪〉及其传统指南》 [Joseph Farrell, Michael C. J. Putnam (eds.), *A Companion to Vergil's Aeneid and Its Tradition*, Hoboken:

---

[1] The Nile-god "would be represented with a watercolorcolorcolorcolored robe, the bosom of which he would throw open" (Conington).

[2] In August, 29 B. C., Augustus celebrated a triple triumph for victories in Dalmatia, at Actium, and at Alexandria.

[3] Here there may be a reference to the two mouths, the Rhine and the Waal.

[4] A bridge over the Araxes, built by Alexander the Great, but later swept away by a flood, was replaced by Augustus.

Wiley-Blackwell, 2010], 以及高峰枫翻译的《维吉尔〈埃涅阿斯纪〉导论》（W. A. 坎普：《维吉尔〈埃涅阿斯纪〉导论》, 高峰枫译, 北京：北京大学出版社, 2019 年）。其他国外论著均可在这些导读性的书籍中找到, 在此不再详列。国内相关研究可参见：

王焕生：《古罗马文学史》, 北京：人民文学出版社, 2006 年；

阿德勒：《维吉尔的帝国——〈埃涅阿斯纪〉中的政治思想》, 王承教、朱战炜译, 北京：华夏出版社, 2012 年；

高峰枫：《维吉尔史诗中的罗马主神》,《外国文学评论》, 2008 年第 4 期；

许鸿：《〈埃涅阿斯记〉乐观与悲观之争》,《史林》, 2016 年第 4 期。

第二章　世界中古史

一、尼基塔斯·侯尼亚迪斯《记事》节选

导读

尼基塔斯·侯尼亚迪斯（Niketas Choniatēs，约 1155—1217）是"仅次于普塞罗斯的中世纪拜占庭最杰出的史家"[1]。尼基塔斯博学多才，在古典学和修辞学方面有很深的造诣。其著作《记事》（又译作《历史》）忠实记录了拜占庭帝国从 1118 年到 1207 年间的历史，涉及科穆宁王朝和安格鲁斯王朝共 8 位皇帝的治世。尼基塔斯曾官拜帝国宰相，不仅能接触到大量政府公文，还是众多事件的目击者和亲历者。尼基塔斯目睹了 1204 年君士坦丁堡的陷落和当时拜占庭人以及首都艺术品遭遇的劫难，是唯一一位将这些事件记录下来的拜占庭史学家。因此，《记事》具有相当的可信度、史料价值与文学价值。

因尼基塔斯在《记事》中记载了拜占庭帝国的政治、军事、文化和社会等方方面面的内容，因此解读文本的角度也是多样的。下面所选的是《记事》前言和涉及 1204 年君士坦丁堡陷落的内容，这一选择有助于读者了解尼基塔斯的史学思想和 1204 年君士坦丁堡陷落这一重大历史事件中拜占庭史学家的视角与观点。

需要注意的有三点：一是拜占庭人称呼自己为罗马人，认为自己的国家就是罗马帝国，"拜占庭"是近代学者为了区分古代和中世纪希腊语典籍而冠以的名称；二是以《记事》为代表的拜占庭史学著作所体现的是古典文化与基督教神学思想的影响；三是对于同一历史事件，不同立场的史学家所记载的历史具有差异性，其分析背后的原因也不相同。

Preface[2]

Historical narratives, indeed, have been invented for the common benefit of mankind, since those who will are able to gather from many of these the most advantageous insights. In recording ancient events and customs, the narratives elucidate human nature and expose men of noble sentiments, those who nourish a natural love for the good, to varied experiences. In

---

[1] 奥斯特洛格尔斯基：《拜占廷帝国》，陈志强译，西宁：青海人民出版社，2006 年，第 300 页。
[2] 此为原著前言，无改动。本书选读材料中的中文注释为本书编者所加。

abasing evil and exalting the noble deed, they introduce us, for the most part, to the temperate and the intemperate who incline to one or the other of these two scales. Men who value the attribute of virtue and eschew shameless conduct and corrupt habitude, although born mortal and subject to death, are immortalized and brought back to life by the writing of history. The same is true for those who, on the contrary, have led depraved lives. It is most fitting that the actions of the virtuous and the shameless be known to posterity. The soul moves onto Hades while the body returns to those elements from which it was constituted.

Whether the actions of a man during his lifetime were holy and righteous or lawless and contemptible, and whether he lived a happy life or gave up the ghost in evildoing, are proclaimed loudly by history. Wherefore, history can be called the book of the living and the written word a clarion trumpet, like a signal from heaven, raising up those long dead and setting them before the eyes of those who desire to see them.

Since such is the value of history, if I may say so in passing, is it not just as pleasing to posterity? Let no one be so mad as to believe that there is anything more pleasurable than history. Decrepit old men, more ancient than Tithonos[1] and thrice a crow's age, familiar with the record of the past, related these things to willing audiences, kindling the fires of their memories and ploughing the furrows of the past. He who loves learning, even though he be but an adolescent, proposes to do the same thing.

For these reasons, therefore, the events which occurred in my times and shortly before, deserving of narration and remembrance, and being of such a multitude and magnitude, I could not allow to pass in silence. It is, then, by way of this history that I make these events known to future generations.

Since others are of the opinion—and I wholly agree—that in the narration of history they should eschew that which is obscure and distorted by discordant and prolix circumlocutions, and should cherish clarity as not only being in accord with the words of the sage but also as being appropriate to them, one shall not find that the events recorded herein fall short of that ideal. Nor have I in any way embraced an affected, recondite, and vulgar vocabulary, even though many are gaping in eager expectation for this; or perhaps it would be more truthful to say that they pass over ancient and contemporary events and bedeck lavishly whatever business suits their interests best. For the most part, however, when it is a matter of setting down in writing those things that are fitting, they choose not to overstep or overleap history's proper limits.

Above all else, as I have said, the phrase which is not straight forward and easy to comprehend has been rejected, and that which is unadorned, natural, and absolutely

---

1. 提托诺斯，特洛伊的创始人拉俄墨冬（Laomedon）之子，普里阿摩斯（Priam）的哥哥，厄俄斯（Eos，黎明女神）的丈夫，门农（Memnen）的父亲。厄俄斯请求宙斯给予提托诺斯永生，但是忘记请求宙斯给予他永久的青春。

unambiguous has been preferred and embraced. This history, having truth as its sole objective, shuns rhetorical artifice and poetic storytelling as being diametrically opposed and disavows, moreover, their characteristics. Furthermore, even when History is composed with solemnity and reverence, she passionately desires to be the reward of diggers and of smiths covered with soot; she is also familiar with the armed company of Ares and is not captious with women who cultivate her; she rejoices at the most elegant of phrases and prefers to adorn herself, not with the pretentious and ostentatious, but with the cloth of plain and simple words.

This history, as far as is possible, will be treated with clarity and succinctness. If it lacks distinction and grace, I humbly request the forbearance of those into whose hands it may fall. Since this is the first time I have undertaken such an endeavor, it is like attempting to traverse a desolate and untrodden road, a much more difficult task than following the footsteps of others who have gone before or than holding to the straight and smooth royal highway without straying.

My history begins with those events which immediately followed the reign and death of Emperor Alexios, the founder of the Komnenian dynasty [1], since those historians who directly preceded us concluded with his reign. My work, then, is a continuation of their written record and is interwoven to resemble a channel whose waters flow from a single source or connecting links which are added to a chain that reaches into infinity. This history will touch briefly upon the reign of John, who succeeded Alexios to the throne, but will not long dwell thereon as it will on succeeding events. Since I was not an eyewitness of that which I have recorded, I could not describe these events extensively but have set down what I heard from those contemporaries who personally knew the emperor and who escorted him on his campaigns against the enemy and accompanied him into battle. It is best that I begin here.

1204 年君士坦丁堡的陷落 [2]

Thereupon [8 April 1204], the enemy's largest ships, carrying the scaling ladders that had been readied and as many of the siege engines as had been prepared, moved out from the shore, and, like the tilting beam of a scale's balance, they sailed over to the walls to take up positions at sufficient intervals from one another. They occupied the region extending in a line from the Monastery of Evergetēs (埃弗杰特斯) to the palace in Blachernai (布拉赫奈皇宫), which had been set on fire, the buildings within razed to the ground, thus stripping it of every pleasant spectacle. Observing these maneuvers, Doukas (杜卡斯皇帝) prepared to resist the enemy. He issued instructions for the imperial pavilion to be set up on the hill of the Pentapoptēs (潘塔波普特斯) monastery whence the warships were visible and the actions of those on board were in full view.

As dawn broke on the ninth day of the month of April in the seven thin diction of the year

---

1　科穆宁王朝。
2　此处标题为本章编者所加。

6712 [9 April 1204] [1], the warships and dromons approached the walls, and certain courageous warriors climbed the scaling ladders and discharged all manner of missiles against the towers' defenders. All through the day, a battle fraught with groanings was waged. The Romans had the upper hand: both the ships carrying the scaling ladders and the dromons transporting the horses were repulsed from the walls they had attacked without success, and many were killed by the stones thrown from the City's engines.

The enemy ceased all hostilities through the next day and the day after, which was the Lord's day [Sunday, 10-11 April 1204]; on the third day, the twelfth day of the month of April, Monday of the sixth week of the Great Lent, they again sailed towards the City and put in along the shore. By midday our forces prevailed, even though the fighting was more intense and furious than on the preceding Friday. Since it was necessary for the queen of cities [2] to put on the slave's yoke, God allowed our jaws to be constrained with bit and curb because all of us, both priest and people, had turned away from him like a stiff-necked and unbridled horse. Two men on one of the scaling ladders nearest the Petria (佩特里亚) Gate, which was raised with great difficulty opposite the emperor, trusting themselves to fortune, were the first from among their comrades to leap down onto the tower facing them. When they drove off in alarm the Roman auxiliaries on watch, they waved their hands from above as a sign of joy and courage to embolden their countrymen. While they were jumping onto the tower, a knight by the name of Peter entered through the gate situated there. He was deemed most capable of driving in rout all the battalions, for he was nearly nine fathoms tall and wore on his head a helmet fashioned in the shape of a towered city. The noblemen about the emperor and the rest of the troops were unable to gaze upon the front of the helm of a single knight so terrible in form and spectacular in size and took to their customary flight as the efficacious medicine of salvation. Thus, by uniting and fusing into one craven soul, the cowardly thousands, who had the advantage of a high hill, were chased by one man from the fortifications they were meant to defend. When they reached the Golden Gate of the Land walls, they pulled down the new-built wall there, ran forth, and dispersed, deservedly taking the road to perdition and utter destruction. The enemy, now that there was no one to raise a hand against them, ran everywhere and drew the sword against every age and sex. Each did not join with the next man to form a coherent battle array, but all poured out and scattered, since everyone was terrified of them.

That evening the enemy set fire to the eastern sections of the City not far from the Monastery of Evergetēs; from there the flames spread to those areas that slope down to the sea and terminate in the vicinity of the Droungarios (士官) Gate. After despoiling the emperor's pavilion and taking the palace in Blachernai by assault without difficulty, they set up their

---

1 "穆6712年第7个税收年的4月9日拂晓【1204年4月9日】",拜占庭纪年法有税收年纪年法、以上帝创世为元年的纪年法等,6712年是以上帝创世开始纪年的。
2 "众城的女皇",特指拜占庭帝国首都君士坦丁堡。

general headquarters at the Pantepoptēs monastery. The emperor went hither and yon through the City's narrow streets, attempting to rally and mobilize the populace who wandered aimlessly about. Neither were they convinced by his exhortations nor did they yield to his blandishments, but the fiercely shaken aegis filled all with despair.

To continue with the remaining portions of my narrative, the day waned and night came on, and each and every citizen busied himself with removing and burying his possessions. Some chose to leave the City [1], and whoever was able hastened to save himself.

When Doukas saw that he could prevail nothing, he was fearful lest he be apprehended and put into the jaws of the Latins as their dinner or dessert, and he entered the Great Palace. He put on board as mall fishing boat the Empress Euphrosynē (尤夫洛希妮), Emperor Alexios's wife, and her daughters, one of whom he loved passionately [Evdokia] (埃弗多基娅) (for he had frequently engaged in sexual intercourse from the first appearance of hair on his cheek, and he was a proven lecher in bed, having put away two wedded wives) and sailed away from the City [night of 12-13 April 1204], having reigned two months and sixteen days.

When the emperor had fled in this manner, a pair of youths sober and most skillful in matters of warfare, these being Doukasand Laskaris (拉斯卡里斯), bearing the same name as the first emperor of our faith [Constantine], contested the captaincy of a tempest-tossed ship, for they viewed the great and celebrated Roman empire as Fortune's prize, depending upon the chance move of a chessman. They entered the Great Church, evenly matched, competing against each other and being compare done with the other, neither one having more or less to offer than the other, and they were deemed equal in the balance because there was no one to examine them and pass judgment.

Receiving the supreme office by lot, Laskaris refused the imperial insignia; escorted by the patriarch to the Milion (米利翁), he continuously exhorted the assembled populace, cajoling them to put up a resistance. He pressed those who lift from the shoulder and brandish the deadly iron ax, sending them off to the imminent struggle, reminding them that they should not fear destruction any less than the Romans should the Roman empire fall to another nation: no longer would they be paid the ample wages of mercenaries or receive the far-famed gifts of honor of the imperial guard, and their pay in the future would be counted at a hair's worth. Thus did Laskaris, but not a single person from the populace responded to his blandishments. The ax-bearers agreed to fight for wages, deceitfully and cunningly exploiting the height of the danger for monetary gain, and when the Latin battalions clad in full armor made their appearance, they took flight to save themselves [early morning of 13 April 1204].

The enemy, who had expected otherwise, found no one openly venturing into battle or taking up arms to resist; they saw that the way was open before them and everything there for the taking. The narrow streets were clear and the crossroads unobstructed, safe from attack, and

---

1 "the City" 特指君士坦丁堡。

advantageous to the enemy. The populace, moved by the hope of propitiating them, had turned out to greet them with crosses and venerable icons of Christ as was customary during festivals of solemn processions. But their disposition was not at all affected by what they saw, nor did their lips break into the slightest smile, nor did the unexpected spectacle transform their grim and frenzied glance and fury into a semblance of cheerfulness. Instead, they plundered with impunity and stripped their victims shamelessly, beginning with their carts. Not only did they rob them of their substance but also the articles consecrated to God; the rest fortified themselves all around with defensive weapons as their horses were roused at the sound of the war trumpet.

What then should I recount first and what last of those things dared at that time by these murderous men?[1] O, the shameful dashing to earth of the venerable icons and the flinging of the relics of the saints, who had suffered for Christ's sake, into defiled places! How horrible it was to seethe Divine Body and Blood of Christ poured out and thrown to the ground! These forerunners of Antichrist, chief agents and harbingers of his anticipated ungodly deeds, seized as plunder the precious chalices and patens; some they smashed, taking possession of the ornaments embellishing them, and they set the remaining vessels on their tables to serve as bread dishes and wine goblets. Just as happened long ago, Christ was now disrobed and mocked, his garments were parted, and lots were cast for them by this race; and although his side was not pierced by the lance, yet once more streams of Divine Blood poured to the earth.

The report of the impious acts perpetrated in the Great Church are unwelcome to the ears. The table of sacrifice, fashioned from every kind of precious material and fused by fire into one whole-blended together into a perfection of one multicolored thing of beauty, truly extraordinary and admired by all nations—was broken into pieces and divided among the despoilers, as was the lot of all the sacred church treasures, countless in number and unsurpassed in beauty. They found it fitting to bring out as so much booty the all-hallowed vessels and furnishings which had been wrought with incomparable elegance and craftsmanship from rare materials. In addition, in order to remove the pure silver which overlay the railing of the bema, the wondrous pulpit and the gates, as well as that which covered a great many other adornments, all of which were plated with gold, they led to the very sanctuary of the temple itself mules and asses with packsaddles; some of these, unable to keep their feet on the smoothly polished marble floors, slipped and were pierced by knives so that the excrement from the bowels and the spilled blood defiled the sacred floor. Moreover, a certain silly woman laden with sins, an attendant of the Erinyes（复仇女神）, the handmaid of demons, the workshop of unspeakable spells and reprehensible charms, waxing wanton against Christ, sat upon the synthronon（宝座）and intoned a song, and then whirled about and kicked up her heels in dance.

It was not that these crimes were committed in this fashion while others were not, or that some acts were more heinous than others, but that the most wicked and impious deeds were

---

1　意为"我该先讲什么，后讲什么"，出自《荷马史诗》。

perpetrated by all with one accord. Did these madmen, raging thus against the sacred, spare pious matrons and girls of marriageable age or those maidens who, having chosen a life of chastity, were consecrated to God? Above all, it was a difficult and arduous task to mollify the barbarians with entreaties and to dispose them kindly towards us, as they were highly irascible and bilious and unwilling to listen to anything. Everything incited their anger, and they were thought fools and became a laughingstock. He who spoke freely and openly was rebuked, and often the dagger would be drawn against him who expressed a small difference of opinion or who hesitated to carry out their wishes.

The whole head was in pain. There were lamentations and cries of woe and weeping in the narrow ways, wailing at the crossroads, moaning in the temples, outcries of men, screams of women, the taking of captives, and the dragging about, tearing in pieces, and raping of bodies heretofore sound and whole. They who were bashful of their sex were led about naked, they who were venerable in their old age uttered plaintive cries, and the wealthy were despoiled of their riches. Thus it was in the squares, thus it was on the corners, thus it was in the temples, thus it was in the hiding places; for there was no place that could escape detection or that could offer asylum to those who came streaming in.

O Christ our Emperor, what tribulation and distress of men at that time! The roaring of the sea, the darkening and dimming of the sun, the turning of the moon into blood, the displacement of the stars—did they not foretell in this way the last evils? Indeed, we have seen the abomination of desolation stand in the holy place, rounding off meretricious and petty speeches and other things which were moving definitely, if not altogether, contrariwise to those things deemed by Christians as holy and ennobling the word of faith.

Such then, to make a long story short, were the outrageous crimes committed by the Western armies against the inheritance of Christ. Without showing any feelings of humanity whatsoever, they exacted from all their money and chattel, dwellings and clothing, leaving to them nothing of all their goods. Thus behaved the brazen neck, the haughty spirit, the high brow, the ever-shaved and youthful cheek, the bloodthirsty right hand, the wrathful nostril, the disdainful eye, the insatiable jaw, the hateful heart, the piercing and running speech practically dancing over the lips. More to blame were the learned and wise among men, they who were faithful to their oaths, who loved the truth and hated evil, who were both more pious and just and scrupulous in keeping the commandments of Christ than we "Greeks". Even more culpable were those who had raised the cross to their shoulders, who had time and again sworn by it and the sayings of the Lord to cross over Christian lands without bloodletting, neither turning aside to the right nor inclining to the left, and to take up arms against the Saracens and to stain red their swords in their blood; they who had sacked Jerusalem, and had taken an oath not to marry or to have sexual intercourse with women as long as they carried the cross on their shoulders, and who were consecrated to God and commissioned to follow in his footsteps.

In truth, they were exposed as frauds. Seeking to avenge the Holy Sepulcher, they raged openly against Christ and sinned by over turning the Cross with the cross they bore on their backs, not even shuddering to trample on it for the sake of a little gold and silver. By grasping pearls, they rejected Christ, the pearl of great price, scattering among the most accursed of brutes the All-Hallowed One. The sons of Ismael did not behave in this way, for when the Latins overpowered Sion the Latins showed no compassion or kindness to their race. Neither did the Ismaelites neigh after Latin women, nor did they turn the cenotaph of Christ into a common burial place of the fallen, nor did they transform the entranceway of the life-bringing tomb into a passageway leading down into Hades, nor did they replace the Resurrection with the Fall. Rather, they allowed everyone to depart in exchange for the payment of a few gold coins; they took only the ransom money and left to the people all their possessions, even though these numbered more than the grains of sand. Thus the enemies of Christ dealt magnanimously with the Latin infidels, inflicting upon them neither sword, nor fire, nor hunger, nor persecution, nor nakedness, nor bruises, nor constraints. How differently, as we have briefly recounted, the Latins treated us who love Christ and are their fellow believers, guiltless of any wrong against them.

O City, City, eye of all cities, universal boast, supra mundane wonder, wet nurse of churches, leader of the faith, guide of Orthodoxy, beloved topic of orations, the abode of every good thing! O City, that hast drunk at the hand of the Lord the cup of his fury! O City, consumed by a fire far more drastic than the fire which of old fell upon the Pentapolis! "What shall I testify to thee? What shall I compare to thee? The cup of thy destruction is magnified," says Jeremias, who was given to tears as he lamented over ancient Sion. What malevolent powers have desired to have you and taken you to be sifted? What jealous and relentless avenging demons have made a riotous assault upon you in wild revel? If these implacable and crazed suitors neither fashioned a bridal chamber for thee, nor lit a nuptial torch for thee, did they not, however, ignite the coals of destruction?

O prolific City, once garbed in royal silk and purple and now filthy and squalid and heir to many evils, having need of true children! O City, formerly enthroned on high, striding far and wide, magnificent in comeliness and more becoming in stature; now thy luxurious garments and elegant royal veils are rent and torn; thy flashing eye has grown dark, and thou art like unto an aged furnace woman all covered with soot, and thy formerly glistening and delightful countenance is now furrowed by loose wrinkles. I shall forego describing those who set words to the music of the lyre and sang of thy calamities and, drunk with wine, turned thy tragedy into a comedy, making a profession out of the farcical recitation of thine afflictions: blows struck with the fist and the foot, bruises, moreover, and black eyes inflicted upon thee every hour of the day; for by God's will thou hast provoked to jealousy the foolish nations, or rather, those people who are not truly nations but obscure and scattered tribes, and if thou didst not give birth to the majority of them, thou didst, however, raise them up and provide them with the fat of wheat.

"Who shall save thee? Or who shall comfort thee? Or who shall turn back to inquire after thy welfare? Thus spake the much-wailing Jeremias. Who shall dress in thy former raiment?

第二章 世界中古史

When shall thou heart hose divinely inspired words: "Awake, awake, stand up, O City, that hast drunk the cup of my fury and the cup of calamity. Put on thy strength, put on thy glory. Shake off the dust and arise. Put off the band of thy neck. Enlarge the place of thy tent, and of thy curtains. Fear not because thou hast been put to shame, neither be confounded because thou wast reproached, and all that go by the way have clapped their hands at thee"; they have hissed and shaken their heads and have said, "This is the city, the crown of glory and of joy of all the earth," and, "How does the city that was filled with people sit as a widow, and how has she, princess among provinces, become tributary?" For thy God has said, "For a little while I left thee, but with great mercy will I have compassion upon thee. In a little wrath I turned away my face, but with everlasting mercy will I have compassion upon thee. "Perhaps, thou shalt sing out to God with David, "O Lord, according to the multitude of my griefs within my heart, thy consolations have gladdened my soul. "

Who shall be set over thee as another Moses to renew all things, or who shall restore thee as another Zorobabel? When shall the time come for thee to gather thy children from the four winds to which we have scattered, even as hens which love their chicks gather them under their wings. And now we cannot freely gaze upon thee, face to face, nor joyously cling to thee as to a mother and openly pour out for thee a libation of tears as many as the eyes wish or can, but flying cautiously around thee like sparrows whose mother and source of nourishment has been taken captive and whose nest has been scattered to the winds, we emit piteous and mournful cries; expelled far from thy nesting places, hungry and thirsty, shivering in squalor, often close shorn because of lice, our souls wasting away because of our afflictions, we are no longer able to find the way back to our homes in the City, but roam far and wide like fickle. migratory birds and the planets. In other words, although we are apart, we are united to thee, and being separated, we are intertwined like those who are joined together in spirit even though removed in body, and suffer, moreover, the same anguish as experienced by some animals when beholding their own kind ensnared by hunters and confined within a glass cage. Those animals, gazing upon the sight of their fellow beast, visible in the clarity and brightness of the vessel, are wholly unable to come into physical contact with it. For this reason they vainly circle the receptacle in dismay, bewildered by the captive beast's countenance so dramatically altered from its former appearance. And we likewise wish to cast our eyes upon thee and to draw near, for we have been altogether deprived of clasping thee wholeheartedly to our breast and of boldly embracing thee as in former times, kept asunder by the barbarian forces as though by a solid body much more impervious than glass.

"Why hast thou smitten us, Lord, and there is no healing for us?" We know, O Lord, our sins, and the iniquities of our fathers. Refrain out of mercy, destroy not the throne of thy glory. Chasten us, O Lord, that our soul may not be removed from thee, but with judgment and not in wrath, lest thou make us few. Pour out thy wrath upon the families that have not called upon thy name. Lord, thou art our Father; we are clay, and thou our potter, and we are all the work of thine hands. Behold, and look on our reproaches. Our inheritance has been turned away to aliens, our houses to strangers. Turn us, O Lord, to thee, and we shall be turned. Most useful and timely are these scriptural verses in describing similar calamities.

But now even my power of speech fails me, like a body which, united to the soul as her attendant, succumbs and dies together with thee, O nurturer of the word! One ought to dedicate to thee copious lamentations with muted tears and stifled groaning and refrain from continuing the sequence of this history. For in a land long alienated from letters and completely barbarized, who dares sing out the Muses' melodies? Nor should I be singing out the accomplishments of the barbarians, nor passing on to posterity military actions in which Hellenes were not victorious. For if Hippocrates of Kos (科斯岛的希波克拉底), who was promised huge sums of money by the king of the Persians to visit the cities under his rule in order to tend to those who were sorely afflicted with disease, absolutely refused to give ear to the summons and allowed the barbarians to go to ruin, how then can I devote the very best thing and the most beautiful invention of the Hellenes-history-to the recounting of barbarian deeds against Hellenes?

But let these, like the incendiary of the temple of Artemis (阿耳忒弥) in Ephesos (以弗所), be gone out of sight and out of hearing[1], not even meriting a greeting from us until the iniquity has passed away and God be entreated concerning his servants. For it cannot be that our God shall forget forever, nor shall he in anger shut up his tender mercies and be well pleased no more, but he both wounds and heals, kills and restores to life. If he does send the teeth of wild beasts with the rage of serpents creeping on the ground, he also breaks the jaw teeth of the lions and crushes the dragon's head. If he breaks the reed, he also rebukes the wild beasts of the reed. If some glory lies in chariots and some in horses, yet a horse is vain for safety, and neither is he well pleased with the legs of a man. If he shows his own people hard things and gives them to drink the wine of astonishment, he also prepares a table in the presence of them that afflict us and offers the cup of gladness which brings cheer like the best wine. If he gathers the scourgers from the ends of the earth and from them that are on the sea afar off, and cries out through the great preacher and prophet, "Giants are coming to fulfill my wrath, rejoicing at the same time and dancing; for they are blessed and I bring them," he inflicts upon them even more violent blows and flogs the worst among them with afflictions, showing no partiality whatsoever. He either uses these as instruments for the ruin of cities and to effect public calamities and as pitiless executioners of men, or, as the physician of souls, he uses the majority of them in nursing the sick and as healing remedies whose nature is evident to the wise. The nurses either perished with the patient, or, once the sick recovered, they withered away for lack of something to do; and the curative medications that healed the infirmity were excreted together.

I affirm that what is needed is not a writing of divorcement given us by God, nor should we

---

1 "无踪无影,音讯荡然",出自《荷马史诗》。

consider the ensuing horrors a grafting of the barbarians as a wild olive tree into our good olive tree. What is needed is a small chastening which God knows how to lay on, in which excess is foregone and all things are not permitted to the tempters, but those who are sorely tried are spared. Indeed, if in their actions they [the Latins] did not know the limits of wickedness and were impiously arrogant towards him from Whom they received the power to flog, like Nabouzardan (纳布扎尔丹), the captain of the guard, they consigned the city of God to the flames and carried away the liturgical vessels as booty, and like Baltasar (巴尔塔萨尔) who reveled in these vessels, profaned the altars and mocked the Holy Mysteries; the suffering [Roman] on the other hand, accusing himself at the beginning of his defense, fervently called upon God to be his comforter.

In expectation of God's love for mankind, we ought to sing out with David, "Remember us, O Lord, with the favor thou hast to thy people; visit us with thy salvation that we may behold the good of thine elect, that we may rejoice in the gladness of thy nation, that we may glory with thine inheritance," knowing full well that in the end the ungodly shall be overlooked and flogged, and that for those who hope in the Lord their chastisement shall be accompanied by the call to repentance and consolation.

选自 Niketas Choniatēs, *O City of Byzantium, Annals of Niketas Choniatēs*, Detroit: Wayne State University Press, 1984.

推荐阅读

1. Robert de Clari, *The Conquest of Constantinople*, translated by Edgar Holmes McNeal, Toronto: University of Toronto Press, in association with the Medieval Academy of America, c. 1996.

2. Alfred J. Andrea, *Contemporary Sources for the Fourth Crusade*, with contributions by Brett E. Whalen, Leiden, Boston: Brill, 2000.

3. 邹薇:《尼基塔斯·侯尼亚迪斯〈记事〉研究》,天津:南开大学博士学位论文,2009 年。

二、1215 年英国《大宪章》

导读

《大宪章》(*Magna Carta*) 又称为《自由大宪章》(*Magna Carta Libertatum*),是英国国王"失地王"约翰(John Lackland,1166—1216)于 1215 年 6 月 15 日在温莎附近的兰尼米德(Runnymede)草地被迫签署的文件,也是英国议会君主制形成过程中的重要产物,最初由坎特伯雷大主教用拉丁文起草,意在缓解国王和叛乱贵族之间的矛盾。《大宪章》是英国封建贵族用于限制国王权力的宪法性文件，国王如违背之，由 25 名贵族组成的委员会则有权对国王使用武力。按照传统观点，《大宪章》主要保障大封建主在经济、司法和政治方面的特权，涉及骑士和市民权利保护的较少。《大宪章》可以被视为英国宪政之滥觞，开创了"法治"之理念。其后，《大宪章》屡次被部分或是全部推翻，又被多次确定，直至 1297 年，《大宪章》以成文法的形式再次颁布，成为"肯定法案"的一部分。时至今日，其部分条款仍旧有效，如确认英国教会的自由，确认伦敦城等城镇的"古代自由"权利，以及所有人都必须经过合法审判才能被监禁等条款。《大宪章》后来成为近代资产阶级建立法治的重要依据之一，也影响了诸如美国、澳大利亚和新西兰等国的法律。因此，《大宪章》具有重要的历史价值和学术意义。

1215 年《大宪章》目前有四个正本幸存于世，两份存于大英图书馆，一份在林肯大教堂，还有一份在索尔兹伯里大教堂。[1] 这些文本在篇幅和文字上都略有不同，但是历史学家认为每个版本都具有同等的权威性。[2] 下面所选的内容为其中一个版本的完整英译本。《大宪章》的主要内容：保障教会选举教职人员的自由；保护贵族和骑士的领地继承权，国王不得违例征收领地继承税；未经由贵族、教士和骑士组成的"王国大会议"的同意，国王不得向直属附庸征派补助金和盾牌钱；取消国王干涉封建主法庭从事司法审判的权力；未经同级贵族的判决，国王不得任意逮捕或监禁任何自由人或没收他们的财产。此外，少数条款涉及城市，如确认城市已享有的权利、保护商业自由、统一度量衡等。其内容的多样性使《大宪章》可从诸多视角解读，也有多种潜在价值可供挖掘。

在阅读《大宪章》时，首先要了解《大宪章》诞生的历史背景；其次需意识到《大宪章》没有从根本上解决国王与封建主之间的矛盾，英国议会君主制的形成还有很长一段路要走；最后需肯定《大宪章》的历史意义，即它标志着中世纪英国封建秩序开始法理化、成文化和制度化。

The Magna Carta
(The Great Charter)

Preamble: John, by the grace of God, king of England, lord of Ireland, duke of Normandy (诺曼底) and Aquitaine (阿奎丹), and count of Anjou (安茹), to the archbishop, bishops, abbots, earls, barons, justiciaries, foresters (森林官), sheriffs, stewards, servants, and to all his bailiffs and liege subjects, greetings. Know that, having regard to God and for the salvation of our soul, and those of all our ancestors and heirs, and unto the honor of God and the advancement of his holy Church and for the rectifying of our realm, we have granted as

---

1　Claire Breay, *Magna Carta: Manuscripts and Myths*, London: The British Library, 2010, p. 35.
2　同上，第 34-36 页。

underwritten by advice of our venerable fathers, Stephen, archbishop of Canterbury（坎特伯雷）, primate of all England and cardinal of the holy Roman Church, Henry, archbishop of Dublin（都柏林）, William of London, Peter of Winchester, Jocelyn of Bath（巴斯）and Glastonbury（格拉斯顿伯里）, Hugh of Lincoln, Walter of Worcester, William of Coventry, Benedict of Rochester（罗切斯特）, bishops; of Master Pandulf, subdeacon and member of the household of our lord the Pope, of brother Aymeric (master of the Knights of the Temple in England), and of the illustrious men William Marshal, earl of Pembroke, William, earl of Salisbury（索尔兹伯里）, William, earl of Warenne（沃恩）, William, earl of Arundel（阿伦德尔）, Alan of Galloway (constable of Scotland), Waren Fitz Gerold, Peter Fitz Herbert, Hubert De Burgh (seneschal of Poitou), Hugh de Neville, Matthew Fitz Herbert, Thomas Basset, Alan Basset, Philip d'Aubigny, Robert of Roppesley, John Marshal, John Fitz Hugh, and others, our liegemen.

1. In the first place we have granted to God, and by this our present charter confirmed for us and our heirs forever that the English Church shall be free, and shall have her rights entire, and her liberties inviolate; and we will that it be thus observed; which is apparent from this that the freedom of elections, which is reckoned most important and very essential to the English Church, we, of our pure and unconstrained will, did grant, and did by our charter confirm and did obtain the ratification of the same from our lord, Pope Innocent III, before the quarrel arose between us and our barons: and this we will observe, and our will is that it be observed in good faith by our heirs forever. We have also granted to all freemen of our kingdom, for us and our heirs forever, all the underwritten liberties, to be had and held by them and their heirs, of us and our heirs forever.

2. If any of our earls or barons, or others holding of us in chief by military service shall have died, and at the time of his death his heir shall be full of age and owe "relief", he shall have his inheritance by the old relief, to wit, the heir or heirs of an earl, for the whole barony of an earl by £ 100; the heir or heirs of a baron, £ 100 for a whole barony; the heir or heirs of a knight, 100s（100先令）, at most, and whoever owes less let him give less, according to the ancient custom of fees.

3. If, however, the heir of any one of the aforesaid has been under age and in wardship, let him have his inheritance without relief and without fine when he comes of age.

4. The guardian of the land of an heir who is thus under age, shall take from the land of the heir nothing but reasonable produce, reasonable customs, and reasonable services, and that without destruction or waste of men or goods; and if we have committed the wardship of the lands of any such minor to the sheriff, or to any other who is responsible to us for its issues, and he has made destruction or waster of what he holds in wardship, we will take of him amends, and the land shall be committed to two lawful and discreet men of that fee, who shall be responsible for the issues to us or to him to whom we shall assign them; and if we have given or sold the wardship of any such land to anyone and he has therein made destruction or waste, he

shall lose that wardship, and it shall be transferred to two lawful and discreet men of that fief, who shall be responsible to us in like manner as aforesaid.

5. The guardian, moreover, so long as he has the wardship of the land, shall keep up the houses, parks, fishponds, stanks, mills, and other things pertaining to the land, out of the issues of the same land; and he shall restore to the heir, when he has come to full age, all his land, stocked with plough sand wainage, according as the season of husbandry shall require, and the issues of the land can reasonable bear.

6. Heirs shall be married without disparagement, yet so that before the marriage takes place the nearest in blood to that heir shall have notice.

7. A widow, after the death of her husband, shall forthwith and without difficulty have her marriage portion and inheritance; nor shall she give anything for her dower, or for her marriage portion, or for the inheritance which her husband and she held on the day of the death of that husband; and she may remain in the house of her husband for forty days after his death, within which time her dower shall be assigned to her.

8. No widow shall be compelled to marry, so long as she prefers to live without a husband; provided always that she gives security not to marry without our consent, if she holds of us, or without the consent of the lord of whom she holds, if she holds of another.

9. Neither we nor our bailiffs will seize any land or rent for any debt, as long as the chattels of the debtor are sufficient to repay the debt; nor shall the sureties of the debtor be distrained so long as the principal debtor is able to satisfy the debt; and if the principal debtor shall fail to pay the debt, having nothing wherewith to pay it, then the sureties shall answer for the debt; and let them have the lands and rents of the debtor, if they desire them, until they are indemnified for the debt which they have paid for him, unless the principal debtor can show proof that he is discharged thereof as against the said sureties.

10. If one who has borrowed from the Jews any sum, great or small, die before that loan be repaid, the debt shall not bear interest while the heir is under age, of whomsoever he may hold; and if the debt fall into our hands, we will not take anything except the principal sum contained in the bond.

11. And if anyone die indebted to the Jews, his wife shall have her dower and pay nothing of that debt; and if any children of the deceased are left under age, necessaries shall be provided for them in keeping with the holding of the deceased; and out of the residue the debt shall be paid, reserving, however, service due to feudal lords; in like manner let it be done touching debts due to others than Jews.

12. No scutage not aid shall be imposed on our kingdom, unless by common counsel of our kingdom, except for ransoming our person, for making our eldest son a knight, and for once marrying our eldest daughter; and for these there shall not be levied more than a reasonable aid. In like manner it shall be done concerning aids from the city of London.

13. And the city of London shall have all it ancient liberties and free customs, as well by

land as by water; furthermore, we decree and grant that all other cities, boroughs, towns, and ports shall have all their liberties and free customs.

14. And for obtaining the common counsel of the kingdom anent the assessing of an aid (except in the three cases aforesaid) or of a scutage, we will cause to be summoned the archbishops, bishops, abbots, earls, and greater barons, severally by our letters; and we will move over cause to be summoned generally, through our sheriffs and bailiffs, and others who hold of us in chief, for a fixed date, namely, after the expiry of at least forty days, and at a fixed place; and in all letters of such summons we will specify the reason of the summons. And when the summons has thus been made, the business shall proceed on the day appointed, according to the counsel of such as are present, although not all who were summoned have come.

15. We will not for the future grant to anyone license to take an aid from his own free tenants, except to ransom his person, to make his eldest sona knight, and once to marry his eldest daughter; and on each of these occasions there shall be levied only a reasonable aid.

16. No one shall be distrained for performance of greater service for a knight's fee, or for any other free tenement, than is due therefrom.

17. Common pleas shall not follow our court, but shall be held in some fixed place.

18. Inquests of novel disseisin, of mort d'ancestor, and of darrein presentment shall not be held elsewhere than in their own county courts, and that in manner following; We, or, if we should be out of the realm, our chief justiciar, will send two justiciaries through every county four times a year, who shall alone with four knights of the county chosen by the county, hold the said assizes in the county court, on the day and in the place of meeting of that court.

19. And if any of the said assizes cannot be taken on the day of the county court, let there remain of the knights and freeholders, who were present at the county court on that day, as many as may be required for the efficient making of judgments, according as the business be more or less.

20. A freeman shall not be amerced for a slight offense, except in accordance with the degree of the offense; and for a grave offense he shall be amerced in accordance with the gravity of the offense, yet saving always his "contentment"; and a merchant in the same way, saving his "merchandise"; and a villein shall be amerced in the same way, saving his "wainage" if they have fallen into our mercy: and none of the aforesaid amercements shall be imposed except by the oath of honest men of the neighborhood.

21. Earls and barons shall not be amerced except through their peers, and only in accordance with the degree of the offense.

22. A clerk shall not be amerced in respect of his lay holding except after the manner of the others aforesaid; further, he shall not be amerced in accordance with the extent of his ecclesiastical benefice.

23. No village or individual shall be compelled to make bridges at river banks, except those who from of old were legally bound to do so.

24. No sheriff, constable, coroners, or others of our bailiffs, shall hold pleas of our Crown.

25. All counties, hundred, wapentakes, and trithings (except our demesne manors) shall remain at the old rents, and without any additional payment.

26. If anyone holding of us a lay fief shall die, and our sheriff or bailiff shall exhibit our letters patent of summons for a debt which the deceased owed us, it shall be lawful for our sheriff or bailiff to attach and enroll the chattels of the deceased, found upon the lay fief, to the value of that debt, at the sight of law worthy men, provided always that nothing whatever be thence removed until the debt which is evident shall be fully paid to us; and the residue shall be left to the executors to fulfill the will of the deceased; and if there be nothing due from him to us, all the chattels shall go to the deceased, saving to his wife and children their reasonable shares.

27. If any freeman shall die intestate, his chattels shall be distributed by the hands of his nearest kinsfolk and friends, under supervision of the Church, saving to every one the debts which the deceased owed to him.

28. No constable or other bailiff of ours shall take corn or other provisions from anyone without immediately tendering money therefor, unless he can have postponement thereof by permission of the seller.

29. No constable shall compel any knight to give money in lieu of castle-guard, when he is willing toper form it in his own person, or (if he himself cannot do it from any reasonable cause) then by another responsible man. Further, if we have led or sent him upon military service, he shall be relieved from guard in proportion to the time during which he has been on service because of us.

30. No sheriff or bailiff of ours, or other person, shall take the horses or carts of any freeman for transport duty, against the will of the said freeman.

31. Neither we nor our bailiffs shall take, for our castles or for any other work of ours, wood which is not ours, against the will of the owner of that wood.

32. We will not retain beyond one year and one day, the lands those who have been convicted of felony, and the lands shall thereafter be handed over to the lords of the fiefs.

33. All kydells for the future shall be removed altogether from Thames and Medway, and throughout all England, except upon the seashore.

34. The writ which is called praecipe shall not for the future be issued to anyone, regarding any tenement whereby a freeman may lose his court.

35. Let there be one measure of wine throughout our whole realm; and one measure of ale; and one measure of corn, to wit, "the London quarter"[1] （伦敦夸尔）; and one width of cloth

---

1　也有人直译为"伦敦四分之一"。"quarter"是葡萄酒、啤酒和谷物的国家度量标准,具体为1/4吨或大桶,为亨利三世时期的规定。

(whether dyed, or russet, or "halberget"[1]), to wit, two ells within the selvedges; of weights also let it be as of measures.

36. Nothing in future shall be given or taken for a writ of inquisition of life or limbs, but freely it shall be granted, and never denied.

37. If anyone holds of us by fee-farm, either by socage or by burage, or of any other land by knight's service, we will not (by reason of that fee-farm, socage, or burgage), have the wardship of the heir, or of such land of his as if of the fief of that other; nor shall we have wardship of that fee-farm, socage, or burgage, unless such fee-farm owes knight's service. We will not by reason of any small serjeancy which anyone may hold of us by the service of rendering to us knives, arrows, or the like, have wardship of his heir or of the land which he holds of another lord by knight's service.

38. No bailiff for the future shall, upon his own unsupported complaint, put anyone to his "law"[2], without credible witnesses brought for this purposes.

39. No freemen shall be taken or imprisoned or disseised or exiled or in any way destroyed, nor will we go upon him nor send upon him, except by the lawful judgment of his peers or by the law of the land.

40. To no one will we sell, to no one will we refuse or delay, right or justice.

41. All merchants shall have safe and secure exit from England, and entry to England, with the right to tarry there and to move about as well by land as by water, for buying and selling by the ancient and right customs, quit from all evil tolls, except (in time of war) such merchants as are of the land at war with us. And if such are found in our land at the beginning of the war, they shall be detained, without injury to their bodies or goods, until information be received by us, or by our chief justiciar, how the merchants of our land found in the land at war with us are treated; and if our men are safe there, the others shall be safe in our land.

42. It shall be lawful in future for anyone (excepting always those imprisoned or outlawed in accordance with the law of the kingdom, and natives of any country at war with us, and merchants, who shall be treated as if above provided) to leave our kingdom and to return, safe and secure by land and water, except for a short period in time of war, on grounds of public policy-reserving always the allegiance due to us.

43. If anyone holding of some escheat [such as the honor of Wallingford (沃灵福德), Nottingham (诺丁汉), Boulogne (布洛涅), Lancaster (兰开斯特), or of other escheats which

---

1 《大宪章》中描述的一种布料，其确切性质尚不确定。《新牛津英语词典》仅将其定义为"一种布"。英国中世纪考古学会1968年的一篇评论提出，这是一种羊毛布，因早期的织机而具有特殊的不规则钻石型花纹而闻名。作为在《大宪章》中和其他各种中世纪文献中出现的三种布之一，它被认为是12世纪和13世纪的主要商品。布料可以染成绿色、孔雀绿、深褐色，并且可以提供粗糙、良好或优良的品质，因此，它可以供穷人使用，也有适合皇室使用的等级。Cf. Eleanora Carus-Wilson, "Haberget: A Medieval Textile Conundrum", *Medieval Archaeology*, Vol. 13, No. 1, 1969.

2 有版本指此处为"神判法"。

are in our hands and are baronies] shall die, his heir shall give no other relief, and perform no other service to us than he would have done to the baron if that barony had been in the baron's hand; and we shall hold it in the same manner in which the baron held it.

44. Men who dwell without the forest need not henceforth come before our justiciaries of the forest upon a general summons, unless they are in plea, or sureties of one or more, who are attached for the forest.

45. We will appoint as justices, constables, sheriffs, or bailiffs only such as know the law of the realm and mean to observe it well.

46. All barons who have founded abbeys, concerning which they hold charters (特许状) from the kings of England, or of which they have long continued possession, shall have the wardship of them, when vacant, as they ought to have.

47. All forests that have been made such in our time shall forthwith be disafforested; and a similar course shall be followed with regard to river banks that have been placed "in defense" by us in our time.

48. All evil customs connected with forests and warrens, foresters and warreners, sheriffs and their officers, river banks and their wardens, shall immediately by inquired into in each county by twelve sworn knights of the same county chosen by the honest men of the same county, and shall, within forty days of the said inquest, be utterly abolished, so as never to be restored, provided always that we previously have intimation thereof, or our justiciar, if we should not be in England.

49. We will immediately restore all hostages and charters delivered to us by Englishmen, as sureties of the peace of faithful service.

50. We will entirely remove from their bailiwicks[1] (百利威克), the relations of Gerard of Athee[2] (阿蒂的杰拉德) (so that in future they shall have no bailiwick in England); namely, Engelard (恩格尔德) of Cigogne (席格涅), Peter, Guy, and Andrew of Chanceaux (尚索), Guy of Cigogne, Geoffrey of Martigny (马蒂尼) with his brothers, Philip Mark with his brothers and his nephew Geoffrey, and the whole brood of the same.

51. As soon as peace is restored, we will banish from the kingdom all foreign born knights, crossbowmen, serjeants, and mercenary soldiers who have come with horses and arms to the kingdom's hurt.

52. If anyone has been dispossessed or removed by us, without the legal judgment of his peers, from his lands, castles, franchises, or from his right, we will immediately restore them to him; and if a dispute arise over this, then let it be decided by the five and twenty barons of whom mention is made below in the clause for securing the peace. Moreover, for all those

---

1 类似辖区。
2 1211年至1215年间由英格兰国王约翰（John）雇佣来控制威尔士南部的雇佣军上尉。他的亲属被授予英格兰的地产，包括被任命为格洛斯特郡和赫里福德郡高级警长（1208—1210）等，该家族在英国官场的崛起引起了不少人的不满。

possessions, from which anyone has, without the lawful judgment of his peers, been disseised or removed, by our father, King Henry, or by our brother, King Richard, and which we retain in our hand (or which as possessed by others, to whom we are bound to warrant them) we shall have respite until the usual term of crusaders; excepting those things about which a plea has been raised, or an inquest made by our order, before our taking of the cross; but as soon as we return from the expedition, we will immediately grant full justice therein.

53. We shall have, moreover, the same respite and in the same manner in rendering justice concerning the disafforestation or retention of those forests which Henry our father and Richard our brother afforested, and concerning the wardship of lands which are of the fief of another (namely, such wardships as we have hitherto had by reason of a fief which anyone held of us by knight's service), and concerning abbeys founded on other fiefs than our own, in which the lord of the fee claims to have right; and when we have returned, or if we desist from our expedition, we will immediately grant full justice to all who complain of such things.

54. No one shall be arrested or imprisoned upon the appeal of a woman, for the death of any other than her husband.

55. All fines made with us unjustly and against the law of the land, and all amercements, imposed unjustly and against the law of the land, shall be entirely remitted, or else it shall be done concerning them according to the decision of the five and twenty barons whom mention is made below in the clause for securing the pease, or according to the judgment of the majority of the same, along with the aforesaid Stephen, archbishop of Canterbury, if he can be present, and such others as he may wish to bring with him for this purpose, and if he cannot be present the business shall nevertheless proceed without him, provided always that if any one or more of the aforesaid five and twenty barons are in a similar suit, they shall be removed as far as concerns this particular judgment, others being substituted in their places after having been selected by the rest of the same five and twenty for this purpose only, and after having been sworn.

56. If we have disseised or removed Welshmen from lands or liberties, or other things, without the legal judgment of their peers in England or in Wales, they shall be immediately restored to them; and if a dispute arise over this, then let it be decided in the marches by the judgment of their peers; for the tenements in England according to the law of England, for tenements in Wales according to the law of Wales, and for tenements in the marches according to the law of the marches. Welshmen shall do the same to us and ours.

57. Further, for all those possessions from which any Welshman has, without the lawful judgment of his peers, been disseised or removed by King Henry our father, or King Richard our brother, and which we retain in our hand (or which are possessed by others, and which we ought to warrant), we will have respite until the usual term of crusaders; excepting those things about which a plea has been raised or an inquest made by our order before we took the cross; but as soon as were turn (or if perchance we desist from our expedition), we will immediately grant full justice in accordance with the laws of the Welsh and in relation to the foresaid regions.

58. We will immediately give up the son of Llywelyn (利维林) and all the hostages of Wales, and the charters delivered to us as security for the peace.

59. We will do towards Alexander, king of Scots, [1] concerning the return of his sisters and his hostages, and concerning his franchises, and his right, in the same manner as we shall do towards our owher barons of England, unless it ought to be otherwise according to the charters which we hold from William his father, formerly king of Scots; and this shall be according to the judgment of his peers in our court.

60. Moreover, all these aforesaid customs and liberties, the observances of which we have granted in our kingdom as far as pertains to us towards our men, shall be observed by all of our kingdom, as well clergy as laymen, as far as pertains to them towards their men.

61. Since, move over, for God and the amendment of our kingdom and for the better allaying of the quarrel that has arisen between us and our barons, we have granted all these concessions, desirous that they should enjoy them in complete and firm endurance forever, we give and grant to them the underwritten security, namely, that the barons choose five and twenty barons of the kingdom, whomsoever they will, who shall be bound with all their might, to observe and hold, and cause to be observed, the peace and liberties we have granted and confirmed to them by this our present Charter, so that if we, or our justiciar, or our bailiffs or anyone of our officers, shall in anything be at fault towards anyone, or shall have broken any one of the articles of this peace or of this security, and the offense be notified to four barons of the foresaid five and twenty, the said four barons shall repair to us (or our justiciar, if we are out of the realm) and, laying the transgression before us, petition to have that transgression redressed without delay. And if we shall not have corrected the transgression (or, in the event of our being out of the realm, if our justiciar shall not have corrected it) within forty days, reckoning from the time it has been intimated to us (or to our justiciar, if we should be out of the realm), the four barons aforesaid shall refer that matter to the rest of the five and twenty barons, and those five and twenty barons shall, together with the community of the whole realm, distrain and distress us in all possible ways, namely, by seizing our castles, lands, possessions, and in any other way they can, until redress has been obtained as they deem fit, saving harmless our own person, and the persons of our queen and children; and when redress has been obtained, they shall resume their old relations towards us. And let whoever in the country desires it, swear to obey the orders of the said five and twenty barons for the execution of all the aforesaid matters, and along with them, to molest us to the utmost of his power; and we publicly and freely grant leave to everyone who wishes to swear, and we shall never forbid anyone to swear. All those, move over, in the land who of themselves and of their own accord are unwilling to swear to the twenty five to help them in constraining and molesting us, we shall by our command compel the same to swear to

---

1 指苏格兰的亚历山大二世(Alexander II of Scotland, 1198—1249),他缔结了《约克条约》(1237),该条约规定了英格兰和苏格兰之间的边界,今天几乎没有变化。

the effect foresaid. And if any one of the five and twenty barons shall have died or departed from the land, or be incapacitated in any other manner which would prevent the foresaid provisions being carried out, those of the said twenty five barons who are left shall choose another in his place according to their own judgment, and he shall be sworn in the same way as the others. Further, in all matters, the execution of which is entrusted, to these twenty five barons, if perchance these twenty five are present and disagree about anything, or if some of them, after being summoned, are unwilling or unable to be present, that which the majority of those present ordain or command shall be held as fixed and established, exactly as if the whole twenty five had concurred in this; and the said twenty five shall swear that they will faithfully observe all that is aforesaid, and cause it to be observed with all their might. And we shall procure nothing from anyone, directly or indirectly, whereby any part of these concessions and liberties might be revoked or diminished; and if any such things has been procured, let it be void and null, and we shall never use it personally or by another.

62. And all the will, hatreds, and bitterness that have arisen between us and our men, clergy and lay, from the date of the quarrel, we have completely remitted and pardoned to everyone. Moreover, all trespasses occasioned by the said quarrel, from Easter in the sixteenth year of our reign till the restoration of peace, we have fully remitted to all, both clergy and laymen, and completely forgiven, as far as pertains to us. And on this head, we have caused to be made for them letters testimonial patent of the lord Stephen, archbishop of Canterbury, of the lord Henry, archbishop of Dublin, of the bishops aforesaid, and of Master Pandulf as touching this security and the concessions aforesaid.

63. Wherefore we will and firmly order that the English Church be free, and that the men in our kingdom have and hold all the aforesaid liberties, rights, and concessions, well and peaceably, freely and quietly, fully and wholly, for themselves and their heirs, of us and our heirs, in all respects and in all places forever, as is aforesaid. An oath, moreover, has been taken, as well on our part as on the art of the barons, that all these conditions aforesaid shall be kept in good faith and without evil intent.

Given under our hand—the above named and many others being witnesses—in the meadow which is called Runnymede, between Windsor and Staines, on the fifteenth day of June, in the seventeenth year of our reign.

选自 https://www.ucg.ac.me/skladiste/blog_21209/objava_66356/fajlovi/MAGNA%20CARTA%20LIBERTATUM.pdf

推荐阅读

1. Claire Breay, *Magna Carta: Manuscripts and Myths*, London: The British Library, 2010.
2. David A. Carpenter, *Struggle for Mastery: The Penguin History of Britain 1066−1284*, London: Penguin, 2004.

3. H. D. Hazeltine, "The Influence of Magna Carta on American Constitutional Development", in Henry Elliot Malden (ed.), *Magna Carta Commemoration Essays*, Charleston: Biblio Bazaar, 1917.

第三章　早期现代史

一、洛伦佐·瓦拉《论拉丁语的优雅》

导读

关于意大利文艺复兴时期的人文主义思潮，在我国学界长期充斥着各种论述，许多人倾向于把人文主义视为文艺复兴时代的"时代精神"——这个时代最核心和最有代表性的思想、而且他们倾向于把这个时代的人文主义思潮解释为一个反对宗教和神性，弘扬人本主义和人性的运动。持这种见解的人显然从未深入研读过当时人文主义者的原著，他们只是想当然地对文艺复兴时期的人文主义思潮进行随心所欲的解读和演绎，并做出各种浮夸和不着边际的曲解。在笔者看来，意大利文艺复兴时期的人文主义思潮是从复兴优美的拉丁文学开始的，对拉丁语文学美的追求是这个文化运动的一个特征。正因如此，能否精通古典拉丁语并用最优雅的古典拉丁语——通常是西塞罗（Cicero）、昆体良（Qintilian）、维吉尔（Virgil）等拉丁语大师的拉丁语——写作，才是衡量"人文主义者"（在当时常被称为"诗人"或"演说家"）一个最基本的标准。洛伦佐·瓦拉（Lorenzo Valla，约1406—1457）的《论拉丁语的优雅》系统地阐述了文艺复兴时期"人文主义者"或"新拉丁语文人"的一个最基本的理想：追求拉丁语的文采（eloquence）和典雅。因为只有纯正的古典拉丁语才是打开文明之门的钥匙，只有通过使用优雅的拉丁语才有可能把自己塑造成有文明教养的自由人。用瓦拉的原话来说，这是因为"拉丁语包含了适合自由人的所有学科……有谁不知，当拉丁语兴盛时，一切学问和学科都兴旺发达；当拉丁语消亡时，一切学问和学科都化为乌有"（the language that embraced all disciplines worthy of a free man. . . . Who does not know that when the Latin language flourishes, all studies and disciplines thrive, as they are ruined when it perishes）。一言蔽之，瓦拉的《论拉丁语的优雅》堪称文艺复兴时期人文主义者的"文化宣言"。

The Glory of the Latin Language
Lorenzo Valla

c. 1430-1440

As our ancestors, winning high praises, surpassed all the men in military affairs, so by the extension of their language, they indeed surpassed themselves, as if, abandoning their dominion on earth, they had attained to the fellowship of gods in Paradise. If Ceres, Liber, and Minerva, who are considered the discoverers of grain, wine, oil, and many others had been placed among the golds for some benefactions of this kind, is it less beneficial to have spread among the nations the Latin language, the noblest and the truly divine fruit, food, not of the body but of the soul? For this language introduced those nations and all peoples to all the art which I called liberal; it taught the best laws, prepared the way for all wisdom; And finally, made it possible for them to no longer to be called barbarians.

Why would anyone who is a fair judge of things not prefer those who were distinguished for their cultivation of the sacred mysteries of literature to those who were celebrated for waging terrible wars? For you may most justly call those men royal, indeed divine, who not only founded the republic and the majesty of the Roman people, insofar as this might be done by men, but, as if they were gods, established also their welfare of the whole world. Their achievement was more amazing because those who are submitted to our rules knew that they have given up their own government, and what is more bitter, had been deprived of liberty, though not perhaps by violence. They recognized, however, that the Latin language had both strengthened and adorned their own, as the later discovery of wine did not drive out the use of water, or silk expel wool and linen, or gold the other metals, but added to these other blessings. And just as the beauty of jewel set in a gold ring is not diminished but enhanced, so our language, in uniting with the vernacular speech of others, conferred splendor: it did not destroy it. For not by arms or bloodshed or wars was its domination achieved, but by benefits, love, and concord. Of this achievement (so far as I can conjecture) the sources have been, as I have said, first, that our ancestors perfected themselves in an incredible degree in all kinds of studies; so that no one seems to have been pre-eminent in military affairs unless he was distinguished also in letters, which was a not inconsiderable stimulus to emulation of other; then, that they wisely offered honorable rewards to the teacher of literature; finally, that encourage all provincials to become accustomed to speak, both in Rome and at home, in the Roman fashion.

But since this is sufficient, I should say no more about the comparison between the Roman empire and its language. The Roman dominion, the people and nations long ago threw off as an unwelcome burden; The language of Rome they have thought sweeter than any nectar, more splendid than any silk, more precious than any gold or gems, and they have embraced it as if it were a god sent from Paradise. Great, therefore, is the sacramental power of the Latin language, truly great is its divinity, which had been preserved these many centuries with religious and holy awe, by strangers, by barbarians, by enemies, so that we Romans should not grieve and rejoice, that the whole listening earth should glory. We have lost the Rome, we have lost authority, we have lost dominion, not by our own fault, but by that of the times, yet we reign still, by this more splendid sovereignty, in a great part of the world. Ours is Italy, ours Gaul, ours Spain, Germany, Pannonia, Dalmatia, Illyricum, and many other lands. For wherever the Roman tongue holds sway, there is the Roman Empire.

But now the Greeks are going around, boasting about abundance of their language. Impoverished as they say it is, our one language is more effective than five of their dialects, which according to them, are so much richer than ours. The Latin language is a single tongue, like one law, for many peoples; in one Greece there is not a single language (which is a scandalous thing), but many dialects like factions in the states. Moreover, foreigners agree with us in speaking as we do. The Greek cannot agree among themselves, much less hope to induce others to speak their language. Among the Greeks, various authors write in Attic, Aeolic, Ionic, Doric, Koiné; with us, that is among many nations, no one writes except in Latin, in the language that embraces all disciplines worthy of a free man, just as among the Greeks, there are diffused in many dialects. Who does not know that when the Latin language flourishes, all studies and disciplines thrive, as they are ruined when it perishes? For who had been the most profound philosophers, the best orators, the most distinguished jurisconsults, and finally the greatest writers, but those indeed who have been most zealous in the speak well?

But when I wish to say more, sorrow hinders and torments me, and forces me to weep as I contemplate the state which eloquence had once attained and the condition into which it has now fallen. For what lovers of the letters and public good can restrain his tears when he sees eloquence now in the street in which it was long ago then Rome was captured by the Gauls; everything was overturned, burned, destroyed, so that Capitoline citadel hardly survived. Indeed, for many centuries not only has no one spoken in the Latin manner, but no one who had read Latin had understood it. Students of the philosophy have not possessed, nor do they possess the works of ancient philosophers; nor do rhetoricians have the orators; nor lawyers the jurisconsults; nor teachers the known works of the ancients, as if after the Roman Empire had fallen, it would not be fitting to speak or understanding in the Roman fashion, and the glory of Latinity was allowed to decay in rust and mould. And many, indeed, and varied are the opinion of the wise man on how this happened. I neither accept nor reject any of these, daring only to declare soberly that those arts which are the most closely related to the liberal arts, the arts of painting, sculpture, modeling, and architecture, had degenerated for so long and so greatly and almost died with letters themselves, and in this age they had been aroused and come to life again, so greatly increased is the number of good artists and men of letters who now flourish.

But truly, as wretched as were those former times in which no learned man was found, so much the more this our age should be congratulated, in which (if we exert ourselves a little more), I am confident that the language of Rome will shortly grow stronger than the city itself, and with it all disciplines will be restored. Therefore, because of my devotion to my native Rome and because of the importance of the matter, I shall arouse and call forth all men who are lovers of the eloquence, as if from a watchtower, and give them, as they say, the signal for battle.

选自 James B. Ross, Mary M. McLaughlin (eds.), *The Portable Renaissance Reader*, New York: Penguin, 1968, pp. 131–135.

二、弗朗切斯科·圭恰尔迪尼《意大利史》

导读

弗朗切斯科·圭恰尔迪尼（Francesco Guicciardini，1483—1540）是 16 世纪意大利最杰出的政治活动家、政治思想家和史学家。他的《意大利史》首次打破了文艺复兴时期人文主义史学的传统：以李维的《建城以来的罗马史》为典范撰写某个城市的叙事史。圭恰尔迪尼的《意大利史》以整个意大利半岛，而非某个城邦的立场叙述 1494 年以来的意大利史，作者以冷静的口吻讲述了这一关键时期意大利动荡不安的历史，准确地记录了意大利各个邦国之间的争斗，以及外敌入侵给意大利造成的灾难。

文艺复兴时期城邦的激烈争斗促进了近代外交的发展，而关于这一点，美国学者甘瑞特·马丁利（Garrett Mattingly）在其《文艺复兴时期的外交》（*Renaissance Diplomacy*）中有全面的论述。近代外交的特征包括常驻大使的设立和外交思想的成熟，后者主要体现在"均势"或"力量平衡"（balance of power）思想的形成，而弗朗切斯科·圭恰尔迪尼在《意大利史》开篇就系统地阐述了"力量平衡"的思想和实践，这一经典分析的结论差不多已经成为史学家公认的定论。下面的选文正是作者论述文艺复兴时期（尤其是 15 世纪）意大利半岛"力量平衡"的内容。

The Balance of Power in Italy

Francesco Guicciardini

1536

I have determined to relate the things which happened in Italy within our memory from the time when the French armies, called by our princes, began to disturb it by their great invasion. This subject, in its variety and grandeur, is most memorable and full of the most atrocious events, because for so many years Italy suffered all those calamities with which wretched mortals are wont to be tormented, sometimes, through the just wrath of God, sometimes from the impiety and wickedness of other men. From the knowledge of these incidents, so various and grievous, everyone will be able to draw salutary precepts both for his own and for public good. It will become clearly apparent from innumerable examples to what great instability human affairs are subject, not unlike a sea stirred by the winds. And it will be seen how destructive, almost always to themselves, but always to the people, are poorly considered counsels of rulers when, bearing only in the mind either vain errors or current greed, they do not remember frequent change of fortune, and, turning to the harm others the power granted them for the common welfare, make themselves the author of the new commotions either from insufficient prudence or excessive ambition.

But the calamities of the Italy (in order that I may note what was then its condition and likewise the causes from which so many evils sprang) inspired so much great grief and fear in the minds of the men because things in general were at that time joyous and happy. It is clear that from the time when the Roman Empire, weakened chiefly by the change in the ancient customs, began to decline—already more than a thousand years ago—from that greatness to which it has risen by marvelous ability and fortune, Italy had never known such great prosperity nor experienced of state of affairs so desirable as that in which she rested securely in the year of our Christian salvation, 1490, and the years just before and after. In the condition of the greatest peace and tranquility, cultivated no less in the mall mountainous and arid places than in the plains and more fertile regions, not subjected to any rules except that of her own, she not only abounded in inhabitants, merchandise, and riches, but was highly renowned for the magnificence of the many princes, for the splendor of the many most noble and beautiful cities, for the seat and the majesty of the religion. She also flourished in men most distinguished in the administration of public affairs, and of noble talents in all the branches of the learning and in every art and skills. Since she did not lack military glory, in accordance with custom of the age, and was adorned by such great gifts, she deservedly bore a most splendid name and fame among all the nations.

In this state of felicity, achieved by the means of the various opportunities, she was preserved by many factors. But among others not a little credit was attributed, by general consent to the industry and ability of Lorenzo de' Medici, a citizen so far above the private rank in the city of Florence that by his counsels there were governed the affairs of that republic, which was powerful more by the advantage of this location, the capacities of its men, and the readiness of its money then by the extent of its dominion. And having recently become related by marriage to Pope Innocent VIII and influenced the pope to trust not a little in his advice. Lorenzo's name was great throughout all Italy and his authority accepted in the deliberations on the common affairs. Knowing that it would be very dangerous to the Florentine republic and to himself if anyone of the greater potentate should extend farther his own power, he strove with great effort to bring it about that affair of Italy were maintained as if in a balance, so that they did not incline more to one side than another. This could not be done without preserving the peace and without been diligently on the alert against every mishap, even the slightest.

There concurred in the same desire for the common tranquility Ferrante of Aragon, Kings of Naples, a prince certainly most prudent and of the highest esteem, despite the fact that many times in the past he had revealed ideas which were ambitious and foreign to the counsels of peace, and at this time was much urged on by Alfonso, Duke of Calabria, his eldest son. The latter took it ill that Giovanni Galeazzo Sforza, Duke of Milan, his son-in-law, more than twenty years old, although very deficient in intellect, held only the ducal name, being humbled and held down by Ludovico Sforza, his uncle. More than ten years before, Ludovico, as a result of the imprudent and dissolute habits of the mother, Lady Bona, had assumed tutelage over his nephew, and thanks to his opportunity had little by little brought under his own power, the fortresses, the armed forces, the treasure, and all the foundations of the state.

Ferrante, nevertheless, having more in mind present advantage than former ambition or indignation, however just, about the youth, desired that Italy should not be changed. Perhaps he feared that Italian discord would afford opportunity to the French to attack the realm of Naples, having experienced a few years before, in the gravest peril, the hatred directed against himself by his barons and his people. Knowing that affection which many of his subjects felt for the name of the French dynasty from the memories of past events. Or perhaps he recognized that union with others was necessary, and especially with states of Milan and Florence, in order to counteract the power of the Venetians, then formidable to the whole of Italy.

Nor could any other counsels appeared Ludovico Sforza, although he was restless and ambitious in spirits, since the danger from the Venetian Senate threatened no less those who ruled Milan than the others, and because it was easier for him to preserve his usurped authority in the tranquility of the peace than in the troubles of the war. And although the intentions of Ferrante and Alfonso of Aragon were always suspect him, nevertheless, recognizing the desire of Lorenzo de' Medici for peace and likewise the fear which Lorenzo also had of the of their greatness, he was persuaded that because of the difference inspirit and the ancient hatred between Ferrante and Venetians, it was vain to fear that any alliance would be established between them. And so he considered it fairly certain that the Aragonese would be not accompanied by others in attempting against him what he they were not competent to achieve alone.

Since, then, there was present in Ferrante, Ludovico, and Lorenzo, partly for the name, partly for different reasons, the same inclination to peace, there was easily maintained an alliance, contracted in the name of Ferrante, King of Naples, Giovanni Galeazzo, Duke of Milan, and the Florentine republic, for the defence of their states. This relationship, begun many years before and interrupted thereafter by various accidents, had been renewed in the year 1480 for twenty-five years, with the adherence of almost all the minor powers of Italy, having as the chief end to prevent the Venetians from becoming more powerful. The latter, greater without doubt than any one of the allies but lesser than all of them together, followed their own counsels, apart from the common counsels, and awaiting the opportunity to derive advantage from the division and troubles of others, stood by attentive and ready to avail themselves of any chance that might open the way to their dominion over the whole of Italy. This aspiration has been very clearly recognized at very times, especially when, seizing the occasion of the death of Filippo Maria Visconti, Duke of Milan, they tried to make themselves lords of that state under pretence of defending the liberty of the Milanese; and more recently, when in open warfare, they strove to occupy the duchy of Ferrara.

This alliance easily held in check the cupidity of the Venetian Senate, but it did not unite the allies in sincere and faithful friendship, inasmuch as, full of competition and jealousy among themselves, they did not cease to watch carefully one another's movements, mutually undermining all the plans by which any one of them might grow in power and reputation. This, however, did not make the peace less stable; on the contrary, it aroused in all of them the great readiness to try to extinguish carefully all the sparks that might prove to be the origin of the new fire.

Such was the state of affairs, such were the foundations of the tranquility of Italy, disposed and balanced in such a way that not only was there no fear of present change, but no one could easily guess from what counsels or through what chances or by what arms such as a great quiet could possibly be disturbed. Then in the month of April 1492, there came about the unexpectedly the death of Lorenzo de' Medici, a death bitter to him on account of his age, because he died before finishing his forty-four years; bitter, too, for the fatherland [Florence], which through his renown and wisdom and through his genius skilled in all worthy and excellent things, flourished marvelously in riches and in all those goods and ornaments with which a long peace is wont to be accompanied in human affairs. But it was a death most unfortunate for the rest of Italy as well, both on account of the activities which he carried on continually for the common security, and because he was the mediator and almost like a brake in the disagreement and suspicions which for various reasons often sprang up between Ferrante and Ludovico Sforza, princes of ambition and almost equal in power.

选自 James B. Ross, Mary M. McLaughlin (eds.), *The Portable Renaissance Reader*, New York: Penguin, 1968, pp. 279-284.

三、乔尔乔·瓦萨里《意大利艺苑名人传》序言

导读

16世纪意大利艺术家和艺术史家乔尔乔·瓦萨里（Giorgio Vasari, 1511—1574）的《意大利艺苑名人传》（以下简称《名人传》，1550, 1568）被誉为西方现代艺术史的奠基之作。作为一位职业艺术家，瓦萨里写作的首要目的是重塑三门艺术和重新确立艺术家的社会文化地位，并为人们保留了关于文艺复兴时期艺术家的一份永久记忆。《名人传》具有宏大的历史视野，该书分为三部分，大致分别对应14、15和16世纪的意大利艺术。主体是200多位画家、

雕塑家和建筑师的传记。瓦萨里的艺术史观、方法和艺术理论主要体现在三部分的序言中。第一部分的序言论述了三门艺术的起源及其在一些古代民族中的发展。瓦萨里与同时代的人文主义史家一样持有一种有机历史观，认为艺术有其诞生、成长、衰落和死亡的过程。他认为艺术在古希腊罗马时期发展到辉煌的顶峰，随后在古代晚期和中世纪日益衰亡，到14世纪才在意大利"再生"并达到完美。第二部分的序言集中表现了瓦萨里的艺术史观念。在这里，瓦萨里详细论述了艺术于14世纪复兴、经过15世纪的发展并在16世纪重达完美的历史。在第三部分的序言中，瓦萨里提出了艺术的五个理想品质：规则（regola）、柱式（ordine，指爱奥尼亚式、多里亚式、科林斯式、托斯卡纳式和混合柱式五种建筑柱式）、比例（misura）、设计（disegno）以及手法或风格（maniera）。瓦萨里的传记艺术史为后世西方艺术史学确立了一些根本原则，包括古希腊罗马和意大利文艺复兴艺术的典范地位，古代、中世纪、意大利文艺复兴的艺术史分期，意大利文艺复兴艺术的三阶段划分以及对三门视觉艺术精神价值的高度肯定。瓦萨里将绘画、雕塑和建筑视为优于应用艺术和装饰艺术的高级精神活动，并用"设计"（disegno）将它们统一起来。瓦萨里的这一认识成为现代"艺术"观念的先声，并成为后世西方艺术史学的一个核心原则。

Preface to the Second Part[1]

When first I undertook to write these Lives, it was not my intention to make a list of the craftsmen, and an inventory, so to speak, of their works, nor did I ever judge it a worthy end for these my labors—I will not call them beautiful, but certainly long and fatiguing—to discover their numbers, their names, and their countries, and to tell in what cities, and in what places exactly in those cities, their pictures, or sculptures, or buildings were now to be found; for this I could have done with a simple table, without interposing my own judgment in any part. But seeing that the writers of history—those of them who, by common consent, are reputed to have written with the best judgment—have not only refused to content themselves with the simple narration of the succession of events, but, with all diligence and with the greatest power of research at their disposal, have set about investigating the methods, the means, and the ways that men of mark have used in the management of their enterprises; and seeing that they have striven to touch on their errors, and at the same time on their fine achievements and on the expedients and resolutions sometimes wisely adopted in their government of affairs, and on everything, in short, that these men have effected therein, sagaciously or negligently, or with prudence, or piety, or magnanimity; which these writers have done as men who knew history to be truly the mirror of human life, not in order to make a succinct narration of the events that befell a Prince

---

1　此为原著第二部分的序言，无改动。

or a Republic, but in order to observe the judgments, the counsels, the resolutions, and the intrigues of men, leading subsequently to fortunate and unfortunate actions; for this is the true soul of history, and is that which truly teaches men to live and makes them wise, and which, besides the pleasure that comes from seeing past events as present, is the true end of that art; for this reason, having undertaken to write the history of the most noble craftsmen,[1] in order to assist the arts in so far as my powers permit, and besides that to honor them, I have held to the best of my ability, in imitation of men so able, to the same method, and I have striven not only to say what these craftsmen have done, but also, in treating of them, to distinguish the better from the good and the best from the better, and to note with no small diligence the methods, the feeling, the manners, the characteristics, and the fantasies of the painters and sculptors; seeking with the greatest diligence in my power to make known, to those who do not know this for themselves, the causes and origins of the various manners and of that amelioration and that deterioration of the arts which have come to pass at diverse times and through diverse persons. And because at the beginning of these Lives I spoke of the nobility and antiquity of these arts, in so far as it was then necessary for our subject, leaving on one side many things from Pliny and other authors whereof I could have availed myself, had I not wished—contrary, perhaps, to the judgment of many—to leave each man free to see the fantasies of others in their proper sources; it appears to me expedient to do at present that which, in avoidance of tedium and prolixity (mortal enemies of attention), it was not permitted me to do then—namely, to declare more diligently my mind and intention, and to demonstrate to what end I have divided this book of the Lives into Three Parts.

  Now it is true that greatness in the arts springs in one man from diligence, in another from study, in this man from imitation[2], in that man from knowledge of the sciences, which all render assistance to the arts, and in some from all the aforesaid sources together, or from the greater part of them; yet I, none the less, having discoursed sufficiently, in the Lives of the individuals, of their methods of art, their manners, and the causes of their good, better, and best work, will discourse of this matter in general terms, and rather of the characteristics of times than of persons; having made a distinction and division, in order not to make too minute a research, into Three Parts, or we would rather call them ages, from the second birth of these arts up to the century wherein we live, by reason of that very manifest difference that is seen between one and another of them. In the first and most ancient age these three arts are seen to have been very

---

1 文艺复兴时期并无现代意义的"艺术家"概念,当时艺术家与其他行业的手工业者统称"手艺人",或按照职业分别称为画家、雕塑家和建筑师。《意大利艺苑名人传》(*Le vite de' più eccellenti pittori, scultori earchitettori*) 的标题就反映了这一点。
2 "imitation",即模仿,是西方艺术理论中最古老的一个概念,可追溯到古希腊哲学家柏拉图和亚里士多德。在文艺复兴时期,随着古代文化的复兴,艺术模仿自然的观念逐渐复兴,并成为人文主义艺术理论和艺术批评的一个核心术语。艺术家准确模仿和表现自然的能力也成为衡量其艺术的一个重要标准。模仿理论在一定程度上促进了文艺复兴时期艺术家对自然的观察和科学研究。到瓦萨里时代,除了自然,古代艺术品也被视为艺术家模仿的重要对象,因为当时的人们相信古代艺术家业已在其作品中实现了对自然的完美模仿。

distant from their perfection, and, although they had something of the good, to have been accompanied by so great imperfection that they certainly do not merit too great praise; although, seeing that they gave a beginning and showed the path and method to the better work that followed later, if for no other reason, we cannot but speak well of them and give them a little more glory than the works themselves have merited, were we to judge them by the perfect standard of art.

Next, in the second, it is manifestly seen that matters were much improved, both in the inventions[1] and in the use of more design[2], better manner[3], and greater diligence, in their execution; and likewise that the rust of age and the rudeness and disproportion, wherewith the grossness of that time had clothed them, were swept away. But who will be bold enough to say that there was to be found at that time one who was in every way perfect, and who brought his work, whether in invention, or design, or coloring, to the standard of to-day, and contrived the sweet gradation of his figures with the deep shades of color, in a manner that the lights remained only on the parts in relief, and likewise contrived those perforations and certain extraordinary refinements in marble statuary that are seen in the statues of to-day? The credit of this is certainly due to the third age, wherein it appears to me that I can say surely that art has done everything that it is possible for her, as an imitator of nature, to do, and that she has climbed so high that she has rather to fear a fall to a lower height than to ever hope for more advancement.

Having pondered over these things intently in my own mind, I judge that it is the peculiar and particular nature of these arts to go on improving little by little from a humble beginning, and finally to arrive at the height of perfection; and of this I am persuaded by seeing that almost the same thing came to pass in other faculties, which is no small argument in favour of its truth, seeing that there is a certain degree of kinship between all the liberal arts.[4] Now this must have happened to painting and sculpture in former times in such similar fashion, that, if the names were changed round, their histories would be exactly the same. For if we can put faith in those who lived near those times and could see and judge the labors of the ancients, it is seen that the statues of Canachus were very stiff and without any vivacity or movement, and therefore very

---

1　"invention"，即创意，是 15 世纪晚期和 16 世纪的艺术批评家和理论家从诗学借用的一个概念，主要指主题的构思，特别是用新颖、独特的方式表现传统的历史、诗歌和宗教故事。

2　"design"，意大利语为"disegno"，中文一般译为设计，这是文艺复兴时期出现的一个艺术概念。在瓦萨里的艺术理论中，设计既指素描（drawing），也指艺术家头脑中的构思（conception）。瓦萨里用这个概念强调了艺术实践的知性性质，并将其视为绘画、雕塑和建筑艺术的共同原则。

3　"manner"，意大利语为"maniera"，即手法或风格。在瓦萨里那里，"manner"的意义复杂多样，根据语境的不同分别指艺术家的个人风格、一种统一的时代风格或一种理想的艺术品质。

4　"自由艺术"与"技工艺术"（mechanical arts）是中世纪和文艺复兴时期流行的两个知识分类范畴，前者对应脑力劳动，后者包括各种涉及手工操作的活动。这个分类范畴显示了自古希腊以来重脑力、轻体力的传统偏见和社会区分。在中世纪，绘画、雕塑和建筑一般被归为"技工艺术"。到文艺复兴时期，人文主义者和艺术家开始打破这一传统划分，并强调三门艺术与自由艺术的密切关系，力图以此提高艺术和艺术家的社会文化地位。瓦萨里将三门艺术归为知性的"设计艺术"，以此将艺术家与其他行业的手艺人区分开。这一区分预示了现代"美术"（Fine Arts）与应用艺术和装饰艺术的等级区分。

distant from the truth; and the same is said of those of Calamis, although they were somewhat softer than those aforesaid. Then came Myron, who was no very close imitator of the truth of nature, but gave so much proportion and grace to his works that they could be reasonably called beautiful. There followed in the third degree Polycletus and the other so famous masters, who, as it is said and must be believed, made them entirely perfect. The same progress must have also come about in painting, because it is said, and it is reasonable to suppose that it was so, that in the works of those who painted with only one color, and were therefore called Monochromatists, there was no great perfection. Next, in the works of Zeuxis, Polygnotus, Timanthes, and the others who used only four colors, there is nothing but praise for their lineaments, outlines, and forms; yet, without doubt, they must have left something to be desired. But in Erion, Nicomachus, Protogenes, and Apelles, everything is perfect and most beautiful, and nothing better can be imagined, seeing that they painted most excellently not only the forms and actions of bodies, but also the emotions and passions of the soul.

But, passing these men by, since for knowledge of them we must refer to others, who very often do not agree in their judgments on them, or even, what is worse, as to the dates, although in this I have followed the best authorities; let us come to our own times, wherein we have the help of the eye, a much better guide and judge than the ear. Is it not clearly seen how great improvement was acquired by architecture—to begin with one starting-point—from the time of the Greek Buschetto to that of the German Arnolfo and of Giotto? See the buildings of those times, and the pilasters, the columns, the bases, the capitals, and all the cornices, with their ill-formed members, such as there are in Florence, in S. Maria del Fiore, in the external incrustations of S. Giovanni, and in S. Miniato sul Monte; in the Vescovado of Fiesole, in the Duomo of Milan, in S. Vitale at Ravenna, in S. Maria Maggiore at Rome, and in the Duomo Vecchio without Arezzo; wherein, excepting that little of the good which survived in the ancient fragments, there is nothing that has good order or form. But these men certainly improved it not a little, and under their guidance it made no small progress, seeing that they reduced it to better proportion, and made their buildings not only stable and stout, but also in some measure ornate, although it is true that their ornamentation was confused and very imperfect, and, so to speak, not greatly ornamental. For they did not observe that measure and proportion in the columns that the art required, or distinguish one Order[1] from another, whether Doric, Corinthian, Ionic, or Tuscan, but mixed them all together with a rule of their own that was no rule, making them very thick or very slender, as suited them best; and all their inventions came partly from their own brains, and partly from the relics of the antiquities that they saw; and they made their plans partly by copying the good, and partly by adding thereunto their own fancies, which, when the walls were raised, had a very different appearance. Nevertheless, whosoever compares their

---

1 "order"，即建筑柱式，是区分古典建筑风格的重要标准。到瓦萨里时代，意大利建筑师已区分和确立了五种柱式，包括三种古希腊柱式、一种托斯卡纳柱式和一种混合柱式。

works with those before them will see in them an improvement in every respect, although he will also see some things that give no little displeasure to our own times; as, for example, some little temples of brick, wrought over with stucco, at S. Giovanni Laterano in Rome.

The same do I say of sculpture, which, in that first age of its new birth, had no little of the good; for after the extinction of the rude Greek manner [1], which was so uncouth that it was more akin to the art of quarrying than to the genius of the craftsmen—their statues being entirely without folds, or attitudes, or movement of any kind, and truly worthy to be called stone images—when design was afterwards improved by Giotto, many men also improved the figures in marble and stone, as did Andrea Pisano and his son Nino and his other disciples, who were much better than the early sculptors and gave their statues more movement and much better attitudes; as also did those two Sienese masters, Agostino and Agnolo, who made the tomb of Guido, Bishop of Arezzo, as it has been said, and those Germans who made the facade at Orvieto. It is seen, then, that during this time sculpture made a little progress, and that there was given a somewhat better form to the figures, with a more beautiful flow of folds in the draperies, and sometimes a better air in the heads and certain attitudes not so stiff; and finally, that it had begun to seek the good, but was nevertheless lacking in innumerable respects, seeing that design was in no great perfection at that time and there was little good work seen that could be imitated. Wherefore those masters who lived at that time, and were put by me in the First Part of the book, deserve to be thus praised and to be held in that credit which the works made by them merit, if only one considers—as is also true of the works of the architects and painters of those times—that they had no help from the times before them, and had to find the way by themselves; and a beginning, however small, is ever worthy of no small praise.

Nor did painting encounter much better fortune in those times, save that, being then more in vogue by reason of the devotion of the people, it had more craftsmen and therefore made more evident progress than the other two. Thus it is seen that the Greek manner, first through the beginning made by Cimabue, and then with the aid of Giotto, was wholly extinguished; and there arose a new one, which I would fain call the manner of Giotto, seeing that it was discovered by him and by his disciples, and then universally revered and imitated by all. By this manner, as we see, there were swept away the outlines that wholly enclosed the figures, and those staring eyes, and the feet stretched on tiptoe, and the pointed hands, with the absence of shadow and the other monstrous qualifies of those Greeks; and good grace was given to the heads, and softness to the coloring. And Giotto, in particular, gave better attitudes to his figures, and revealed the first effort to give a certain liveliness to the heads and folds to his draperies, which drew more towards nature than those of the men before him; and he discovered, in part, some thing of the gradation and foreshortening of figures. Besides this, he made a beginning with the

---

1 瓦萨里所说的"希腊风格"指中世纪拜占庭的艺术风格。瓦萨里对中世纪艺术,包括拜占庭艺术和欧洲哥特艺术都持批评态度,这既是出于文化和宗教偏见,也是为了强调文艺复兴时期托斯卡纳艺术家的创新性成就。

expression of emotions, so that fear, hope, rage, and love could in some sort be recognized; and he reduced his manner, which at first was harsh and rough, to a certain degree of softness; and although he did not make the eyes with that beautiful roundness that makes them lifelike, and with the tear-channels that complete them, and the hair soft, and the beards feathery, and the hands with their due joints and muscles, and the nudes true to life, let him find excuse in the difficulty of the art and in the fact that he saw no better painters than himself; and let all remember, amid the poverty of art in those times, the excellence of judgment in his stories, the observation of feeling, and the subordination of a very ready natural gift, seeing that his figures were subordinate to the part that they had to play. And thereby it is shown that he had a very good, if not a perfect judgment; and the same is seen in the others after him, as in the coloring of Taddeo Gaddi, who is both sweeter and stronger, giving better tints to the flesh and better color to the draperies, and more boldness to the movements of his figures. In Simone Sanese there is seen dignity in the composition of stories; and Stefano the Ape and his son Tommaso brought about great improvement and perfection in design, invention in perspective, and harmony and unity in coloring, ever maintaining the manner of Giotto. The same was done for mastery and dexterity of handling by Spinello Aretino and his son Parri, Jacopo di Casentino, Antonio Viniziano, Lippo, Gherardo Stamina, and the other painters who labored after Giotto, following his feeling, lineaments, coloring, and manner, and even improving them somewhat, but not so much as to make it appear that they were aiming at another goal. Whosoever considers this my discourse, therefore, will see that these three arts were up to this time, so to speak, only sketched out, and lacking in much of that perfection that was their due; and in truth, without further progress, this improvement was of little use and not to be held in too great account. Nor would I have anyone believe that I am so dull and so poor in judgment that I do not know that the works of Giotto, of Andrea Pisano, of Nino, and of all the others, whom I have put together in the First Part by reason of their similarity of manner, if compared with those of the men who labored after them, do not deserve extraordinary or even mediocre praise; or that I did not see this when I praised them. But whosoever considers the character of those times, the dearth of craftsmen, and the difficulty of finding good assistance, will hold them not merely beautiful, as I have called them, but miraculous, and will take infinite pleasure in seeing the first beginnings and those sparks of excellence that began to be rekindled in painting and sculpture. The victory of Lucius Marcius in Spain was certainly not so great that the Romans did not have many much greater; but in consideration of the time, the place, the circumstances, the men, and the numbers, it was held stupendous, and even to-day it is held worthy of the infinite and most abundant praises that are given to it by writers. To me, likewise, by reason of all the aforesaid considerations, it has appeared that these masters deserve to be not only described by me with all diligence, but praised with that love and confidence wherewith I have done it. Nor do I think that it can have been wearisome to my brother craftsmen to read these their Lives, and to consider their manners and methods, and from this, perchance, they will derive no little profit; which will be right pleasing to me, and I will esteem it a good reward for my labors, wherein I have sought to do nought else but give them profit and delight to the best of my power.

And now that we have weaned these three arts, to use such a fashion of speaking, and brought them through their childhood, there comes their second age, wherein there will be seen infinite improvement in everything; invention more abundant in figures, and richer in ornament; more depth and more lifelike reality in design; some finality, moreover, in the works, which are executed thoughtfully and with diligence, although with too little mastery of handling; with more grace in manner and more loveliness in coloring, so that little is wanting for the reduction of everything to perfection and for the exact imitation of the truth of nature. Wherefore, with the study and the diligence of the great Filippo Brunelleschi, architecture first recovered the measures and proportions of the ancients, both in the round columns and in the square pilasters, and in the corner-stones both rough and smooth; and then one Order was distinguished from another, and it was shown what differences there were between them. It was ordained that all works should proceed by rule, should be pursued with better ordering, and should be distributed with due measure. Design grew in strength and depth; good grace[1] was given to buildings; the excellence of that art made itself known; and the beauty and variety of capitals and cornices were recovered in such a manner that the ground-plans of his churches and of his other edifices are seen to have been very well conceived, and the buildings themselves ornate, magnificent, and beautifully proportioned, as it may be seen in the stupendous mass of the cupola of S. Maria del Fiore in Florence, and in the beauty and grace of its lantern; in the ornate, varied, and graceful Church of S. Spirito, and in the no less beautiful edifice of S. Lorenzo; in the most bizarre invention of the octagonal Temple of the Angeli; in the most fanciful Church and Convent of the Abbey of Fiesole, and in the magnificent and vast beginning of the Pitti Palace; besides the great and commodious edifice that Francesco di Giorgio made in the Palace and Church of the Duomo at Urbino, and the very strong and rich Castle of Naples, and the impregnable Castle of Milan, not to mention many other notable buildings of that time. And although there were not therein that delicacy and a certain exquisite grace and finish in the mouldings, and certain refinements, and beauties in the carving of the leafage, and in making-certain extremities in the foliage, and other points of perfection, which all came later, as it will be seen in the Third Part, wherein there will follow those who will attain to all that perfection, whether in grace, or refinement, or abundance, or dexterity, to which the old architects did not attain; none the less, they can be safely called beautiful and good. I do not call them yet perfect, because later there was seen something better in that art, and it appears to me that I can reasonably affirm that there was something wanting in them. And although there are in them some parts so miraculous that

---

1 "grace",意大利语为"grazia",一般理解为优美或优雅,瓦萨里认为这是16世纪艺术家才获得的一种理想品质。这个概念的含义非常复杂,与宗教的神恩(grace)和当时宫廷社会推崇的优雅的行为规范都有关联。瓦萨里认为优雅超越一切客观的比例和规则,是一种与生俱来的神圣天赋,但同时,艺术家要使其作品表现出"优雅"也离不开长期刻苦的训练。

nothing better has yet been done in our own times, nor will be, peradventure, in times to come, such as, for example, the lantern of the cupola of S. Maria del Fiore, and, in point of grandeur, the cupola itself, wherein Filippo was emboldened not only to equal the ancients in the extent of their structures, but also to excel them in the height of the walls[1]; yet we are speaking generically and universally, and we must not deduce the excellence of the whole from the goodness and perfection of one thing alone.

This I can also say of painting and sculpture, wherein very rare works of the masters of that second age may still be seen to-day, such as those in the Carmine by Masaccio, who made a naked man shivering with cold, and lively and spirited figures in other pictures; but in general they did not attain to the perfection of the third, whereof we will speak at the proper time, it being necessary now to discourse of the second, whose craftsmen, to speak first of the sculptors, advanced so far beyond the manner of the first and improved it so greatly, that they left little to be done by the third. They had a manner of their own, so much more graceful and more natural, and so much richer in order, in design, and in proportion, that their statues began to appear almost like living people, and no longer figures of stone, like those of the first age; and to this those works bear witness that were wrought in that new manner, as it will be seen in this Second Part; among which the figures of Jacopo della Quercia have more movement, more grace, more design, and more diligence; those of Filippo, a more beautiful knowledge of muscles, better proportion, and more judgment; and so, too, those of their disciples. But the greatest advance came from Lorenzo Ghiberti in the work of the gates of S. Giovanni, wherein he showed such invention, order, manner, and design, that his figures appear to move and to have souls. But as for Donato[2], although he lived in their time, I am not wholly sure whether I ought not to place him in the third age, seeing that his works challenge comparison with the good works of the ancients; but this I will say, that he can be called the pattern of the others in this second age, having united in his own self all the qualities that were divided singly among many, for he brought his figures to actual motion, giving them such vivacity and liveliness that they can stand beside the works of to-day, and, as I have said, beside the ancient as well.

The same advance was made at this time by painting, from which that most excellent Masaccio swept away completely the manner of Giotto in the heads, the draperies, the buildings, the nudes, the coloring, and the foreshortenings, all of which he made new, bringing to light that modern manner which was followed in those times and has been followed up to our own day by all our craftsmen, and enriched and embellished from time to time with better grace, invention, and ornament; as it will be seen more particularly in the Life of each master, wherein there will appear a new manner of coloring, of foreshortenings, and of natural attitudes, with much better expression for the emotions of the soul and the gestures of the body, and an attempt to approach

---

1 瓦萨里认为艺术的发展是循环的，也是不断进步的，并认为16世纪的意大利艺术家业已超过了古人。
2 指意大利文艺复兴时期著名的雕塑家多纳泰罗（Donatello）。

closer to the truth of nature in draughtsmanship, and an effort to give to the expressions of the faces so complete a resemblance to the living men, that it might be known for whom they were intended. Thus they sought to imitate that which they saw in nature, and no more, and thus their works came to be better planned and better conceived; and this emboldened them to give rules to their perspectives and to foreshorten them in a natural and proper form, just as they did in relief; and thus, too, they were ever observing lights and shades, the projection of shadows, and all the other difficulties, and the composition of stories with more characteristic resemblance, and attempted to give more reality to landscapes, trees, herbs, flowers, skies, clouds, and other objects of nature, insomuch that we may boldly say that these arts were not only reared but actually carried to the flower of their youth, giving hope of that fruit which afterwards appeared, and that, in short, they were about to arrive at their most perfect age.

With the help of God, then, we will begin the Life of Jacopo della Quercia of Siena, and afterwards those of the other architects and sculptors, until we come to Masaccio, who, having been the first to improve design in the art of painting, will show how great an Obligation is owed to him for the new birth that he gave to her. Having chosen the aforesaid Jacopo for the honor of beginning this Second Part, I will follow the order of the various manners, and proceed to lay open, together with the Lives themselves, the difficulties of arts so beautiful, so difficult, and so highly honored.

选自 Giorgio Vasari, *Lives of the Most Eminent Painters, Sculptors & Architects*, London: Macmillan, 1912-1915, pp. 245-255.

推荐阅读

1. Giorgio Vasari, *Le vite de' più eccellenti pittori, scultori e architettori*, Fiorenza: Torrentino, 1550; Fiorenza: Appresso i Givnti, 1568.

2. Giorgio Vasari, *Lives of the Painters, Sculptors, and Architects*, in 10 Volumes, translated by Gaston du C. de Vere, New York: Everyman's Library, 1912.

3. 乔尔乔·瓦萨里：《意大利艺苑名人传》（四卷），刘耀春、徐波、刘君等译，武汉：湖北美术出版社，长江文艺出版社，2003年。

第四章 世界近现代史

一、1688 年英国《权利法案》

导读

《权利法案》是英国重要的法律性文件，奠定了英国君主立宪政体的理论和法律基础，确立了议会权力高于王权的原则，标志着君主立宪制开始在英国建立。它与《王位继承法》共同标志着英国内战的结束，为英国带来了较为安定的国内政治环境。

在成功地推翻了英国天主教国王詹姆斯二世之后，1689 年 4 月 11 日，奥兰治的威廉（William of Orange）和妻子玛丽（Mary）在威斯敏斯特大教堂（Westminster Abbey）加冕为英格兰国王和女王。其间，议会向威廉和玛丽提出了一个"权利宣言"，提出了诸如国王未经议会同意不能停止法律的效力，不经议会同意不能征收赋税，今后任何天主教徒不得担任英国国王，任何国王不能与罗马天主教徒结婚等要求。威廉接受了这些要求，即位为英国国王，是为威廉三世。玛丽即位为英国女王，是为玛丽二世。1689 年 10 月，议会通过了"权利宣言"。1689 年 12 月 16 日，国王和女王授予了皇家同意书，使之成为法律，是为《权利法案》。《权利法案》旨在控制国王的权力，并使之服从议会的法律。上述事件被称为"不流血的革命"或"光荣的革命"，标志着国王权力至上的终结。

这项议会法案奠定了英国宪政制度的基础，事实上确立了议会主权的原则。一方面，确立了各项"议会特权"，如确立了经常举行议会、自由选举和议会内言论自由的原则。另一方面，对王室的法律特权做了严格的限制，如禁止任意中止议会法律、未经议会同意不征税、和平时期不得维持常备军、国王政府不得干预民众的自由、请愿权等。

《权利法案》的主要原则至今在英国和一些英联邦国家仍然有效，仍可在法律案件中被引用。它的国际影响还体现在其被用作 1789 年美国《权利法案》的范本，也体现在其他确立人权的文件中，如《联合国人权宣言》和《欧洲人权公约》。

Bill of Rights [1688]
1688 CHAPTER 21 Will and Mar Sess 2 [1]

An Act declareing the Rights and Liberties of the Subject and Setleing the Succession of the Crowne.

X1 Whereas the Lords Spirituall and Temporall [2] and Comons assembled at Westminster lawfully fully and freely representing all the Estates of the People of this Realme did upon the thirteenth day of February in the yeare of our Lord one thousand six hundred eighty eight present unto their Majesties then called and known by the Names and Stile of William and Mary Prince and Princesse of Orange being present in their proper Persons a certaine Declaration in Writing made by the said Lords and Comons in the Words following viz

The Heads of Declaration of Lords and Commons, recited.

Whereas the late King James the Second by the Assistance of diverse evill Councellors Judges and Ministers imployed by him did endeavour to subvert and extirpate the Protestant Religion and the Lawes and Liberties of this Kingdome.

Dispensing and Suspending Power.

By Assumeing and Exerciseing a Power of Dispensing with and Suspending of Lawes and the Execution of Lawes without Consent of Parlyament.

Committing Prelates.

By Committing and Prosecuting diverse Worthy Prelates for humbly Petitioning to be excused from Concurring to the said Assumed Power.

Ecclesiastical Commission [3].

By issueing and causeing to be executed a Commission under the Great Seale [4] for Erecting a Court called The Court of Commissioners for Ecclesiasticall Causes.

Levying Money.

By Levying Money for and to the Use of the Crowne by pretence of Prerogative for other time and in other manner then the same was granted by Parlyament.

Standing Army.

By raising and keeping a Standing Army within this Kingdome in time of Peace without Consent of Parlyament and Quartering Soldiers contrary to Law.

Disarming Protestants, &c.

By causing severall good Subjects being Protestants to be disarmed at the same time when Papists were both Armed and Imployed contrary to Law.

---

1 英国法案的命名方式，此处指 1688 年《权利法案》在议会被命名为"威廉和玛丽元年第二章议会第二会期法令"。
2 教会和世俗贵族，此处指英国议会上院。
3 指宗教事务法院。
4 指国玺，是王权的象征，由大法官或掌玺大臣掌管。

Violating Elections.

By Violating the Freedome of Election of Members to serve in Parlyament.

Illegal Prosecutions.

By Prosecutions in the Court of Kings Bench[1] for Matters and Causes cognizable onely in Parlyament and by diverse other Arbitrary and Illegall Courses.

Juries.

And whereas of late yeares Partiall Corrupt and Unqualifyed Persons have beene returned and served on Juryes in Tryalls and particularly diverse Jurors in Tryalls for High Treason[2] which were not Freeholders,

Excessive Bail.

And excessive Baile hath beene required of Persons committed in Criminall Cases to elude the Benefitt of the Lawes made for the Liberty of the Subjects.

Fines.

And excessive Fines have beene imposed.

Punishments.

And illegall and cruell Punishments inflicted.

Grants of Fines, &c. before Conviction, &c.

And severall Grants and Promises made of Fines and Forfeitures before any Conviction or Judgement against the Persons upon whome the same were to be levyed. All which are utterly directly contrary to the knowne Lawes and Statutes and Freedome of this Realme.

Recital that the late King James II had abdicated the Government, and that the Throne was vacant, and that the Prince of Orange[3] had written Letters to the Lords and Commons for the choosing Representatives in Parliament.

And whereas the said late King James the Second haveing Abdicated the Government and the Throne being thereby Vacant His [**X2** Hignesse] the Prince of Orange (whome it hath pleased Almighty God to make the glorious Instrument of Delivering this Kingdome from Popery and Arbitrary Power) did (by the Advice of the Lords Spirituall and Temporall and diverse principall Persons of the Commons) cause Letters to be written to the Lords Spirituall and Temporall being Protestants and other Letters to the severall Countyes Cityes Universities Burroughs and Cinque Ports for the Choosing of such Persons to represent them as were of right to be sent to Parlyamentto meete and sitt at Westminster upon the two and twentyeth day of January in this Yeare one thousand six hundred eighty and eight in order to such an Establishment as that their Religion Lawes and Liberties might not againe be in danger of being Subverted, Upon which Letters Elections haveing beene accordingly made.

1　指王座法庭。
2　指重叛逆罪。
3　指荷兰的奥兰治亲王，即后来的英格兰国王威廉三世。

The Subject's Rights.

And thereupon the said Lords Spirituall and Temporall and Commons pursuant to their respective Letters and Elections being now assembled in a full and free Representative of this Nation takeing into their most serious Consideration the best meanes for attaining the Ends aforesaid Doe in the first place (as their Auncestors in like Case have usually done) for the Vindicating and Asserting their auntient Rights and Liberties, Declare

Dispensing Power.

That the pretended Power of Suspending of Laws or the Execution of Laws by Regall Authority without Consent of Parlyament is illegall.

Late dispensing Power.

That the pretended Power of Dispensing with Laws or the Execution of Laws by Regall Authoritie as it hath beene assumed and exercised of late is illegall.

Ecclesiastical Courts illegal.

That the Commission for erecting the late Court of Commissioners for Ecclesiasticall Causes and all other Commissions and Courts of like nature are Illegall and Pernicious.

Levying Money.

That levying Money for or to the Use of the Crowne by pretence of Prerogative without Grant of Parlyament for longer time or in other manner then the same is or shall be granted is Illegall.

Right to petition.

That it is the Right of the Subjects to petition the King and all Commitments and Prosecutions for such Petitioning are Illegall.

Standing Army.

That the raising or keeping a standing Army within the Kingdome in time of Peace unlesse it be with Consent of Parlyament is against Law.

Subjects' Arms.

That the Subjects which are Protestants may have Arms for their Defence suitable to their Conditions and as allowed by Law.

Freedom of Election.

That Election of Members of Parlyament ought to be free.

Freedom of Speech.

That the Freedome of Speech and Debates or Proceedings in Parlyament ought not to be impeached or questioned in any Court or Place out of Parlyament.

Excessive Bail.

That excessive Baile ought not to be required nor excessive Fines imposed nor cruell and unusuall Punishments inflicted.

Juries.

That Jurors ought to be duely impannelled and returned. . . **F1**

Grants of Forfeitures. [1]

That all Grants and Promises of Fines and Forfeitures of particular persons before Conviction are illegall and void.

Frequent Parliaments.

And that for Redresse of all Grievances and for the amending strengthening and preserveing of the Lawes Parlyaments ought to be held frequently.

The said Rights claimed. Tender of the Crown. Regal Power exercised. Limitation of the Crown.

And they doe Claime Demand and Insist upon all and singular the Premises as their undoubted Rights and Liberties and that noe Declarations Judgements Doeings or Proceedings to the Prejudice of the People in any of the said Premisses ought in any wise to be drawne hereafter into Consequence or Example. To which Demand of their Rights they are particularly encouraged by the Declaration of this Highnesse the Prince of Orange as being the onely meanes for obtaining a full Redresse and Remedy therein. Haveing therefore an intire Confidence That his said Highnesse the Prince of Orange will perfect the Deliverance soe farr advanced by him and will still preserve them from the Violation of their Rights which they have here asserted and from all other Attempts upon their Religion Rights and Liberties. The said Lords Spirituall and Temporall and Commons assembled at Westminster doe Resolve That William and Mary Prince and Princesse of Orange be and be declared King and Queene of England France and Ireland and the Dominions thereunto belonging to hold the Crowne and Royall Dignity of the said Kingdomes and Dominions to them the said Prince and Princesse dureing their Lives and the Life of the Survivour of them And that the sole and full Exercise of the Regall Power be onely in and executed by the said Prince of Orange in the Names of the said Prince and Princesse dureing their joynt Lives And after their Deceases the said Crowne and Royall Dignitie of the said Kingdoms and Dominions to be to the Heires of the Body of the said Princesse And for default of such Issue to the Princesse Anne of Denmarke and the Heires of her Body And for default of such Issue to the Heires of the Body of the said Prince of Orange. And the Lords Spirituall and Temporall and Commons doe pray the said Prince and (**X3**) Princesse to accept the same accordingly.

New Oaths of Allegiance, &c.

And that the Oathes hereafter mentioned be taken by all Persons of whome the Oathes of Allegiance and Supremacy might be required by Law instead of them And that the said Oathes of Allegiance and Supremacy be abrogated.

Allegiance.

I A B doe sincerely promise and sweare That I will be faithfull and beare true Allegiance to their Majestyes King William and Queene Mary Soehelpe me God.

---

1 指没收的授权。

Supremacy.

I A B doe sweare That I doe from my Heart Abhorr, Detest and Abjure as Impious and Hereticall this damnable Doctrine and Position That Princes Excommunicated or Deprived by the Pope or any Authority of the See of Rome may be deposed or murdered by their Subjects or any other whatsoever. And I doe declare That noe Forreigne Prince Person Prelate, State or Potentate hath or ought to have any Jurisdiction Power Superiority Preeminence or AuthoritieEcclesiasticall or Spirituall within this Realme Soe helpe me God.

Acceptance of the Crown. The Two Houses to sit. Subjects' Liberties to be allowed, and Ministers hereafter to serve according to the same. William and Mary declared King and Queen. Limitation of the Crown. Papists debarred the Crown. Every King, &c. shall make the Declaration of 30 Car. II. If under 12 Years old, to be done after Attainment thereof. King's and Queen's Assent

Upon which their said Majestyes did accept the Crowne and Royall Dignitie of the Kingdoms of England France and Ireland and the Dominions thereunto belonging according to the Resolution and Desire of the said Lords and Commons contained in the said Declaration. And thereupon their Majestyes were pleased That the said Lords Spirituall and Temporall and Commons being the two Houses of Parlyament should continue to sitt and with their Majesties Royall Concurrence make effectuall Provision for the Setlement of the Religion Lawes and Liberties of this Kingdome soe that the same for the future might not be in danger againe of being subverted, To which the said Lords Spirituall and Temporall and Commons did agree and proceede to act accordingly. Now in pursuance of the Premisses the said Lords Spirituall and Temporall and Commons in Parlyament assembled for the ratifying confirming and establishing the said Declaration and the Articles Clauses Matters and Things therein contained by the Force of a Law made in due Forme by Authority of Parlyament doe pray that it may be declared and enacted That all and singular the Rights and Liberties asserted and claimed in the said Declaration are the true auntient and indubitable Rights and Liberties of the People of this Kingdome and soe shall be esteemed allowed adjudged deemed and taken to be and that all and every the particulars aforesaid shall be firmly and strictly holden and observed as they are expressed in the said Declaration And all Officers and Ministers whatsoever shall serve their Majestyes and their Successors according to the same in all times to come. And the said Lords Spirituall and Temporall and Commons seriously considering how it hath pleased Almighty God in his marvellous Providence and mercifull Goodness to this Nation to provide and preserve their said Majestyes Royall Persons most happily to Raigne over us upon the Throne of their Auncestors for which they render unto him from the bottome of their Hearts their humblest Thanks and Praises doe truely firmely assuredly and in the Sincerity of their Hearts thinke and doe hereby recognize acknowledge and declare That King James the Second haveing abdicated the Government and their Majestyes haveing accepted the Crowne and Royall Dignity [**X4** as] aforesaid Their said Majestyes did become were are and of right ought to be by the Lawes of this

Realme our Soveraigne Liege Lord and Lady King and Queene of England France and Ireland and the Dominions thereunto belonging in and to whose Princely Persons the Royall State Crowne and Dignity of the said Realmes with all Honors Stiles Titles Regalities Prerogatives Powers Jurisdictions and Authorities to the same belonging and appertaining are most fully rightfully and intirely invested and incorporated united and annexed And for preventing all Questions and Divisions in this Realme by reason of any pretended Titles to the Crowne and for preserveing a Certainty in the Succession thereof in and upon which the Unity Peace Tranquillity and Safety of this Nation doth under God wholly consist and depend The said Lords Spirituall and Temporall and Commons doe beseech their Majestyes That it may be enacted established and declared That the Crowne and Regall Government of the said Kingdoms and Dominions with all and singular the Premisses thereunto belonging and appertaining shall bee and continue to their said Majestyes and the Survivour of them dureing their Lives and the Life of the Survivour of them And that the entire perfect and full Exercise of the Regall Power and Government be onely in and executed by his Majestie in the Names of both their Majestyes dureing their joynt Lives And after their deceases the said Crowne and Premisses shall be and remaine to the Heires of the Body of her Majestie and for default of such Issue to her Royall Highnesse the Princess Anne of Denmarke and the Heires of her Body and for default of such Issue to the Heires of the Body of his said Majestie And thereunto the said Lords Spirituall and Temporall and Commons doe in the Name of all the People aforesaid most humbly and faithfully submit themselves their Heires and Posterities for ever and doe faithfully promise That they will stand to maintaine and defend their said Majesties and alsoe the Limitation and Succession of the Crowne herein specified and contained to the utmost of their Powers with their Lives and Estates against all Persons whatsoever that shall attempt any thing to the contrary. And whereas it hath beene found by Experience that it is inconsistent with the Safety and Welfaire of this Protestant Kingdome to be governed by a Popish Prince **F2**. . . the said Lords Spirituall and Temporall and Commons doe further pray that it may be enacted That all and every person and persons that is are or shall be reconciled to or shall hold Communion with the See or Church of Rome or shall professe the Popish Religion **F3**. . . shall be excluded and be for ever uncapeable to inherit possesse or enjoy the Crowne and Government of this Realme and Ireland and the Dominions thereunto belonging or any part of the same or to have use or exercise any Regall Power Authoritie or Jurisdiction within the same [**X5** And in all and every such Case or Cases the People of these Realmes shall be and are hereby absolved of their Allegiance] And the said Crowne and Government shall from time to time descend to and be enjoyed by such person or persons being Protestants as should have inherited and enjoyed the same in case the said person or persons soe reconciled holding Communion or Professing **F4**. . . as aforesaid were naturally dead [**X6** And that every King and Queene of this Realme who at any time hereafter shall come to and succeede in the Imperiall Crowne of this Kingdome shall on the first day of the meeting of the first Parlyament next after his or her comeing to the Crowne sitting in his or her Throne in the House of Peeres[1] in the presence of the Lords and Commons therein assembled or at his or her Coronation before such person or persons who shall administer the Coronation Oath to him or her at the time of his or her takeing the said Oath (which shall first happen) make subscribe and audibly repeate the Declaration mentioned in the Statute made in the thirtyeth yeare of the Raigne of King Charles the Second Entituled An Act for the more effectuall Preserveing the Kings Person and Government by disableing Papists from sitting in either House of Parlyament But if it shall happen that such King or Queene upon his or her Succession to the Crowne of this Realme shall be under the Age of twelve yeares then every such King or Queene shall make subscribe and audibly repeate the said Declaration at his or her Coronation or the first day of the meeting of the first Parlyament as aforesaid which shall first happen after such King or Queene shall have attained the said Age of twelve yeares.] All which Their Majestyes are contented and pleased shall be declared enacted and established by authoritie of this present Parliament and shall stand remaine and be the Law of this Realmefor ever And the same are by their said Majesties by and with the advice and consent of the Lords Spirituall and Temporall and Commons in Parlyament assembled and by the authoritie of the same declared enacted and established accordingly.

Editorial Information

X1 The Bill of Rights is assigned to the year 1688 on legislation. gov. uk (as it was previously in successive official editions of the revised statutes from which the online version is derived) although the Act received Royal Assent on 16th December 1689. This follows the practice adopted in The Statutes of the Realm, Vol. VI (1819), in the Chronological Table in that volume and all subsequent Chronological Tables of the Statutes, which attach all the Acts in 1 Will and Mar sess 2 to the year 1688. The first Parliament of William and Mary (the Convention Parliament) convened on 13th February 1689 (1688 in the old style calendar—until 1st Jan 1752 the calendar year began on March 25th). It appears that all the Acts of that Parliament (both sessions) were treated as being Acts of 1688 using the old method of reckoning, according to which, until 1793, all Acts passed in a session of Parliament with no specified commencement date were deemed to be passed in the year in which that session began [see Acts of Parliament (Commencement) Act 1793 (c. 13)]. The Short Titles Act 1896 (c. 14) gave to chapter 2 of 1 Will and Mar sess 2 the title "The Bill of Rights", without attributing it to any calendar year. In the Republic of Ireland, the Short Titles Act 1896 (c. 14) has been amended to add "1688" to the short title of The Bill of Rights as it continues to have effect there [see Statute Law Revision Act 2007, Act of the Oireachtas No 28 of 2007, s 5 (a)].

X2 Variant reading of the text noted in The Statutes of the Realm as follows: Highnesse

---

1　指英国议会上院。

O. [O. refers to a collection in the library of Trinity College, Cambridge]

X3　Variant reading of the text noted in The Statutes of the Realm as follows: and O. [O. refers to a collection in the library of Trinity College, Cambridge]

X4　interlined on the Roll.

X5　annexed to the Original Act in a separate Schedule.

X6　annexed to the Original Act in a separate Schedule.

Textual Amendments

F1　Words repealed by (E. W.) Juries Act 1825 (c. 50), s. 62 and (N. I.) Statute Law Revision Act 1950 (c. 6), Sch. 1

F2　Words in s. 1 omitted (26. 3. 2015) by virtue of Succession to the Crown Act 2013 (c. 20), s. 5, Sch. para. 2 (a) (with Sch. para. 5); S. I. 2015/894, art. 2

F3　Words in s. 1 omitted (26. 3. 2015) by virtue of Succession to the Crown Act 2013 (c. 20), s. 5, Sch. para. 2 (b) (with Sch. para. 5); S. I. 2015/894, art. 2

F4　Words in s. 1 omitted (26. 3. 2015) by virtue of Succession to the Crown Act 2013 (c. 20), s. 5, Sch. para. 2 (c) (with Sch. para. 5); S. I. 2015/894, art. 2

Modifications etc. (not altering text)

C1　Short title "The Bill of Rights" given by Short Titles Act 1896 (c. 14), Sch. 1

C2　Act declared to be a Statute by Crown and Parliament Recognition Act 1689 (c. 1)

C3　S. 1 amended by Accession Declaration Act 1910 (c. 29), s. 1

选自英国政府立法网，http://www.legislation.gov.uk/aep/WillandMarSess2/1/2/introduction # reference-M_F_889d968f-39fa-4d24-d246-0a00eb355b6d.

注：
1. 正文中粗体字为后来加入的概括性和解释性文字，非正文内容。
2. 注意文中一些单词与现代英语单词拼写方式的区别。

推荐阅读

1. 靳克斯：《英国法》，张季忻译，北京：中国政法大学出版社，2007年。

2. 威廉·布莱克斯通：《英国法释义》（第一卷），游云庭、缪苗译，上海：上海人民出版社，2006年。

3. 沃尔特·白芝浩：《英国宪法》，夏彦才译，北京：商务印书馆，2017年。

4. 韦农·波格丹诺：《新英国宪法》，李松峰译，北京：法律出版社，2014年。

5. 钱乘旦：《英国通史》（第一至六卷），南京：江苏人民出版社，2016年。

二、《北爱尔兰和平协议》导言

导读

《北爱尔兰和平协议》即《耶稣受难日协议》(The Good Friday Agreement)，又被称为《贝尔法斯特协议》(Belfast Agreement)，是20世纪90年代北爱尔兰在和平进程中签署的重要政治文件。协议于1998年4月10日——耶稣受难日当天在贝尔法斯特签署。参与该协议制定的主要是英国和爱尔兰政府以及北爱尔兰八个政党，由美国总统克林顿的特使乔治·米切尔(George J. Mitchell)主持双方的谈判。

协议包括两个相互关联的文件，分别是北爱尔兰主要政党达成的多党协议（北爱尔兰八个政党与英国、爱尔兰两国政府之间达成的实质性协定）以及英国和爱尔兰政府之间的一项国际协议（由两国政府领导人签署）。主要内容包括英国北爱尔兰政府的地位和制度、北爱尔兰与爱尔兰共和国之间的关系、爱尔兰共和国和联合王国之间的关系。与主权、公民和文化权利，武器销毁，非军事化，正义和维持治安有关的问题是该协定的核心内容。

协议本着异中求同、非零和博弈的精神，提出了保障和平的四大重要原则：同意(Consent)原则、平等尊重(Parity of Esteem)原则、权力分享(Power-sharing)原则和包容性原则(Inclusion)。四大原则确保了协定签署20年来北爱尔兰地区总体上维持了和平稳定的局面，社会经济得以迅速发展。

协议的一个重要特点是包含某些被称为"建设性歧义"的含糊不清的措辞。这种处理一方面有助于确保该协定被各方接受，并有助于推迟对一些更具争议性问题的辩论，主要包括准军事组织的复原、警察制度改革以及北爱尔兰历史问题的处置等方面；另一方面，协议的模糊性也导致了在其具体实施过程中的大量争议以及和平进程的波折。

协议塑造了北爱尔兰目前的政府体制，北爱尔兰和爱尔兰共和国以及爱尔兰共和国和英国之间的一系列合作机构也是基于该协定建立的。由于《耶稣受难日协议》在北爱尔兰的若干法律问题上对英国政府具有约束力，因此它事实上已成为英国宪法的一部分。甚至有学者认为它是"英国和爱尔兰的核心宪法文本，比诸如1215年的《大宪章》或1689年的《人权法案》之类的神圣文书具有更高的日常重要性"。此外，该协议提到英国和爱尔兰为"欧洲联盟的伙伴"，在英国脱欧背景下，北爱尔兰问题特别是北爱尔兰边界问题成为欧盟与英国之间一个重要的争议点。

The Northern Ireland Peace Agreement
The Agreement reached in the multi-party negotiations
10 April 1998

CONTENTS

1. Declaration of Support
2. Constitutional Issues
    Annex A: Draft Clauses/Schedules for Incorporation in British Legislation
    Annex B: Irish Government Draft Legislation
3. Strand One:
    Democratic Institutions in Northern Ireland
4. Strand Two:
    North/South Ministerial Council
5. Strand Three:
    British-Irish Council
    British-Irish Intergovernmental Conference
6. Rights, Safeguards and Equality of Opportunity
    Human Rights
    United Kingdom Legislation
    New Institutions in Northern Ireland
    Comparable Steps by the Irish Government A Joint Committee
    Reconciliation and Victims of Violence Economic, Social and Cultural Issues
7. Decommissioning
8. Security
9. Policing and Justice
    Annex A: Commission on Policing for Northern Ireland
    Annex B: Review of the Criminal Justice System
10. Prisoners
11. Validation, Implementation and Review
    Validation and Implementation
    Review Procedures Following Implementation
ANNEX: Agreement between the Government of the United Kingdom of Great Britain and Northern Ireland and the Government of Ireland

DECLARATION OF SUPPORT

1. We, the participants in the multi-party negotiations, believe that the agreement we have negotiated offers a truly historic opportunity for a new beginning.

2. The tragedies of the past have left a deep and profoundly regrettable legacy of suffering.

We must never forget those who have died or been injured, and their families. But we can best honor them through a fresh start, in which we firmly dedicate ourselves to the achievement of reconciliation, tolerance, and mutual trust, and to the protection and vindication of the human rights of all.

3. We are committed to partnership, equality and mutual respect as the basis of relationships within Northern Ireland, between North and South, and between these islands.

4. We reaffirm our total and absolute commitment to exclusively democratic and peaceful means of resolving differences on political issues, and our opposition to any use or threat of force by others for any political purpose, whether in regard to this agreement or otherwise.

5. We acknowledge the substantial differences between our continuing, and equally legitimate, political aspirations. However, we will endeavour to strive in every practical way towards reconciliation and rapprochement within the framework of democratic and agreed arrangements. We pledge that we will, in good faith, work to ensure the success of each and every one of the arrangements to be established under this agreement. It is accepted that all of the institutional and constitutional arrangements-an Assembly in Northern Ireland, a North/South Ministerial Council, implementation bodies, a British-Irish Council and a British-Irish Intergovernmental Conference and any amendments to British Acts of Parliament and the Constitution of Ireland—are interlocking and interdependent and that in particular the functioning of the Assembly and the North/South Council are so closely inter-related that the success of each depends on that of the other.

6. Accordingly, in a spirit of concord, we strongly commend this agreement to the people, North and South, for their approval.

STRAND ONE
DEMOCRATIC INSTITUTIONS IN NORTHERN IRELAND

1. This agreement provides for a democratically elected Assembly in Northern Ireland which is inclusive in its membership, capable of exercising executive and legislative authority, and subject to safeguards to protect the rights and interests of all sides of the community.

The Assembly

2. A 108 member Assembly will be elected by PR (STV)[1] from existing Westminster constituencies.

3. The Assembly will exercise full legislative and executive authority in respect of those matters currently within the responsibility of the six Northern Ireland Government Departments, with the possibility of taking on responsibility for other matters as detailed elsewhere in this agreement.

4. The Assembly—operating where appropriate on a cross-community basis—will be the

---

1 比例代表制,详见聂露:《论英国选举制度》,北京:中国政法大学出版社,2006年,第249-252页。

prime source of authority in respect of all devolved responsibilities.

Safeguards

5. There will be safeguards to ensure that all sections of the community can participate and work together successfully in the operation of these institutions and that all sections of the community are protected, including:

(a) allocations of Committee Chairs, Ministers and Committee membership in proportion to party strengths;

(b) the European Convention on Human Rights (ECHR)[1] and any Bill of Rights for Northern Ireland supplementing it, which neither the Assembly nor public bodies can infringe, together with a Human Rights Commission;

(c) arrangements to provide that key decisions and legislation are proofed to ensure that they do not infringe the ECHR and any Bill of Rights for Northern Ireland;

(d) arrangements to ensure key decisions are taken on a cross-community basis;

(1) either parallel consent[2], i.e. a majority of those members present and voting, including a majority of the unionist and nationalist designations present and voting;

(2) or a weighted majority[3] (60%) of members present and voting, including at least 40% of each of the nationalist and unionist designations present and voting.

Key decisions requiring cross-community support will be designated in advance, including election of the Chair of the Assembly, the First Minister and Deputy First Minister, standing orders and budget allocations. In other cases such decisions could be triggered by a petition of concern brought by a significant minority of Assembly members (30/108).

(e) an Equality Commission to monitor a statutory obligation to promote equality of opportunity in specified areas and parity of esteem between the two main communities, and to investigate individual complaints against public bodies.

Operation of the Assembly

6. At their first meeting, members of the Assembly will register a designation of identity—nationalist, unionist or other—for the purposes of measuring cross-community support in Assembly votes under the relevant provisions above.

7. The Chair and Deputy Chair of the Assembly will be elected on a cross-community basis, as set out in paragraph 5 (d) above.

8. There will be a Committee for each of the main executive functions of the Northern Ireland Administration. The Chairs and Deputy Chairs of the Assembly Committees will be allocated proportionally, using the d'Hondt system[4]. Membership of the Committees will be in

---

1 欧洲人权公约。
2 可译为"平行同意"。
3 可译为"加权多数"。
4 东特选举法,详见聂露:《论英国选举制度》,北京:中国政法大学出版社,2006年,第249-252页。

broad proportion to party strengths in the Assembly to ensure that the opportunity of Committee places is available to all members.

9. The Committees will have a scrutiny, policy development and consultation role with respect to the Department with which each is associated, and will have a role in initiation of legislation. They will have the power to:

- consider and advise on Departmental budgets and Annual Plans in the context of the overall budget allocation;
- approve relevant secondary legislation and take the Committee stage of relevant primary legislation;
- call for persons and papers;
- initiate enquiries and make reports;
- consider and advise on matters brought to the Committee by its Minister.

10. Standing Committees other than Departmental Committees may be established as may be required from time to time.

11. The Assembly may appoint a special Committee to examine and report on whether a measure or proposal for legislation is in conformity with equality requirements, including the ECHR/Bill of Rights. The Committee shall have the power to call people and papers to assist in its consideration of the matter. The Assembly shall then consider the report of the Committee and can determine the matter in accordance with the cross-community consent procedure.

12. The above special procedure shall be followed when requested by the Executive Committee, or by the relevant Departmental Committee, voting on a cross-community basis.

13. When there is a petition of concern as in 5 (d) above, the Assembly shall vote to determine whether the measure may proceed without reference to this special procedure. If this fails to achieve support on a cross-community basis, as in 5 (d) (i) above, the special procedure shall be followed.

Executive Authority

14. Executive authority to be discharged on behalf of the Assembly by a First Minister and Deputy First Minister and up to ten Ministers with Departmental responsibilities.

15. The First Minister and Deputy First Minister shall be jointly elected into office by the Assembly voting on a cross-community basis, according to 5 (d) (i) above.

16. Following the election of the First Minister and Deputy First Minister, the posts of Ministers will be allocated to parties on the basis of the d'Hondt system by reference to the number of seats each party has in the Assembly.

17. The Ministers will constitute an Executive Committee, which will be convened, and presided over, by the First Minister and Deputy First Minister.

18. The duties of the First Minister and Deputy First Minister will include, inter alia, dealing with and co-ordinating the work of the Executive Committee and the response of the Northern Ireland administration to external relationships.

19. The Executive Committee will provide a forum for the discussion of, and agreement on, issues which cut across the responsibilities of two or more Ministers, for prioritising executive and legislative proposals and for recommending a common position where necessary (e. g. in dealing with external relationships).

20. The Executive Committee will seek to agree each year, and review as necessary, a programme incorporating an agreed budget linked to policies and programmes, subject to approval by the Assembly, after scrutiny in Assembly Committees, on a cross-community basis.

21. A party may decline the opportunity to nominate a person to serve as a Minister or may subsequently change its nominee.

22. All the Northern Ireland Departments will be headed by a Minister. All Ministers will liaise regularly with their respective Committee.

23. As a condition of appointment, Ministers, including the First Minister and Deputy First Minister, will affirm the terms of a Pledge of Office (Annex A) undertaking to discharge effectively and in good faith all the responsibilities attaching to their office.

24. Ministers will have full executive authority in their respective areas of responsibility, within any broad programme agreed by the Executive Committee and endorsed by the Assembly as a whole.

25. An individual may be removed from office following a decision of the Assembly taken on a cross-community basis, if (s) he loses the confidence of the Assembly, voting on a cross-community basis, for failure to meet his or her responsibilities including, inter alia, those set out in the Pledge of Office. Those who hold office should use only democratic, non-violent means, and those who do not should be excluded or removed from office under these provisions.

Legislation

26. The Assembly will have authority to pass primary legislation for Northern Ireland in devolved areas, subject to:

   (a) the ECHR and any Bill of Rights for Northern Ireland supplementing it which, if the courts found to be breached, would render the relevant legislation null and void;

   (b) decisions by simple majority of members voting, except when decision on a cross-community basis is required;

   (c) detailed scrutiny and approval in the relevant Departmental Committee;

   (d) mechanisms, based on arrangements proposed for the Scottish Parliament, to ensure suitable co-ordination, and avoid disputes, between the Assembly and the Westminster Parliament;

   (e) option of the Assembly seeking to include Northern Ireland provisions in United Kingdom-wide legislation in the Westminster Parliament, especially on devolved issues where parity is normally maintained (e. g. social security, company law).

27. The Assembly will have authority to legislate in reserved areas with the approval of the

Secretary of State and subject to Parliamentary [1] control.

28. Disputes over legislative competence will be decided by the Courts.

29. Legislation could be initiated by an individual, a Committee or a Minister.

Relations with other institutions

30. Arrangements to represent the Assembly as a whole, at Summit level and in dealings with other institutions, will be in accordance with paragraph 18, and will be such as to ensure cross-community involvement.

31. Terms will be agreed between appropriate Assembly representatives and the Government of the United Kingdom to ensure effective co-ordination and input by Ministers to national policy-making, including on EU issues.

32. Role of Secretary of State:

(a) to remain responsible for NIO matters not devolved to the Assembly, subject to regular consultation with the Assembly and Ministers;

(b) to approve and lay before the Westminster Parliament any Assembly legislation on reserved matters;

(c) to represent Northern Ireland interests in the United Kingdom Cabinet;

(d) to have the right to attend the Assembly at their invitation.

33. The Westminster Parliament (whose power to make legislation for Northern Ireland would remain unaffected) will:

(a) legislate for non-devolved issues, other than where the Assembly legislates with the approval of the Secretary of State and subject to the control of Parliament;

(b) to legislate as necessary to ensure the United Kingdom's international obligations are met in respect of Northern Ireland;

(c) scrutinise, including through the Northern Ireland Grand and Select Committees, the responsibilities of the Secretary of State.

34. A consultative Civic Forum will be established. It will comprise representatives of the business, trade union and voluntary sectors, and such other sectors as agreed by the First Minister and the Deputy First Minister. It will act as a consultative mechanism on social, economic and cultural issues. The First Minister and the Deputy First Minister will by agreement provide administrative support for the Civic Forum and establish guidelines for the selection of representatives to the Civic Forum.

Transitional Arrangements

35. The Assembly will meet first for the purpose of organisation, without legislative or executive powers, to resolve its standing orders and working practices and make preparations for the effective functioning of the Assembly, the British-Irish Council and the North/South Ministerial Council and associated implementation bodies. In this transitional period, those

---

1 此处指英国的威斯敏斯特议会。

members of the Assembly serving as shadow Ministers shall affirm their commitment to nonviolence and exclusively peaceful and democratic means and their opposition to any use or threat of force by others for any political purpose; to work in good faith to bring the new arrangements into being; and to observe the spirit of the Pledge of Office applying to appointed Ministers.

Review

36. After a specified period there will be a review of these arrangements, including the details of electoral arrangements and of the Assembly's procedures, with a view to agreeing any adjustments necessary in the interests of efficiency and fairness.

Annex A

Pledge of Office

To pledge:

(a) to discharge in good faith all the duties of office;

(b) commitment to non-violence and exclusively peaceful and democratic means;

(c) to serve all the people of Northern Ireland equally, and to act in accordance with the general obligations on government to promote equality and prevent discrimination;

(d) to participate with colleagues in the preparation of a programme for government;

(e) to operate within the framework of that programme when agreed within the Executive Committee and endorsed by the Assembly;

(f) to support, and to act in accordance with, all decisions of the Executive Committee and Assembly;

(g) to comply with the Ministerial Code of Conduct.

CODE OF CONDUCT

Ministers must at all times:

- observe the highest standards of propriety and regularity involving impartiality, integrity and objectivity in relationship to the stewardship of public funds;
- be accountable to users of services, the community and, through the Assembly, for the activities within their responsibilities, their stewardship of public funds and the extent to which key performance targets and objectives have been met;
- ensure all reasonable requests for information from the Assembly, users of services and individual citizens are complied with; and that Departments and their staff conduct their dealings with the public in an open and responsible way;
- follow the seven principles of public life set out by the Committee on Standards in Public Life;
- comply with this code and with rules relating to the use of public funds;
- operate in a way conducive to promoting good community relations and equality of treatment;

- not use information gained in the course of their service for personal gain; nor seek to use the opportunity of public service to promote their private interests;
- ensure they comply with any rules on the acceptance of gifts and hospitality that might be offered;
- declare any personal or business interests which may conflict with their responsibilities. The Assembly will retain a Register of Interests. Individuals must ensure that any direct or indirect pecuniary interests which members of the public might reasonably think could influence their judgement are listed in the Register of Interests.

STRAND TWO
NORTH/SOUTH MINISTERIAL COUNCIL

1. Under a new British/Irish Agreement dealing with the totality of relationships, and related legislation at Westminster and in the Oireachtas[1], a North/South Ministerial Council to be established to bring together those with executive responsibilities in Northern Ireland and the Irish Government, to develop consultation, co-operation and action within the island of Ireland-including through implementation on an all-island and cross-border basis—on matters of mutual interest within the competence of the Administrations, North and South.

2. All Council decisions to be by agreement between the two sides. Northern Ireland to be represented by the First Minister, Deputy First Minister and any relevant Ministers, the Irish Government by the Taoiseach and relevant Ministers, all operating in accordance with the rules for democratic authority and accountability in force in the Northern Ireland Assembly and the Oireachtas respectively. Participation in the Council to be one of the essential responsibilities attaching to relevant posts in the two Administrations. If a holder of a relevant post will not participate normally in the Council, the Taoiseach in the case of the Irish Government and the First and Deputy First Minister in the case of the Northern Ireland Administration to be able to make alternative arrangements.

3. The Council to meet in different formats:
 (i) in plenary format twice a year, with Northern Ireland representation led by the First Minister and Deputy First Minister and the Irish Government led by the Taoiseach;
 (ii) in specific sectoral formats on a regular and frequent basis with each side represented by the appropriate Minister;
 (iii) in an appropriate format to consider institutional or cross-sectoral matters (including in relation to the EU) and to resolve disagreement.

4. Agendas for all meetings to be settled by prior agreement between the two sides, but it will be open to either to propose any matter for consideration or action.

5. The Council:

---

1 指爱尔兰议会（由总统和两院组成）。

(i) to exchange information, discuss and consult with a view to co-operating on matters of mutual interest within the competence of both Administrations, North and South;

(ii) to use best endeavours to reach agreement on the adoption of common policies, in areas where there is a mutual cross-border and all-island benefit, and which are within the competence of both Administrations, North and South, making determined efforts to overcome any disagreements;

(iii) to take decisions by agreement on policies for implementation separately in each jurisdiction, in relevant meaningful areas within the competence of both Administrations, North and South;

(iv) to take decisions by agreement on policies and action at an all-island and cross-border level to be implemented by the bodies to be established as set out in paragraphs 8 and 9 below.

6. Each side to be in a position to take decisions in the Council within the defined authority of those attending, through the arrangements in place for co-ordination of executive functions within each jurisdiction. Each side to remain accountable to the Assembly and Oireachtas respectively, whose approval, through the arrangements in place on either side, would be required for decisions beyond the defined authority of those attending.

7. As soon as practically possible after elections to the Northern Ireland Assembly, inaugural meetings will take place of the Assembly, the British/Irish Council and the North/South Ministerial Council in their transitional forms. All three institutions will meet regularly and frequently on this basis during the period between the elections to the Assembly, and the transfer of powers to the Assembly, in order to establish their modus operandi.

8. During the transitional period between the elections to the Northern Ireland Assembly and the transfer of power to it, representatives of the Northern Ireland transitional Administration and the Irish Government operating in the North/South Ministerial Council will undertake a work programme, in consultation with the British Government, covering at least 12 subject areas, with a view to identifying and agreeing by 31 October 1998 areas where co-operation and implementation for mutual benefit will take place. Such areas may include matters in the list set out in the Annex.

9. As part of the work programme, the Council will identify and agree at least 6 matters for cooperation and implementation in each of the following categories:

(i) Matters where existing bodies will be the appropriate mechanisms for cooperation in each separate jurisdiction;

(ii) Matters where the co-operation will take place through agreed implementation bodies on a cross-border or all-island level.

10. The two Governments will make necessary legislative and other enabling preparations to ensure, as an absolute commitment, that these bodies, which have been agreed as a result of the work programme, function at the time of the inception of the British-Irish Agreement and the transfer of powers, with legislative authority for these bodies transferred to the Assembly as soon

as possible thereafter. Other arrangements for the agreed co-operation will also commence contemporaneously with the transfer of powers to the Assembly.

11. The implementation bodies will have a clear operational remit. They will implement on an all-island and cross-border basis policies agreed in the Council.

12. Any further development of these arrangements to be by agreement in the Council and with the specific endorsement of the Northern Ireland Assembly and Oireachtas, subject to the extent of the competences and responsibility of the two Administrations.

13. It is understood that the North/South Ministerial Council and the Northern Ireland Assembly are mutually inter-dependent, and that one cannot successfully function without the other.

14. Disagreements within the Council to be addressed in the format described at paragraph 3 (iii) above or in the plenary format. By agreement between the two sides, experts could be appointed to consider a particular matter and report.

15. Funding to be provided by the two Administrations on the basis that the Council and the implementation bodies constitute a necessary public function.

16. The Council to be supported by a standing joint Secretariat, staffed by members of the Northern Ireland Civil Service and the Irish Civil Service.

17. The Council to consider the European Union dimension of relevant matters, including the implementation of EU policies and programmes and proposals under consideration in the EU framework. Arrangements to be made to ensure that the views of the Council are taken into account and represented appropriately at relevant EU meetings.

18. The Northern Ireland Assembly and the Oireachtas to consider developing a joint parliamentary forum, bringing together equal numbers from both institutions for discussion of matters of mutual interest and concern.

19. Consideration to be given to the establishment of an independent consultative forum appointed by the two Administrations, representative of civil society, comprising the social partners and other members with expertise in social, cultural, economic and other issues.

ANNEX

Areas for North-South co-operation and implementation may include the following:

1. Agriculture—animal and plant health.
2. Education—teacher qualifications and exchanges.
3. Transport—strategic transport planning.
4. Environment—environmental protection, pollution, water quality, and waste management.
5. Waterways—inland waterways.
6. Social Security/Social Welfare—entitlements of cross-border workers and fraud control.
7. Tourism—promotion, marketing, research, and product development.
8. Relevant EU Programmes such as SPPR, INTERREG, Leader II and their successors.

9. Inland Fisheries.

10. Aquaculture and marine matters

11. Health: accident and emergency services and other related cross-border issues.

12. Urban and rural development.

Others to be considered by the shadow North/South Council.

STRAND THREE
BRITISH-IRISH COUNCIL

1. A British-Irish Council (BIC) will be established under a new British-Irish Agreement to promote the harmonious and mutually beneficial development of the totality of relationships among the peoples of these islands.

2. Membership of the BIC will comprise representatives of the British and Irish Governments, devolved institutions in Northern Ireland, Scotland and Wales, when established, and, if appropriate, elsewhere in the United Kingdom, together with representatives of the Isle of Man and the Channel Islands.

3. The BIC will meet in different formats: at summit level, twice per year; in specific sectoral formats on a regular basis, with each side represented by the appropriate Minister; in an appropriate format to consider cross-sectoral matters.

4. Representatives of members will operate in accordance with whatever procedures for democratic authority and accountability are in force in their respective elected institutions.

5. The BIC will exchange information, discuss, consult and use best endeavours to reach agreement on co-operation on matters of mutual interest within the competence of the relevant Administrations. Suitable issues for early discussion in the BIC could include transport links, agricultural issues, environmental issues, cultural issues, health issues, education issues and approaches to EU issues. Suitable arrangements to be made for practical co-operation on agreed policies.

6. It will be open to the BIC to agree common policies or common actions. Individual members may opt not to participate in such common policies and common action.

7. The BIC normally will operate by consensus. In relation to decisions on common policies or common actions, including their means of implementation, it will operate by agreement of all members participating in such policies or actions.

8. The members of the BIC, on a basis to be agreed between them, will provide such financial support as it may require.

9. A secretariat for the BIC will be provided by the British and Irish Governments in coordination with officials of each of the other members.

10. In addition to the structures provided for under this agreement, it will be open to two or more members to develop bilateral or multilateral arrangements between them. Such arrangements could include, subject to the agreement of the members concerned, mechanisms to

enable consultation, co-operation and joint decision-making on matters of mutual interest; and mechanisms to implement any joint decisions they may reach. These arrangements will not require the prior approval of the BIC as a whole and will operate independently of it.

11. The elected institutions of the members will be encouraged to develop interparliamentary links, perhaps building on the British-Irish Interparliamentary Body.

12. The full membership of the BIC will keep under review the workings of the Council, including a formal published review at an appropriate time after the Agreement comes into effect, and will contribute as appropriate to any review of the overall political agreement arising from the multi-party negotiations.

BRITISH-IRISH INTERGOVERNMENTAL CONFERENCE

1. There will be a new British-Irish Agreement dealing with the totality of relationships. It will establish a standing British-Irish Intergovernmental Conference, which will subsume both the Anglo-Irish Intergovernmental Council and the Intergovernmental Conference established under the 1985 Agreement.

2. The Conference will bring together the British and Irish Governments to promote bilateral co-operation at all levels on all matters of mutual interest within the competence of both Governments.

3. The Conference will meet as required at Summit level (Prime Minister and Taoiseach). Otherwise, Governments will be represented by appropriate Ministers. Advisers, including police and security advisers, will attend as appropriate.

4. All decisions will be by agreement between both Governments. The Governments will make determined efforts to resolve disagreements between them. There will be no derogation from the sovereignty of either Government.

5. In recognition of the Irish Government's special interest in Northern Ireland and of the extent to which issues of mutual concern arise in relation to Northern Ireland, there will be regular and frequent meetings of the Conference concerned with non-devolved Northern Ireland matters, on which the Irish Government may put forward views and proposals. These meetings, to be co-chaired by the Minister for Foreign Affairs and the Secretary of State for Northern Ireland, would also deal with all-island and cross-border co-operation on non-devolved issues.

6. Co-operation within the framework of the Conference will include facilitation of co-operation in security matters. The Conference also will address, in particular, the areas of rights, justice, prisons and policing in Northern Ireland (unless and until responsibility is devolved to a Northern Ireland administration) and will intensify co-operation between the two Governments on the all-island or cross-border aspects of these matters.

7. Relevant executive members of the Northern Ireland Administration will be involved in meetings of the Conference, and in the reviews referred to in paragraph 9 below to discuss non-devolved Northern Ireland matters.

8. The Conference will be supported by officials of the British and Irish Governments, including by a standing joint Secretariat of officials dealing with non-devolved Northern Ireland matters.

9. The Conference will keep under review the workings of the new British-Irish Agreement and the machinery and institutions established under it, including a formal published review three years after the Agreement comes into effect. Representatives of the Northern Ireland Administration will be invited to express views to the Conference in this context. The Conference will contribute as appropriate to any review of the overall political agreement arising from the multi-party negotiations but will have no power to override the democratic arrangements set up by this Agreement.

AGREEMENT

BETWEEN THE GOVERNMENT OF

THE UNITED KINGDOM OF GREAT BRITAIN AND NORTHERN IRELAND

AND

THE GOVERNMENT OF IRELAND [1]

The British and Irish Governments:

Welcoming the strong commitment to the Agreement reached on 10th April 1998 by themselves and other participants in the multi-party talks and set out in Annex 1 to this Agreement (hereinafter "the Multi-Party Agreement");

Considering that the Multi-Party Agreement offers an opportunity for a new beginning in relationships within Northern Ireland, within the island of Ireland and between the peoples of these islands;

Wishing to develop still further the unique relationship between their peoples and the close co-operation between their countries as friendly neighbours and as partners in the European Union;

Reaffirming their total commitment to the principles of democracy and non-violence which have been fundamental to the multi-party talks;

Reaffirming their commitment to the principles of partnership, equality and mutual respect and to the protection of civil, political, social, economic and cultural rights in their respective jurisdictions;

Have agreed as follows:

ARTICLE 1

The two Governments:

(i) recognise the legitimacy of whatever choice is freely exercised by a majority of the

---

1　此处标题排列方式遵照协议原文。

people of Northern Ireland with regard to its status, whether they prefer to continue to support the Union with Great Britain or a sovereign united Ireland;

(ii) recognise that it is for the people of the island of Ireland alone, by agreement between the two parts respectively and without external impediment, to exercise their right of self-determination on the basis of consent, freely and concurrently given, North and South, to bring about a united Ireland, if that is their wish, accepting that this right must be achieved and exercised with and subject to the agreement and consent of a majority of the people of Northern Ireland;

(iii) acknowledge that while a substantial section of the people in Northern Ireland share the legitimate wish of a majority of the people of the island of Ireland for a united Ireland, the present wish of a majority of the people of Northern Ireland, freely exercised and legitimate, is to maintain the Union and accordingly, that Northern Ireland's status as part of the United Kingdom reflects and relies upon that wish; and that it would be wrong to make any change in the status of Northern Ireland save with the consent of a majority of its people;

(iv) affirm that, if in the future, the people of the island of Ireland exercise their right of selfdetermination on the basis set out in sections (i) and (ii) above to bring about a united Ireland, it will be a binding obligation on both Governments to introduce and support in their respective Parliaments legislation to give effect to that wish;

(v) affirm that whatever choice is freely exercised by a majority of the people of Northern Ireland, the power of the sovereign government with jurisdiction there shall be exercised with rigorous impartiality on behalf of all the people in the diversity of their identities and traditions and shall be founded on the principles of full respect for, and equality of, civil, political, social and cultural rights, of freedom from discrimination for all citizens, and of parity of esteem and of just and equal treatment for the identity, ethos and aspirations of both communities;

(vi) recognise the birthright of all the people of Northern Ireland to identify themselves and be accepted as Irish or British, or both, as they may so choose, and accordingly confirm that their right to hold both British and Irish citizenship is accepted by both Governments and would not be affected by any future change in the status of Northern Ireland.

ARTICLE 2

The two Governments affirm their solemn commitment to support, and where appropriate implement, the provisions of the Multi-Party Agreement. In particular there shall be established in accordance with the provisions of the Multi-Party Agreement immediately on the entry into force of this Agreement, the following institutions:

(i) a North/South Ministerial Council;

(ii) the implementation bodies referred to in paragraph 9 (ii) of the section entitled "Strand Two" of the Multi-Party Agreement;

(iii) a British-Irish Council;

(iv) a British-Irish Intergovernmental Conference.

ARTICLE 3

(1) This Agreement shall replace the Agreement between the British and Irish Governments done at Hillsborough on 15th November 1985 which shall cease to have effect on entry into force of this Agreement.

(2) The Intergovernmental Conference established by Article 2 of the aforementioned Agreement done on 15th November 1985 shall cease to exist on entry into force of this Agreement.

ARTICLE 4

(1) It shall be a requirement for entry into force of this Agreement that:

(a) British legislation shall have been enacted for the purpose of implementing the provisions of Annex A to the section entitled "Constitutional Issues" of the Multi-Party Agreement;

(b) the amendments to the Constitution of Ireland set out in Annex B to the section entitled "Constitutional Issues" of the Multi-Party Agreement shall have been approved by Referendum;

(c) such legislation shall have been enacted as may be required to establish the institutions referred to in Article 2 of this Agreement.

(2) Each Government shall notify the other in writing of the completion, so far as it is concerned, of the requirements for entry into force of this Agreement. This Agreement shall enter into force on the date of the receipt of the later of the two notifications.

(3) Immediately on entry into force of this Agreement, the Irish Government shall ensure that the amendments to the Constitution of Ireland set out in Annex B to the section entitled "Constitutional Issues" of the Multi-Party Agreement take effect.

In witness thereof the undersigned, being duly authorised thereto by the respective Governments, have signed this Agreement.

Done in two originals at Belfast on the 10th day of April 1998.

ANNEX 1

The Agreement Reached in the Multi-Party Talks

ANNEX 2

Declaration on the Provisions of

Paragraph (vi) of Article 1

In Relationship to Citizenship

The British and Irish Governments declare that it is their joint understanding that the term "the people of Northern Ireland" in paragraph (vi) of Article 1 of this Agreement means, for the purposes of giving effect to this provision, all persons born in Northern Ireland and having, at the time of their birth, at least one parent who is a British citizen, an Irish citizen or is otherwise entitled to reside in Northern Ireland without any restriction on their period of residence.

选自 United Nations (UN) Peacemaker, https://peacemaker.un.org/sites/peacemaker.un.org/files/

IE%20GB_ 980410_ Northern%20Ireland%20Agreement. pdf.

推荐阅读

1. 比尔·考克瑟、林顿·罗宾斯、罗伯特·里奇：《当代英国政治》，孔新峰、蒋鲲译，北京：北京大学出版社，2009年。
2. 钱乘旦、许洁明：《英国通史》，上海：上海社会科学院出版社，2017年。

三、阿瑟·扬《1787、1788、1789年法国游记》节选

导读

阿瑟·扬（1741—1820），英国农学家。自1768年《英格兰与威尔士南部各郡六周环游记》起，他开创了一种新的游记写作方式。怀着科学调查的目的，他对经过地区的农业实践进行调查并获取有益的教训。1787年、1788年和1789年他在法国三次旅行时也抱着同样的目的，并希望对英法两国进行系统比较。仔细设计线路，获取介绍信后，他的每一站都进入了法国文人和科学精英的网络之中。阿瑟·扬的游记深刻表现了他对技术进步是解决一切经济问题，特别是农业领域的经济问题的万灵药的信念，这也是启蒙时代很多精英的态度。因此，游记特别关注农业生产及相应技术的改良、道路交通状况等。当然，他也记载了沿途的乡村、城市景观和民众生活、生产情况，尤其喜爱记录沿途小客栈的情况。尽管阿瑟·扬的评价不乏成见，但也总有一针见血的见解。由于当时正值法国革命爆发前夕，《1787、1788和1789年法国游记》的作者阿瑟·扬以其严谨的调查态度、严肃冷静的记述风格、旁观者的角度，成了这段历史的最佳见证者。

下面的内容节选自游记中1789年6月30日至7月28日的记载。阿瑟·扬在巴黎见证了国民议会在局势动荡、群情激愤中成立，他认为"一切事务看起来都结束了，革命完成了"，于6月28日离开巴黎，经过香巴尼地区、洛林地区，于7月20日在斯特拉斯堡听到了攻占巴士底狱的消息，随后向南前往弗朗什-孔泰地区。这部分游记记载了法国革命爆发时法国的政治氛围、社会状况、民情舆情、民众心态等各方面情况，观察细致入微，值得认真研读。

Arthur Young, Travels in France during the Years 1787, 1788, 1789
From Paris to Strasbourg (from 30th June to 28th July 1789)

The 30th.[1] My friend's chateau is a considerable one, and much better built than was common in England in the same period, 200 years ago; I believe, however, that this superiority was universal in France, in all the arts. They were, I apprehend, in the reign of Henry IV far beyond us in towns, houses, streets, roads, and in short, in every thing. We have since, thanks to liberty, contrived to turn the tables on them. Like all the chateaus I have seen in France, it stands close to the town, indeed joining the end of it; but the back front[2], by some very judicious plantations, has entirely the air of the country, without the sight of any buildings. There the present marquis has formed an English lawn, with some agreeable winding walks of gravel, and other decorations, to skirt it. In this lawn they are making hay; and I have had the marquis, Mons. l'Abbé[3], and some others on the stack to shew them how to make and tread it: such hot politicians! —it is well they did not set the stack on fire. Nangis is near enough to Paris for the people to be politicians; the perruquier[4] that dressed me this morning tells me, that every body is determined to pay no taxes, should the National Assembly so ordain. But the soldiers will have something to say. No, Sir, never: —be assured as we are, that the French soldiers will never fire on the people; but, if they should, it is better to be shot than starved. He gave me a frightful account of the misery of the people; whole families in the utmost distress; those that work have a pay insufficient to feed them—and many that find it difficult to get work at all. I enquired of Mons. de Guerchy concerning this, and found it true. By order of the magistrates no person is allowed to buy more than two bushels of wheat at a market, to prevent monopolizing. It is dear to common sense, that all such regulations have a direct tendency to increase the evil, but it is in vain to reason with people whose ideas are immoveably fixed. Being here on a market-day, I attended, and saw the wheat sold out under this regulation, with a party of dragoons[5] drawn up before the market-cross to prevent violence. The people quarrel with the bakers, asserting the prices they demand for bread are beyond the proportion of wheat, and proceeding from words to scuffling, raise a riot, and then run away with bread and wheat for nothing: this has happened at Nangis, and many other markets; the consequence was, that neither farmers nor bakers would supply them till they were in danger of starving, and, when they did come, prices under such circumstances must necessarily rise enormously, which

---

1　6月28日，阿瑟·扬离开巴黎，到巴黎以东的小镇南吉（Nangis）拜访盖尔希（Guerchy）男爵的庄园。30日，他正在盖尔希男爵家中。

2　指建筑的正面。

3　在18世纪，"abbé"只是一类教士的头衔，并不是真正的修道院院长。"Mons."是"先生"（Monsieur）的简写形式，现代缩写形式为"M."。

4　假发师。

5　龙骑兵，法国旧制度时期的一种军事组织。

aggravated the mischief, till troops became really necessary to give security to those who supplied the markets. I have been sifting Madame de Guerchy on the expences of living; our friend Mons. l'Abbé joined the conversation, and I collect from it, that to live in a chateau like this, with six men-servants, five maids, eight horses, a garden, and a regular table, with company, but never to go to Paris, might be done for 1000 louis [1] a year. It would in England cost 2000; the mode of living (not the price of things) is therefore cent. per cent. different. — There are gentlemen (noblesse) that live in this country on 6 or 8000 liv. [2] (2621. to 3501.), that keep two men, two maids, three horses, and a cabriolet; there are the same in England, but they are fools. Among the neighbours that visited Nangis was Mons. Trudaine de Montigny, with his new and pretty wife, to return the first visit of ceremony: he has a fine chateau at Montigny, and an estate of 4000 louis a year. This lady was Mademoiselle de Cour Breton, niece to Madame Calonne; she was to have been married to the son of Mons. Lamoignon [3], but much against her inclinations; finding that common refusals had no avail, she determined on a very uncommon one, which was to go to church, in obedience to her father's orders, and give a solemn NO instead of a yea. She was afterwards at Dijon, and never stirred but she was received with huzzas and acclamations by the people for refusing to be allied with la Cour Pleniere [4]; and her firmness was every where spoken of much to her advantage. Mons. la Luzerne was with them, nephew to the French ambassador at London, who, in some broken English, informed me, that he had learned to box of Mendoza [5]. No one can say that he has travelled without making acquisitions. Has the due d'Orleans learned to box also? The news from Paris is bad: the commotions increase greatly: and such an alarm has spread, that the Queen has called the marechal de Broglio [6] to the king's closet; he has had several conferences: the report is, that an army will be collected under him. It may be now necessary; but woeful management to have made it so.

JULY 2. . . .

The 3d. Meaux [7] was by no means in my direct road; but its district, Brie [8], is so highly celebrated for fertility, that it was an object not to omit. I was provided with letters for M. Bernier, a considerable farmer, at Chaucaunin, near Meaux; and for M. Gibert, of Neuf Moutier,

---

1　法国旧制度时期的货币，1 路易 = 24 利弗尔（livre）。
2　"liv." 为法国旧制度时期货币单位利弗尔 "livre" 的缩写，在法国货币体系中的地位相当于 "英镑"。
3　即拉穆瓦尼翁·德·巴维尔（Chrétien François de Lamoignon de Bâville, 1735—1789）。
4　本义是法国国王在节庆召集的盛大集会。1787 年 4 月，新任司法大臣拉穆瓦尼翁·德·巴维尔试图进行司法改革，以 "la cour plénière"（中文译作 "全能法院" 或 "全能法庭"）的名义建立一种最高法院，由高官显贵组成，集中司法权力，被视为专制之举，引发普遍反对。
5　英国拳击手达尼埃尔·门多萨（Daniel Mendoza, 1764—1836）。在阿瑟·扬写作的这个时期，拳击在英国成了一种常规的表演。
6　布罗伊元帅（Victor François de Broglie, 1718—1804），法国军事贵族，法兰西元帅。
7　莫城，位于巴黎东北部约 40 公里处，属塞纳-马恩省。
8　以土壤肥沃、布里奶酪出名的历史地区，大部分位于如今的塞纳-马恩省。

a considerable cultivator, whose father and himself had between them made a fortune by agriculture. The former gentleman was not at home; by the latter I was received with great hospitality; and I found in him the strongest desire to give me every information I wished. Mons. Gibert has built a very handsome and commodious house, with farming-offices, on the most ample and solid scale. I was pleased to find his wealth, which is not inconsiderable, to have arisen all from the plough. He did not forget to let me know, that he was noble; and exempted from all tailles[1]; and that he had the honors of the chace[2], his father having purchased the charge of Secretaire du Roi[3]: but he very wisely lives en fermier[4]. His wife made ready the table for dinner, and his bailiff, with the female domestic, who has the charge of the dairy, &c. both dined with us. This is in a true farming style; it has many conveniences, and looks like a plan of living, which does not promise, like the foppish modes of little gentlemen, to run through a fortune, from false shame and silly pretensions. I can find no other fault with his system than having built a house enormously beyond his plan of living, which can have no other effect than tempting some successor, less prudent than himself into expences that might dissipate all his and his father's savings. In England that would certainly be the case: the danger, however, is not equal in France.

The 4th. To Chateau Thiery[5], following the course of the Marne. The country is pleasantly varied, and hilly enough to render it a constant picture, were it inclosed. Thiery is beautifully situated on the same river. I arrived there by five o'clock, and wished, in a period so interesting to France, and indeed to all Europe, to see a newspaper. I asked for a coffee-house, not one in the town. Here are two parishes, and some thousands of inhabitants, and not a newspaper to be seen by a traveller, even in a moment when all ought to be anxiety. —What stupidity, poverty, and want of circulation! This people hardly deserve to be free; and should there be the least attempt with vigour to keep them otherwise, it can hardly fail of succeeding. To those who have been used to travel amidst the energetic and rapid circulation of wealth, animation, and intelligence of England, it is not possible to describe, in words adequate to one's feelings, the dulness and stupidity of France. I have been to day on one of their greatest roads, within thirty miles of Paris, yet I have not seen one diligence, and met but a single gentleman's carriage, nor anything else on the road that looked like a gentleman. —30 miles.

The 5th. . . .

The 7th. To Epernay[6], famous for its wines. I had letters for Mons. Paretilaine, one of the

---

1 军役税，法国旧制度时期的一种赋税。由于贵族、城市居民以各种理由享有免交此税的特权，军役税的重负基本完全由农民承担，是农民最沉重的负担。
2 法国旧制度时期，狩猎属于贵族特权。
3 "国王秘书"，法国旧制度时期卖官鬻爵的一种头衔，没有实务。
4 "作为农场主"。
5 沙托-蒂埃里，位于埃纳省，属于历史上的香巴尼（香槟）地区。
6 埃佩尔奈，位于埃纳省东边的马恩省，属于历史上的香巴尼地区，距离巴黎130公里，位于从巴黎前往斯特拉斯堡的大道上，以美酒闻名，号称香槟酒的"仓库"。

most considerable merchants, who was so obliging as to enter, with two other gentlemen, into a minute disquisition of the produce and profit of the fine vineyards. The hotel de Rohan here is a very good inn, where I solaced myself with a bottle of excellent vin mousseux [1] for 40ʃ. [2] and drank prosperity to true liberty in France. —12 miles.

The 8th. . . .

The 9th. To Chalons [3], through a poor country and poor crops. M. de Broussonet had given me a letter to Mons. Sabbatier, secretary to the academy of sciences, but he was absent. A regiment passing to Paris, an officer at the inn addressed me in English: —He had learned, he said, in America, damme! —He had taken lord Cornwallis, damme! —Marechal Broglio was appointed to command an army of 50,000 men near Paris—it was necessary—the tiers état [4] were running mad—and wanted some wholesome correction;—they want to establish a republic—absurd! Pray, Sir, what did you fight for in America? To establish a republic. What was so good for the Americans, is it so bad for the French? Aye, damme! that is the way the English want to be revenged. It is, to be sure, no bad opportunity. Can the English follow a better example? He then made many enquiries about what we thought and said upon it in England: and I may remark, that almost every person I meet has the same idea—The English must be very well contented at our confusion. They feel pretty pointedly what they deserve. —12$\frac{1}{2}$ miles.

The 10th. . . .

The 11th. . . .

The 12th. Walking up a long hill, to ease my mare, I was joined by a poor woman, who complained of the times, and that it was a sad country; demanding her reasons, she said her husband had but a morsel of land, one cow, and a poor little horse, yet they had a franchar (42 lb.) of wheat, and three chickens, to pay as a quit-rent to one Seigneur; and four franchar of oats, one chicken and 1ʃ. to pay to another, besides very heavy tailles and other taxes. She had seven children, and the cow's milk helped to make the soup. But why, instead of a horse, do not you keep another cow? Oh, her husband could not carry his produce so well without a horse; and asses are little used in the country. It was said, at present, that something was to be done by some great folks for such poor ones, but she did not know who nor how, but God send us better, car les tailles & les droits nous ecrasent. [5] —This woman, at no great distance, might have been

---

1 起泡葡萄酒。香槟酒是最著名的一种起泡葡萄酒，且受产区保护，即只有在法国香巴尼地区采用特定的葡萄品种，并运用传统香槟工艺酿成的起泡酒才叫香槟酒。
2 "ʃ"是小写字母"s"的一种印刷体，本用于单词开头或两个"s"连写中的第一个，由于容易与小写字母"f"混淆，19世纪以后逐渐废弃不用。本文中"ʃ"是法国旧制度时期的货币单位"苏"（sou 或 sol）的缩写，20 苏 = 1 利弗尔。
3 指马恩河畔的沙隆，现已更名为香巴尼的沙隆，为马恩省省府。
4 第三等级。
5 "因为军役税和其他税费压垮了我们。"

taken for sixty or seventy, her figure was so bent, and her face so furrowed and hardened by labor, —but she said she was only twenty-eight. An Englishman who has not travelled, cannot imagine the figure made by infinitely the greater part of the countrywomen in France; it speaks, at the first sight, hard and severe labor: I am inclined to think, that they work harder than the men, and this, united with the more miserable labor of bringing a new race of slaves into the world, destroys absolutely all symmetry of person and every feminine appearance. To what are we to attribute this difference in the manners of the lower people in the two kingdoms? To GOVERNMENT. —23 miles.

The 13th. Leave Mar-le-Tour[1] at four in the morning: the village herdsman was sounding his horn; and it was droll to see every door vomiting out its hogs or sheep, and some a few goats, the flock collecting as it advances. Very poor sheep, and the pigs with mathematical backs, large segments of small circles. They must have abundance of commons here, but, if I may judge by the report of the animals carcases, dreadfully overstocked. To Metz[2], one of the strongest places in France; pass three draw-bridges, but the command of water must give a strength equal to its works. The common garrison is 10,000 men, but there are fewer at present. Waited on M. de Payen, secretary of the academy of sciences; he asked my plan, which I explained; he appointed me at four in the afternoon at the academy, as there would be seance[3] held; and he promised to introduce me to some persons who could answer my enquiries. I attended accordingly, when I found the academy assembled at one of their weekly meetings. Mons. Payen introduced me to the members, and, before they proceeded to their business, they had the goodness to sit in council on my enquiries, and to resolve many of them. In the "Almanach des Trois Evechés,"[4] 1789, this academy is said to have been instituted particularly for agriculture; I turned to the list of their honorary members to see what attention they had paid to the men who, in the present age, have advanced that art. I found an Englishman, Dom Cowley, of London. Who is Dom Cowley?—Dined at the table d'hôte[5], with seven officers, out of whose mouths, at this important moment, in which conversation is as free as the press, not one word issued for which I would give a straw, nor a subject touched on of more importance, than a coat, or a puppy dog. At table d'hôtes of officers, you have a voluble garniture of bawdry or nonsense; at those of merchants, a mournful and stupid silence. Take the mass of mankind, and you have more good sense in half an hour in England than in half a year in France—Government! Again: —all—all—is government. —15 miles.

---

1 马尔拉图尔（Mars-la-Tour），位于法国东北部的默尔特-摩泽尔省，属于历史上的洛林地区。
2 梅斯，位于法国、德国和卢森堡三国的交界处，莫泽尔省省府，洛林地区的中心城市。
3 科学院的集会。
4 《三主教区历书》。三主教区指16世纪宗教改革时期，德意志新教王公为获取法国的支持而归并给法国的三个主教区梅斯、图勒和凡尔登。
5 指旅馆中，在规定的时间里客人共享的、价格固定的餐食。

The 14th. They have a cabinet literaire [1] at Metz, something like that I described at Nantes, but not on so great a plan; and they admit any person to read or go in and out for a day, on paying 4ʃ. To this I eagerly resorted, and the news from Paris, both in the public prints, and by the information of a gentleman, I found to be interesting. Versailles and Paris are surrounded by troops: 35,000 men are assembled, and 20,000 more on the road, large trains of artillery collected, and all the preparations of war. The assembling of such a number of troops has added to the scarcity of bread; and the magazines that have been made for their support, are not easily by the people distinguished from those they suspect of being collected by monopolists. This has aggravated their evils almost to madness; so that the confusion and tumult of the capital are extreme. A gentleman of an excellent understanding, and apparently of consideration, from the attention paid him, with whom I had some conversation on the subject, lamented in the most pathetic terms, the situation of his country; he considers a civil war as impossible to be avoided. There is not, he added, a doubt but the court, finding it impossible to bring the National Assembly to terms, will get rid of them; a bankruptcy at the same moment is inevitable; the union of such confusion must be a civil war; and it is now only by torrents of blood that we have any hope of establishing a freer constitution: yet it must be established; for the old government is rivetted to abuses that are insupportable. He agreed with me entirely, that the propositions of the seance royale, though certainly not sufficiently satisfactory, yet, were the ground for a negociation, that would have secured by degrees all even that the sword can give us, let it be as successful as it will. The purse—the power of the purse is every thing; skilfully managed, with so necessitous a government as ours, it would, one after another, have gained all we wished. As to a war, Heaven knows the event; and if we have success, success itself may ruin us; France may have a Cromwell in its bosom, as well as England. Metz is, without exception, the cheapest town I have been in. The table d'hôte is 36ʃ. a head, plenty of good wine included. We were ten, and had two courses and a dessert of ten dishes each, and those courses plentiful. The supper is the same; I had mine, of a pint of wine and a large plate of chaudiés [2], in my chamber, for 10ʃ. a horse, hay, and corn 25ʃ. and nothing for the apartment; my expence was therefore 71ʃ. a day, or 2s. $11\frac{1}{2}$ d. [3]; and with the table d'hôte for supper, would have been but 97ʃ. or 4s. $0\frac{1}{2}$ d. —In addition, much civility and good attendance. It is at the Faisan. Why are the cheapest inns in France the best?—The country to Pont-à-Mousson [4] a is all of bold feature. —The river Moselle, which is considerable, runs in the vale, and the hills on either

---

1 阅览室。

2 一种饼干类的糕点。

3 2s. $11\frac{1}{2}$ d.：2先令11.5便士。

4 蓬阿穆松（Pont-à-Mousson），位于默尔特-摩泽尔省，梅斯与南锡之间。

side are high. Not far from Metz there are the remains of an ancient aqueduct for conducting the waters of a spring across the Moselle: there are many arches left on this side, with the houses of poor people built between them. At Pont-à-Mousson Mons. Pichon, the sub-delegué of the intendant[1], to whom I had letters, received me politely, satisfied my enquiries, which he was well able to do from his office, and conducted me to see whatever was worth viewing in the town. It does not contain much; the école militaire[2], for the sons of the poor nobility, also the convent de Premonte, which has a very fine library, 107 feet long and 25 broad. I was introduced to the abbot as a person who had some knowledge in agriculture. —17 miles.

The 15th. I went to Nancy, with great expectation, having heard it represented as the prettiest town in France. I think, on the whole, it is not undeserving the character in point of building, direction, and breadth of streets. —Bourdeaux is far more magnificent; Bayonne and Nantes are more lively; but there is more equality in Nancy; it is almost all good; and the public buildings are numerous. The place royale, and the adjoining area are superb. Letters from Paris! all confusion! the ministry removed: Mons. Necker[3] ordered to quit the kingdom without noise. The effect on the people of Nancy was considerable. —I was with Mons. Willemet when his letters arrived, and for some time his house was full of enquirers; all agreed, that it was fatal news, and that it would occasion great commotions. What will be the result at Nancy? The answer was in effect the same from all I put this question to: We are a provincial town, we must wait to see what is done at Paris; but every thing is to be feared from the people, because bread is so dear, they are half starved, and are consequently ready for commotion. —This is the general feeling; they are as nearly concerned as Paris; but they dare not stir; they dare not even have an opinion of their own till they know what Paris thinks; so that if a starving populace were not in question, no one would dream of moving. This confirms what I have often heard remarked, that the deficit would not have produced the revolution but in concurrence with the price of bread. Does not this shew the infinite consequence of great cities to the liberty of mankind? Without Paris, I question whether the present revolution, which is fast working in France, could possibly have had an origin. It is not in the villages of Syria or Diarbekir that the Grand Seigneur meets with a murmur against his will; it is at Constantinople that he is obliged to manage and mix caution even with despotism. Mr. Willemet, who is demonstrator of botany, shewed me the botanical garden, but it is in a condition that speaks the want of better funds. He introduced me to a Mons. Durival, who has written on the vine, and gave me one of his

---

1 督办，也译作总督，国王委派至地方的最高长官，相当于省长；督办代理人（sub-delegué），督办委派至下一级的官员，相当于市长。

2 军事学校。

3 雅克·内克（1732—1804），瑞士银行家，1777 年至 1781 年出任法国财政总管，致力整顿财政，实现政府收支平衡。1788 年 8 月，法国面临严重的经济危机和财政危机，内克再次被召回，出任财政总管，试图将法国从崩溃的边缘拯救回来。内克积极筹备三级会议，并支持三级会议的投票方式改革。1789 年 7 月 11 日，内克被解职，激起了法国人的愤怒，谣言四起，认为国王要进攻巴黎或逮捕三级会议的代表，最终引发了 7 月 14 日攻占巴士底狱的风暴。

treatises, and two of his own on botanical subjects. He also conducted me to Mons. l'Abbé Grandpère, a gentleman curious in gardening, who, as soon as he knew that I was an Englishman, whimsically took it into his head to introduce me to a lady, my countrywoman, who hired, he said, the greatest part of his house. I remonstrated against the impropriety of this, but all in vain; the Abbé had never travelled, and thought that if he were at the distance of England from France (the French are not commonly good geographers) he should be very glad to see a Frenchman; and that, by parity of reasoning, this lady must be the same to meet a countryman she never saw or heard of. Away he went, and would not rest till I was conducted into her apartment. It was the dowager Lady Douglas; she was unaffected, and good enough not to be offended at such a strange intrusion. —She had been here but a few days; had two fine daughters with her, and a beautiful Kamchatka dog; she was much troubled with the intelligence her friends in the town had just given her, that she would, in all probability, be forced to move again, as the news of Mons. Necker's removal, and the new ministry being appointed, would certainly occasion such dreadful tumults, that a foreign family would probably find it equally dangerous and disagreeable. —18 miles.

The 16th. All the houses at Nancy have tin eave troughs and pipes, which render walking the streets much more easy and agreeable; it is also an additional consumption, which is politically useful. Both this place and Luneville[1] are lighted in the English manner, instead of the lamps being strung across the streets as in other French towns. Before I quit Nancy, let me caution the unwary traveller, if he is not a great lord, with plenty of money that he does not know what to do with, against the hotel d'Angleterre; a bad dinner 3 liv. and for the room as much more. A pint of wine, and a plate of chaudié 20∫. which at Metz was 10∫. and in addition, I liked so little my treatment, that I changed my quarters to the hotel de Halle, where, at the table d'hôte, I had the company of some agreeable officers, two good courses, and a dessert, for 36∫. with a bottle of wine. The chamber 20∫. ; for building, however, the hotel d'Angleterre is much superior, and is the first inn. In the evening to Luneville. The country about Nancy is pleasing. —17 miles.

The 17th. . . .

The 18th. . . .

The 19th. . . .

The 20th. To Strasbourg, through one of the richest scenes of soil and cultivation to be met with in France, and rivalled only by Flanders, which however, exceeds it. I arrived there at a critical moment, which I thought would have broken my neck; a detachment of horse, with their trumpets on one side, a party of infantry, with their drums beating on the other, and a great mob hallooing, frightened my French mare; and I could scarcely keep her from trampling on Messrs.[2]

1　吕内维尔，位于南锡与斯特拉斯堡之间的城市。

2　"先生"（Monsieur）的复数形式"Messieurs"的缩写，现代缩写形式为"MM."。

the tiers etat. On arriving at the inn, hear the interesting news of the revolt of Paris. —The Guardes Francoises[1] joining the people; the little dependence on the rest of the troops; the taking the Bastile; and the institution of the milice bourgeoise[2]; in a word, of the absolute overthrow of the old government. Every thing being now decided, and the kingdom absolutely in the hands of the assembly, they have the power to make a new constitution, such as they think proper; and it will be a great spectacle for the world to view, in this enlightened age, the representatives of twenty-five millions of people sitting on the construction of a new and better order and fabric of liberty, than Europe has yet offered. It will now be seen, whether they will copy the constitution of England, freed from its faults, or attempt, from theory, to frame something absolutely speculative: in the former case, they will prove a blessing to their country; in the latter they will probably involve it in inextricable confusions and civil wars, perhaps not in the present period, but certainly at some future one. I hear nothing of their removing from Versailles; if they stay there under the controul of an armed mob, they must make a government that will please the mob; but they will, I suppose, be wise enough to move to some central town Tours, Blois, or Orleans, where their deliberations may be free. But the Parisian spirit of commotion spreads quickly; it is here; the troops that were near breaking my neck, are employed, to keep an eye on the people who shew signs of an intended revolt. They have broken the windows of some magistrates that are no favourites; and a great mob of them is at this moment assembled demanding clamourously to have meat at 5ʃ. a pound. They have a cry among them that will conduct them to good lengths, —Point d'impôt & vivent les etâts.[3]— Waited on Mons. Herman, professor of natural history in the University here, to whom I had letters; he replied to some of my questions, and introduced me for others to Mons. Zimmer, who having been in some degree a practitioner, had understanding enough of the subject to afford me some information that was valuable. View the public buildings, and cross the Rhine passing for some little distance into Germany, but no new features to mark a change; Alsace is Germany, and the change great on descending the mountains. The exterior of the cathedral is fine, and the tower singularly light and beautiful; it is well known to be one of the highest in Europe; commands a noble and rich plain, through which the Rhine, from the number of its islands, has the appearance of a chain of lakes rather than of a river. —Monument of marechal Saxe, &c. &c. I am puzzled about going to Carlsrhue[4], the residence of the Margrave of Baden: it was an old intention to do it, if ever I was within an hundred miles; for there are some features in the reputation of that sovereign, which made me wish to be there. He fixed Mr. Taylor, of Bifrons in

---

1 法兰西卫队，旧制度时期法国国王的护卫部队之一。这支部队的大部分军队转向革命，引领了巴士底狱风暴，并构成了革命时期国民卫队的骨干。
2 资产阶级民兵。7月13日第三等级代表发布决议，建立一支资产者组成的民兵队伍。
3 "不纳捐税，三级会议万岁！"
4 德国巴登-符腾堡州的第二大城市卡尔斯鲁厄（Karlsruhe）的旧式拼写，在巴登州与符腾堡州合并之前，曾为巴登州的首府。

Kent, whose husbandry I describe in my Eastern Tour, on a large farm; and the œconomistes[1], in their writings, speak much of an experiment he made in their Physiocratical rubbish, which, however erroneous their principles might be, marked much merit in the prince. Mons. Herman tells me also, that he has sent a person into Spain to purchase rams for the improvement of wool, I wish he had fixed on somebody likely to understand a good ram, which a professor of botany is not likely to do too well. This botanist is the only person Mons. Herman knows at Carlsrhue, and therefore can give me no letter thither, and how can I go, unknown to all the world, to the residence of a sovereign prince, for Mr. Taylor has left him, is a difficulty apparently insurmountable. —$22\frac{1}{2}$ miles.

The 21st. I have spent some time this morning at the cabinet literaire, reading the gazettes and journals that give an account of the transactions at Paris: and I have had some conversation with several sensible and intelligent men on the present revolution. The spirit of revolt is gone forth into various parts of the kingdom; the price of bread has prepared the populace every where for all sorts of violence; at Lyons there have been commotions as furious as at Paris, and the same at a great many other places: Dauphiné is in arms; and Bretagne in absolute rebellion. The idea is, that the people will, from hunger, be driven to revolt; and when once they find any other means of subsistence than that of honest labor, every thing will be to be feared. Of such consequence it is to a country, and indeed to every country, to have a good police of corn; a police that shall by securing a high price to the farmer, encourage his culture enough to secure the people at the same time from famine. My anxiety about Carlsrhue is now at an end; the Margrave is at Spaw; I shall not therefore think of going. —Night—I have been witness to a scene curious to a foreigner; but dreadful to Frenchmen that are considerate. Passing through the square of the hotel de ville[2], the mob were breaking the windows with stones, notwithstanding an officer and a detachment of horse was in the square. Perceiving that their numbers not only increased, but that they grew bolder and bolder every moment, I thought it worth staying to see what it would end in, and clambered on to the roof of a row of low stalls opposite the building, against which their malice was directed. Here I beheld the whole commodiously. Perceiving that the troops would not attack them, except in words and menaces, they grew more violent, and furiously attempted to beat the door in pieces with iron crows; placing ladders to the windows. In about a quarter of an hour, which gave time for the assembled magistrates to escape by a back door, they burst all open, and entered like a torrent with a universal shout of the spectators. From that minute a shower of casements, sashes, shutters, chairs, tables, sophas, books, papers, pictures, &c., rained incessantly from all the windows of the house, which is seventy or eighty feet long, and which was then succeeded by tiles, skirting

---

1 指 18 世纪后期以魁奈为首的重农学派。在 18、19 世纪的多数文献中，这个学派的成员统称 "经济学家"。
2 市政厅。

boards, bannisters, frame-work, and every part of the building that force could detach. The troops, both horse and foot, were quiet spectators. They were at first too few to interpose, and, when they became more numerous, the mischief was too far advanced to admit of any other conduct than guarding every avenue around, permitting none to go to the scene of action, but letting every one that pleased retire with his plunder; guards being at the same time placed at the doors of the churches, and all public buildings. I was for two hours a spectator at different places of the scene, secure myself from the falling furniture, but near enough to see a fine lad of about 14 crushed to death by something as he was handing plunder to a woman, I suppose his mother, from the horror pictured in her countenance. I remarked several common soldiers, with their white cockades, among the plunderers, and instigating the mob even in sight of the officers of the detachment. There were amongst them people so decently dressed, that I regarded them with no small surprize: —they destroyed all the public archives; the streets for some way around strewed with papers; this has been a wanton mischief; for it will be the ruin of many families unconnected with the magistrates.

The 22d. . . .

The 23d. . . .

The 24th. . . .

The 25th. . . .

The 26th. . . .

The 27th. To Besançon[1]; the country mountain, rock, and wood, above the river; some scenes are fine. I had not arrived an hour before I saw a peasant pass the inn on horseback, followed by an officer of the guard bourgeois, of which there are 1200 here, and 200 under arms, and his party-colored detachment, and these by some infantry and cavalry. I asked, why the militia took the pas of the king's troops? For a very good reason, they replied, the troops would be attacked and knocked on the head, but the populace will not resist the milice. This peasant, who is a rich proprietor, applied for a guard to protect his house, in a village where there is much plundering and burning. The mischiefs which have been perpetrated in the country, towards the mountains and Vesoul[2], are numerous and shocking. Many chateaus have been burnt, others plundered, the seigneurs hunted down like wild beasts, their wives and daughters ravished, their papers and titles burnt, and all their property destroyed: and these abominations not inflicted on marked persons, who were odious for their former conduct or principles, but an indiscriminating blind rage for the love of plunder. Robbers, galley-slaves, and villains of all denominations, have collected and instigated the peasants to commit all sorts of outrages. Some gentlemen at the table d'hôte informed me, that letters were received from the

---

1 贝桑松，杜省首府，历史上弗朗什-孔泰（Franche-Comté）地区的首府。
2 沃苏勒，弗朗什-孔泰大区上索恩省省府，法国重要的农畜业区。

Maconois, the Lyonois, Auvergne, Dauphné¹, &c. and that similar commotions and mischiefs were perpetrating every where; and that it was expected they would pervade the whole kingdom. The backwardness of France is beyond credibility in every thing that pertains to intelligence. From Strasbourg hither, I have not been able to see a newspaper. Here I asked for the Cabinet Literaire? None. The gazettes? At the coffee-house. Very easily replied; but not so easily found. Nothing but the *Gazette de France*²; for which at this period, a man of common sense would not give one sol. To four other coffee-houses; at some no paper at all, not even the Mercure³; at the Caffé Militaire, the *Courier de l'Europe*⁴ a fortnight old; and well dressed people are now talking of the news of two or three weeks past, and plainly by their discourse know nothing of what is passing. The whole town of Besançon has not been able to afford me a sight of the *Journal de Paris*⁵, nor of any paper that gives a detail of the transactions of the states; yet it is the capital of a province, large as half a dozen English counties, and containing 25,000 souls,—with strange to say! the post coming in but three times a week. At this eventful moment, with no licence, nor even the least restraint on the press, not one paper established at Paris for circulation in the provinces, with the necessary steps taken by affiche⁶, or placard⁷, to inform the people in all the towns of its establishment. For what the country knows to the contrary, their deputies are in the Bastile, instead of the Bastile being razed; so the mob plunder, burn, and destroy, in complete ignorance: and yet, with all these shades of darkness, these clouds of tenebrity, this universal mass of ignorance, there are men every day in the states, who are puffing themselves off for the FIRST NATION IN EUROPE! the GREATEST PEOPLE IN THE UNIVERSE! as if the political juntos, or literary circles of a capital constituted a people; instead of the universal illumination of knowledge, acting by rapid intelligence on minds prepared by habitual energy of reasoning to receive, combine, and comprehend it. That this dreadful ignorance of the mass of the people, of the events that most intimately concern them, is owing to the old government, no one can doubt; it is however curious to remark, that if the nobility of other provinces are hunted like those of Franche Compté, of which there is little reason to doubt, that whole order of men undergo a proscription, suffer like sheep, without making the least effort to resist the attack. This appears marvellous, with a body that have an army of 150,000 men in their hands; for though a part of those troops would certainly disobey their leaders, yet let it be remembered, that out of the 40,000, or possibly 100,000 noblesse of France, they might, if they had intelligence and union amongst themselves, fill half the ranks of

---

1 马孔人，里昂人，奥弗涅，多菲内。
2 《法兰西公报》。
3 《法兰西信使报》(*Mercure de France*) 的简称，法国最古老的报纸，创刊于 17 世纪。
4 《欧洲邮报》。
5 《巴黎日报》，法国最早的日报，创刊于 1777 年。
6 法语，布告。
7 布告。

more than half the regiments of the kingdom, with men who have fellow-feelings and fellow-sufferings with themselves; but no meetings, no associations among them; no union with military men; no taking refuge in the ranks of regiments to defend or avenge their cause; fortunately for France they fall without a struggle, and die without a blow. That universal circulation of intelligence, which in England transmits the least vibration of feeling or alarm, with electric sensibility, from one end of the kingdom to another, and which unites in bands of connection men of similar interests and situations, has no existence in France. Thus it may be said, perhaps with truth, that the fall of the king, court, lords, nobles, army, church, and parliaments [1] is owing to a want of intelligence being quickly circulated, consequently is owing to the very effects of that thraldom in which they held the people: it is therefore a retribution rather than a punishment. —18 miles.

The 28th. At the table d'hôte last night a person gave an account of being stopped at Salins [2] for want of a passport, and suffering the greatest inconveniencies; I found it necessary, therefore, to demand one for myself, and went accordingly to the Bureau; this was the house of a Mons. Bellamy, an attorney; with whom the following dialogue ensued:

Mais, Monsieur, qui me repondra de vous? Est ce que personne vous connoit? Connaissez vous quelqun a Besançon?

Non personne, mon dessein etoit d'aller a Vesoul d'oü j'aurois eu des lettres, mais j'ai changê de route a cause de ces tumultes.

Monsieur je ne vous connois pas, & si vous etes inconnu a Besançon vous ne pouvez avoir de passport.

Mais voici mes lettres j'en ai plusieurs pour d'autres villes en France, il y a en même d'adressêes a Vesoul e a Arbois, ouvrez & lisez les, & vous trouverez que je ne suis pas inconnu ailleurs quoique je le sois a Besançon.

N'importe; je ne vous connois pas, il n'y a personne ici qui vous connoisse ainsi vous n'aurez point de passport.

Je vous dit Monsieur que ces lettres vous expliqueront.

Il me faut des gens, et non pas des lettres pour m'expliquer qui vous etes; ces lettres ne me valent rien.

Cette façon d'agir me parôit assez singuliere; apparaement que vous la croyez tres honnête; pour moi, Monsieur, j'en pense bien autrement.

Eh Monsieur je ne m'en soucie de ce que vous en pensez.

En verité voici ce qui s'appelle, avoir des manieres gracieuses envers un etranger; c'est la premiere, fois que j'ai eu a faire avec ces Messieurs du tiers etat, & vous m'avourez qu'il n'y a rien ici qui puisse me donner une haute idée du caracteré de ces Messieurs là.

---

1 此处指高等法院，不是议会。
2 萨兰莱班（Salins-les-Bains），位于弗朗什-孔泰大区的汝拉省。此地字面意义为"洗浴用的盐水"，以用于洗浴和制盐的盐水出名。

Monsieur, cela m'est fort égal.

Je donnerai a mon retour en Angleterre le detail de mon voyage au publique, & assurement Monsieur je n'oublirai pas d'enregistrer ce trait de vôtre politesse, il vous fait tant d'honneure, & à ceux pour qui vous agissez.

Monsieur je regarde tout cela avec la derniere indifference. [1]

My gentleman's manner was more offensive than his words; he walked backward and forward among his parchments, with an air veritablement d'un commis de bureau [2]. —These passports are new things from new men, in new power, and show that they do not bear their new honors too meekly. Thus it is impossible for me, without running my head against a wall, to go see the Salins, or to Arbois [3], where I have a letter from M. de Broussonet, but I must take my chance and get to Dijon as fast as I can, where the president de Virly knows me, having spent some days at Bradfield, unless indeed being a president and a nobleman he has got knocked on the head by the tiers état. At night to the play; miserable performers; the theatre, which has not been built many years, is heavy; the arch that parts the stage from the house is like the entrance of a cavern, and the line of the amphitheatre, that of a wounded eel; I do not like the air and manners of the people here—and I would see Besançon swallowed up by an earthquake before I would live in it. The music, and bawling, and squeaking of *l'Epreuve Villageoise* [4] of Gretry, which is wretched, had no power to put me in better humour. I will not take leave of this place, to which I never desire to come again, without saying that they have a fine promenade; and that Mons. Arthaud, the arpenteur [5], to whom I applied for information, without any letter of recommendation was liberal and polite, and answered my enquiries satisfactorily.

The 29th. . . .

选自 Arthur Young, *Travels in France during the Years 1787, 1788, 1789*, London：George Bell and Sons，1909, pp. 188-218.

1　——但是，先生，谁为您做担保呢？您认识哪个人呢？您认识贝桑松的哪个人吗？——没人，我的计划是到沃苏勒去，我有去那里的介绍信，但因为这些骚乱我改变了路线。——先生，我不认识您，如果贝桑松没人认识您，您就不能拿到通行证。——但这是我的介绍信，我有好几封去法国其他城市的介绍信，其中还有一封去沃苏勒和阿尔布瓦的，您打开读一读，您就会发现尽管在贝桑松没人认识我，但在其他地方有人认识我。——没用。我不认识您，这里也没有人认识您，所以您拿不到通行证。——我告诉您了，先生，这些信能给您解释清楚。——我需要有人，而不是信件给我解释您是谁，这些信对我一文不值。——我觉得这种方式太奇怪了，看来您非常信任这种方式，但我呢，先生，我想得不一样。——咳，先生，我不在乎您怎么想。——说真的，这是人们所说的对外国人的亲切有礼的方式了。这是我第一次与第三等级的这些先生们打交道，您承认这里没有任何人能够对这些先生们的特点提供一个精确的看法。——先生，这对我来说是无所谓的。——回到英格兰之后，我会把我的旅行的细节公之于众。先生，我肯定不会忘了将您这些礼貌的话记下来的，这些话真给您和您对待的人带来荣耀。——先生，我对这些完全不在乎。

2　真正的办公室职员的表情。

3　阿尔布瓦，位于弗朗什-孔泰大区的汝拉省。

4　《乡村里的考验》，安德雷-埃内斯特-莫德斯特·格雷特里（André-Ernest-Modeste Grétry）创作的两幕滑稽剧，1784 年首次在凡尔赛宫上演，接下来一个世纪传遍欧洲各地。

5　土地测量员。

四、一封被篡改的伏尔泰致达朗贝尔的信

导读

自 1685 年废除《南特敕令》之后，法国新教徒（胡格诺派）一直受到严重的宗教迫害。1761 年 10 月 13 日晚至 14 日凌晨，图卢兹布商让·卡拉斯之子马克·安托万·卡拉斯死亡。图卢兹人纷纷传闻，马克·安托万·卡拉斯是由于想改宗天主教而被其新教家庭，特别是其父亲谋杀的。1762 年 3 月 9 日，图卢兹高等法院判处让·卡拉斯有罪，并以轮刑处决了他。随后，让·卡拉斯的家人遭到驱逐，两个女儿也被关进修道院。卡拉斯案是当时连续发生的因宗教偏见未得到司法公正处理的案件之一，是伏尔泰插手并帮助平反的司法案件中最著名的一个。此案使伏尔泰获得了整个欧洲"公众的喝彩"，被视为正义和人道的捍卫者。

给好友达朗贝尔写这封信时，伏尔泰刚刚获悉此案。当时天主教徒指责让·卡拉斯出于宗教狂热而杀子，新教徒则认为让·卡拉斯是无辜的，图卢兹高等法院出于宗教狂热而制造冤案。伏尔泰当时正委托朋友们调查案件详情，在此信中表达了对宗教狂热的憎恶。

然而，1762 年 7 月，此信被翻译为英文并被大肆篡改，增加了对法国国王、当权大臣、贵族以及法兰西民族侮辱谩骂的内容，发表在《圣詹姆斯纪事》(*St. James's Chronicle*) 上，紧接着又被《绅士杂志》(*Gentleman's Magazine*) 转载。1762 年秋季，正当伏尔泰为给卡拉斯案平反而游说法国的高官显贵时，这封伪信传播至法国，给伏尔泰的活动造成不少麻烦。与真信相比，这封伪信不仅是了解当时处于七年战争之中的英法对敌宣传的有趣资料，也可用于一窥当时英国媒体的职业操守。

A Falsified Letter from Voltaire to Jean Le Rond d'Alembert

My very dear, and very great Philosopher,

So you have finished the Reading of that impertinent little Libel, of that impertinent little Rogue of a Priest, who has so often been at my Country House, and been there made much of. *The Journal of the Encyclopaedia*, the best of his Works, is what preserves that Crackling, frittering Morsel from Infamy. Thus you see, my dear Friend, that the Presbyterians are not a Bit better than the Jesuits; and that these do not deserve to beg their Bread more than the Jansenists.

You have done to the little dirty City of Geneva an Honor it did not deserve. They performed CASSANDRA on my Stage at Ferney agreeable to your Taste. The grave and austere Ministers did not dare to appear there, but they sent their Daughters. I saw both Men and Women melt into Tears; and indeed never was Piece so well performed: afterwards a Supper for 200 Spectators, and a grand Ball. This is the Manner I have my Revenge, as often as I can, of these good People.

At Thoulouse they lately hanged one of their Preachers: this rendered them a little more gentle. But one of their Brethren is just now broke upon the Wheel, being falsely accused of having hanged his Son out of Spite to our Holy Religion; to which, as supposed, the good Father suspected his Son has a secret Inclination.

Thoulouse more foolish yet, more fanatic than Geneva, deemed the hanged Youth a Martyr. They never thought of examining if he had hanged himself, according to the pious Custom of the Sage Children of Albion: They buried him however pompously: The Parliament was present at the Ceremony, barefooted. The new Saint was invoked: After which, the Court, for criminal affairs, by a Plurality of Voices, eight against six, sentenced the Father to be broke on the Wheel. This Judgement was so much the more Catholic, as there was no Proof against him. He was a good Citizen, and a prolific Father, having had five Children, including him that was hanged. He bemoaned, in his dying Hours, his executed Son; and, under each stroke of the Wheel, protested his own Innocence: He cited the Parliament to the Tribunal of God!

All the heretic Cantons, all tender Christian Hearts, cry out aloud against this Execution! All pronounce us a Nation as barbarous as we are frivolous; that knows how to Torture, and cut Capers—but have forgot how to fight; that can go from a Massacre of Saint Bartholomew to a Comic Opera; and are become the Horror and Contempt of all Europe. What an Age do we live in! It is the Dregs of all Ages. What Ministers! what Generals! what Nobility! what Nation! We are immersed in Debauchery and in Infamy: Court and City are all one: Citizens, Courtiers, Priests, Women—all are Prostitutes. It is a Gulph of Meanness and Prostitution! I am sorry for it; for we were formed to be agreeable Stage-Dancers, fitted to divert; but we are now become the poltroon Prostitutes, the Scum of the World.

I promise you, my Friend, not to go to Geneva, because only small Fools and petty Tyrants dwell there: —nor to Thoulouse, because they have none but Knaves, Fools, and Fanatics: —nor to Paris, because, very soon, none but Whores, Rogues, and Beggars, will live there.

For God's Sake, and for the Sake of that little God Humanity, which still just vegetates, but with little Regard, on Earth, be pleased to make as execrable as you can that barbarous and shocking Fanaticism that has condemned a Father for hanging his Son, or that has broke on the Wheel an innocent Father, by eight rascally Counsellors and Tutors to a King of Cards.

If I was a Minister of State like Richlieu I would send these eight assassins of the Fleur de Lis [1], attended by all the Rabble of Thoulouse, with the Parliament in their Front and Rear, to the Gallies; and there, barefooted, with Torch in Hand, they should annually prostitute themselves before the Shrine of this innocently executed Father, to ask Pardon of God, and solemnly implore him, soon or late, to annihilate this cursed and perverse Race of Roman Catholicks.

1　百合花纹饰，法国王室的徽章图案。

Tell me, prithee, what Corps in France you despise the most. Nota, I just hear from Marseilles, that a Criminal, condemned there for Murder, with Tears in his Eyes, Repentance in his Looks, and Contrition in his Heart, has confessed himself to be the Murder of the Soon of the Protestant of Thoulouse, whom the Parliament sentenced to the Wheel for that Crime.

A Book lately appears here the most singular, and another the most astonishing. The first is an Heroic Poem, intitled, *The Broom, or Broomstick* [1]. Rabelais, Scarron, or La Fontaine, had not more Wit, a better Stile, or finer Imagination. Moreover, it is the Work of an apostate Abbe, namely, Laurence; he published, about eighteen Months since, a Work intitled, *The Jesuisticals*. He is a Poet formed by Nature.

The other is called *Oriental Despotism* [2], by M. Boulanger. It is a Book worthy of a Montesquieu: I know you are acquainted with the Editor: The Police has let loose all her Furies to discover them, but to no Purpose, and I am glad of it.

Within a Month we have had sixty Assassinations, or frightful Murders, considered in their Circumstances. War, Luxury, and Extravagance, destroy this Place.

You know the Jesuits have no longer their Colleges; that we are at the Eve of banishing them out of the Kingdom. We begin, tho' tremblingly, to shew our Teeth at old Grey Beard of Rome.

Send me as soon as you can, your fourth Canto of the Dispensary. If my Christiana appears to you deserving the Notice of your glorious, piratical Gentry, get it translated as faithfully as possible.

Adieu! bestir yourselves, ingrates; praise God for all Things; admire Nature; it is the only Way I know to live sometimes contentedly.

选自 *The St. James's Chronicle*, London, 15–17 July 1762, no. 211, p. 4a–4b.

附1：伏尔泰致达朗贝尔的信（法文原版）

Voltaire à Jean Le Rond d'Alembert

à Ferney 29 Mars 1762

Mon cher et grand Philosophe, vous avez donc lu cet impertinent petit libelle d'un impertinent petit Prêtre qui était venu souvent aux Délices et à qui nous avions daigné faire trop bonne chère. Le sot libelle de ce misérable était si méprisé, si inconnu à Genève que je ne vous en avais point parlé. Je viens de lire dans le Journal Encyclopédique un article où l'on fait l'honneur à ce croquant de relever son infamie. Vous voyez que les presbitériens ne valent pas mieux que les Jesuites, et que ceux cy ne sont pas plus dignes du carcan que les Jansenistes.

Vous aviez fait à la ville de Genève un honneur qu'elle ne méritait pas. Je ne me suis

---

1 亨利·约瑟夫·杜洛朗：《扫帚》，君士坦丁堡，1762年。这首"英雄史诗"是题献给伏尔泰的。
2 尼古拉-安托万·布朗热：《探寻东方专制主义的起源》，日内瓦，1761年。

vengé qu'en amusant ses citoyens. On joua Cassandre ces jours passés sur mon Théâtre de Ferney, non le Cassandre que vous avez vu croquis, mais celui dont j'ai fait un tableau suivant votre goût. Les ministres n'ont osé y aller, mais ils y ont envoyé leurs filles. J'ai vu pleurer Genevois & Genevoises pendant cinq actes, et je n'ai jamais vu pièce si bien jouée, et puis un souper pour deux cent spectateurs, et puis le bal. C'est ainsi que je me suis vengé.

On venait de pendre un de leurs prédicants à Toulouze, cela les rendait plus doux, mais on vient de rouer un de leurs frères accusé d'avoir pendu son fils en haine de notre sainte religion pour laquelle ce bon père soupçonnait dans son fils un secret penchant. La ville de Toulouze, beaucoup plus sotte et plus fanatique que Genève, prit ce jeune pendu pour un martyr. On ne s'avisa pas d'examiner s'il s'était pendu lui même, comme la chose est très vraisemblable. On l'enterra pompeusement dans la cathédrale, une partie du Parlement assista pieds nuds à la cérémonie, on invoqua le nouveau saint, après quoi la Chambre criminelle fit roüer le père à la pluralité de huit voix contre cinq. Ce jugement était d'autant plus chrétien qu'il n'y avait aucune preuve contre le Roüé. Ce roué était un bon bourgeois, bon père de famille, ayant cinq enfants en comptant le pendu. Il a pleuré son fils en mourant, il a protesté de son innocence sous comptant le pendu. Il a pleuré son fils en mourant, il a protesté de son innocence sous les coups de Barre. Il a cité le Parlement au Jugement de Dieu. Tous nos cantons hérétiques jettent les hauts cris, tous disent que nous sommes une nation aussi barbare que frivole, qui sait rouer et qui ne sait pas combattre et qui passe de la S. Barthelemy à l'opéra comique. Nous devenons l'horreur et le mépris de l'Europe. J'en suis fâché car nous étions fait pour être aimables.

Je vous promets de n'aller n'y à Genève n'y à Toulouze. On n'est bien que chez soi.

Pour l'amour de Dieu, rendez moi aussi exécrable que vous le pourrez le fanatisme qui a fait pendre un fils par son père, ou qui a fait rouer un innocent par huit conseillers du Roy.

Mandez moi je vous prie, quel est le corps que vous méprisez le plus, je suis empêché à résoudre ce problème.

Interim vous savez combien je vous aime, estime et révère.

选自 Voltaire, *Oeuvres complètes de Voltaire*, Paris: Louis Moland, 1877−1885, t. 42, lettre 4872.

第四章 世界近现代史

附2：伏尔泰致达朗贝尔的信（中译版）

伏尔泰致达朗贝尔

1762年3月29日，费尔奈

亲爱的、伟大的哲人，这么说您读过那个放肆的小教士写的那份放肆的小谤文[1]了。他以前常常到欢愉府[2]来，我们还屈尊对他非常热情。这个可鄙的人的愚蠢谤文在日内瓦极受鄙视、不为人知，我都没跟您提过。我刚刚在《百科全书报》上看到一篇文章[3]，给了这个乡巴佬荣耀，升级了他的无耻行为。您看到了，这些长老会派的人并不比耶稣会士更好，而后者也不比冉森派分子更配得上铁项圈。

您给了日内瓦一项荣耀[4]，而它根本配不上。我对日内瓦的报复方式就让其公民感到开心。[5] 过去几天我们在我的费尔奈剧院中上演了《珈桑德拉》，不是您曾经读过的那份草稿，而是我根据您的口味编写大纲的那一份。日内瓦的牧师们不敢前来观看演出，但他们把自己的女儿们送来了。我看到日内瓦的男男女女们在这五幕剧的演出过程中哭泣，我从来没看到演得这么好的一部剧。戏剧演出后我为这两百个观众提供了夜宵，之后又举行了舞会。我就是这么复仇的。

在图卢兹，他们的一个牧师刚刚被吊死了[6]，这使他们更加温和了。但是他们的一个信徒兄弟被指控出于对我们的神圣宗教[7]的仇恨，吊死了自己的儿子，因为他怀疑他的儿子对我们的神圣宗教有秘密倾向。这个人被轮刑处死了。图卢兹比日内瓦更加愚蠢、更加狂热，将这个吊死的年轻人当作一位殉教者。人们并没有想起调查一下他是否是自己上吊自杀的，好像这是非常有可能的。人们用很大排场将他安葬在主教座堂，高等法院的一部分人光着脚参加了这场仪式，人们向这个新圣人祈求保佑。之后，刑事法庭以八对五的多数将那位父亲以轮刑处死。这场判决，由于没有证据指证被轮刑处死的那个人，因而更具基督教特征了。那个被处以轮刑的人是个好资产者，家庭的好父亲，算上吊死的那一个，共有五个孩子。垂死之时，他为他的儿子哭泣，在棍棒的重击下他宣称自己是无辜的。他被传唤高等法院接受上帝的审判。我们这里所有异端州[8]的人都声讨我们，都说我们是一个既野蛮又轻浮的民族，能把人处以轮刑却不能打仗，从圣巴

---

1 "小谤文"指的是《一个英国旅行者关于〈百科全书〉的"日内瓦"词条、关于达朗贝尔先生致卢梭先生的信的批判信件》，乌特勒支，1761年。真实作者为J. J. 韦尔奈，但这部著作的前言署名是罗伯特·布朗，伏尔泰以为这篇"小谤文"就是罗伯特·布朗写的，这里的"小教士"指的就是罗伯特·布朗。
2 伏尔泰位于日内瓦的住宅。
3 《百科全书报》1762年3月刊（由皮埃尔·卢梭在比利时主办的报刊）发了一篇对韦尔奈的著作的书评。
4 指达朗贝尔为《百科全书》写的词条"日内瓦"。此文引起很大争议，卢梭写了《致达朗贝尔的信》一书公开反驳，反对在日内瓦上演戏剧，认为戏剧会败坏日内瓦的共和道德。
5 伏尔泰热爱戏剧，在其位于日内瓦境内的宅邸欢愉府上演戏剧遭到日内瓦牧师的反对。与日内瓦人发生冲突之后，伏尔泰在法国与日内瓦边境的法国境内购买了新的宅邸费尔奈府，并在那里修建了私人剧院。确如伏尔泰信中所言，在费尔奈上演的戏剧吸引了一些日内瓦人前去观看。
6 1762年2月19日，于蒙托邦被捕的新教牧师弗朗索瓦·罗谢特被处死。
7 伏尔泰对天主教的嘲讽。
8 指瑞士各州，都信奉新教，伏尔泰用"异端"这个词并非敌视新教，而是嘲讽宗教狂热。

特罗缪大屠杀就谈到喜歌剧了。我们令欧洲感到恐惧，受到他们的鄙视。我很不快，因为我们其实天生被塑造为友好的人。

我答应您，我既不到日内瓦去，也不到图卢兹去。我们待在自己家里就好。

为了天主之爱，请尽您所能让狂热主义变得可憎，它要么使一个儿子被父亲吊死，要么使一个无辜的人被国王的八个法官判处轮刑。

请告诉我，哪一具尸体才是您更加蔑视的，我无法解决这个问题。

同时，您知道我多么热爱您、器重您、尊敬您。

五、新渡户稻造笔下的"武士道"

导读

提及日本，武士道总被认为代表了日本文化中尚武的一面。在西方学者认识日本的经典著作《菊与刀》中，本尼迪克特就有类似表述，足见这种认识的影响之深远。然而，西方世界对于日本的认识也存在一个被建构的过程。

其实，在西方世界对日本的早期认知中，与武士道伴生的往往是强悍与残忍，造成这种印象的恰恰是日本人自己。1868年，新生的明治政府在处理堺事件时，为展示自身的强硬以及交好西方列强的决心，勒令涉事者在法国代表面前切腹谢罪。切腹自杀的残酷场面深深震撼了法方，日本人强悍与残忍的形象由此在西方人中流传开来。但这种形象也把日本隔绝于近代西方社会的主流价值观之外，给日本融入西方世界带来了困扰。当日本人希望通过重塑武士道在西方世界中的形象以弥合日本与西方的差别之际，也就诞生了《武士道》这本书。

作者新渡户稻造在《武士道》的序言中直言不讳：创作本书是要以被告人的身份在包括其妻子在内的西方人面前为日本辩护。在这场辩护中，作者采用的最主要的手段就是通过类比使听众产生如下印象：日本的武士道与西方的骑士精神遵循的都是某种共通的崇高理念，只是表现形式不同而已。

在某种意义上，学习历史就是一个与史料"肉搏"的过程。比起材料的字面意思和语法表现形式，历史研究者更看重的是材料对时代背景的反映。单纯从语言审美的角度着眼，日本学者的著述大概不必出现在一部专业英语教材里。但如果把材料作为理解一个时代的窗口，那么新渡户稻造在《武士道》中具有鲜明倾向性的文字，作为学术训练的标本倒是非常适合。这也是编者选取本段材料的初衷。

Bushido: The Soul of Japan

Chapter I Bushido as an Ethical System

...The Japanese word which I have roughly rendered Chivalry, is, in the original, more expressive than Horsemanship. Bu-shi-do means literally Military-Knight-Ways—the ways which fighting nobles should observe in their daily life as well as in their vocation; in a word, the "Precepts of Knighthood," the noblesse oblige of the warrior class. Having thus given its literal significance, I may be allowed henceforth to use the word in the original. The use of the original term is also advisable for this reason, that a teaching so circumscribed and unique, engendering a cast of mind and character so peculiar, so local, must wear the badge of its singularity on its face; then, some words have a national timbre so expressive of race characteristics that the best of translators can do them but scant justice, not to say positive injustice and grievance. Who can improve by translation what the German "Gemüth" signifies, or who does not feel the difference between the two words verbally so closely allied as the English gentleman and the French gentilhomme?

Bushido, then, is the code of moral principles which the knights were required or instructed to observe. It is not a written code; at best it consists of a few maxims handed down from mouth to mouth or coming from the pen of some well-known warrior or savant. More frequently it is a code unuttered and unwritten, possessing all the more the powerful sanction of veritable deed, and of a law written on the fleshly tablets of the heart. It was founded not on the creation of one brain, however able, or on the life of a single personage, however renowned. It was an organic growth of decades and centuries of military career. It, perhaps, fills the same position in the history of ethics that the English Constitution does in political history; yet it has had nothing to compare with the Magna Charta or the Habeas Corpus Act. True, early in the seventeenth century Military Statutes (Buké Hatto) were promulgated; but their thirteen short articles were taken up mostly with marriages, castles, leagues, etc., and didactic regulations were but meagerly touched upon. We cannot, therefore, point out any definite time and place and say, "Here is its fountain head." Only as it attains consciousness in the feudal age, its origin, in respect to time, may be identified with feudalism. But feudalism itself is woven of many threads, and Bushido shares its intricate nature. As in England the political institutions of feudalism may be said to date from the Norman Conquest, so we may say that in Japan its rise was simultaneous with the ascendency of Yoritomo, late in the twelfth century. As, however, in England, we find the social elements of feudalism far back in the period previous to William the Conqueror, so, too, the germs of feudalism in Japan had been long existent before the period I have mentioned.

Again, in Japan as in Europe, when feudalism was formally inaugurated, the professional class of warriors naturally came into prominence. These were known as samurai, meaning literally, like the old English cniht (knecht, knight), guards or attendants—resembling in character the soldurii whom Caesar mentioned as existing in Aquitania, or the comitati, who, according to Tacitus, followed Germanic chiefs in his time; or, to take a still later parallel, the milites medii that one reads about in the history of Mediaeval Europe. A Sinico-Japanese word Bu-ké or Bu-shi (Fighting Knights) was also adopted in common use. They were a privileged class, and must originally have been a rough breed who made fighting their vocation. This class was naturally recruited, in a long period of constant warfare, from the manliest and the most adventurous, and all the while the process of elimination went on, the timid and the feeble being sorted out, and only "a rude race, all masculine, with brutish strength," to borrow Emerson's phrase, surviving to form families and the ranks of the samurai. Coming to profess great honor and great privileges, and correspondingly great responsibilities, they soon felt the need of a common standard of behavior, especially as they were always on a belligerent footing and belonged to different clans. Just as physicians limit competition among themselves by professional courtesy, just as lawyers sit in courts of honor in cases of violated etiquette, so must also warriors possess some resort for final judgment on their misdemeanors.

选自 INAZO NITOBÉ, *Bushido: The Soul of Japan*, Author's Edition, Revised and Enlarged 13th edition, 1908.

六、冈仓天心《茶之书》节选

导读

　　此书题为"茶之书",读者望文生义,想必会将其视为一本关于茶道的专著。事实也大略如此,仔细阅读了本书的读者对于日本茶道的基本情况可窥一斑。然而,如果认识仅止于此,恐要错失作者冈仓天心的真意。《茶之书》1906年在纽约出版时,冈仓天心因供职于波士顿美术馆而频繁穿梭于日美之间。因此,本书虽然以茶为名,其着眼点却是茶道背后日本人的审美意识。但在笔者看来,日本人的审美意识仍非冈仓天心问题意识的最终指向。对于《茶之书》的理解不能忽略其历史语境。

　　"脱亚入欧"是概括明治维新后日本国家战略时的一种常见说法,但"脱亚"与"入欧"之间的差距却往往被人忽视。一系列侵略战争的胜利使得日本树立起了与亚洲诸国不同的近代国家形象,"脱亚"大致完成。可是在欧美人眼里,日本仍然是一种异质的存在,"入欧"仍然遥遥无期。在明治时代日本精英的留洋体验中,遭受到排斥的个案屡见不鲜,冈仓天心对此大概也颇有感受。正因如此,他深刻地意识到匍匐在西洋文明的脚下永远无法换来西方的尊重。所以我们可以看到,在《茶之书》中,冈仓天心把东方文明置于和西方文明对等的地位,这种对等意识在本书节选的第一章中表现得尤为明显。冈仓天心甚至对西方文明的傲慢进行了辛辣的嘲讽。

　　与西方文明对话意识的存在,令冈仓天心在行文中不拘泥于英语的既有表现形式，而大胆地使用了自创的英语单词。比如为了表现禅宗的文化特质，他创造了"Zennism"，将其与佛教"Buddhism"区别开来。另外如"Swordsoul"也颇能反映日本的文化特色。

实际上，直到今天，我们仍面临如何看待西方文明这个问题。"平等视之"，或许是冈仓天心最想通过《茶之书》来表达的吧！

The Book of Tea
Chapter I The Cup of Humanity

Those who cannot feel the littleness of great things in themselves are apt to overlook the greatness of little things in others. The average Westerner, in his sleek complacency, will see in the tea ceremony but another instance of the thousand and one oddities which constitute the quaintness and childishness of the East to him. He was wont to regard Japan as barbarous while she indulged in the gentle arts of peace: he calls her civilised since she began to commit wholesale slaughter on Manchurian battlefields. Much comment has been given lately to the Code of the Samurai, —the Art of Death which makes our soldiers exult in self-sacrifice; but scarcely any attention has been drawn to Teaism, which represents so much of our Art of Life. Fain would we remain barbarians, if our claim to civilisation were to be based on the gruesome glory of war. Fain would we await the time when due respect shall be paid to our art and ideals.

When will the West understand, or try to understand, the East? We Asiatics are often appalled by the curious web of facts and fancies which has been woven concerning us. We are pictured as living on the perfume of the lotus, if not on mice and cockroaches. It is either impotent fanaticism or else abject voluptuousness. Indian spirituality has been derided as ignorance, Chinese sobriety as stupidity, Japanese patriotism as the result of fatalism. It has been said that we are less sensible to pain and wounds on account of the callousness of our nervous organisation!

Why not amuse yourselves at our expense? Asia returns the compliment. There would be further food for merriment if you were to know all that we have imagined and written about you. All the glamour of the perspective is there, all the unconscious homage of wonder, all the silent resentment of the new and undefined. You have been loaded with virtues too refined to be envied, and accused of crimes too picturesque to be condemned. Our writers in the past—the wise men who knew—informed us that you had bushy tails somewhere hidden in your garments, and often dined off a fricassee of newborn babes! Nay, we had something worse against you: we used to think you the most impracticable people on the earth, for you were said to preach what you never practised.

Such misconceptions are fast vanishing amongst us. Commerce has forced the European tongues on many an Eastern port. Asiatic youths are flocking to Western colleges for the equipment of modern education. Our insight does not penetrate your culture deeply, but at least we are willing to learn. Some of my compatriots have adopted too much of your customs and too much of your etiquette, in the delusion that the acquisition of stiff collars and tall silk hats comprised the attainment of your civilisation. Pathetic and deplorable as such affectations are, they evince our willingness to approach the West on our knees. Unfortunately the Western attitude is unfavourable to the understanding of the East. The Christian missionary goes to impart, but not to receive. Your information is based on the meagre translations of our immense literature, if not on the unreliable anecdotes of passing travellers. It is rarely that the chivalrous pen of a Lafcadio Hearn or that of the author of "The Web of Indian Life" enlivens the Oriental darkness with the torch of our own sentiments.

Perhaps I betray my own ignorance of the Tea Cult by being so outspoken. Its very spirit of politeness exacts that you say what you are expected to say, and no more. But I am not to be a polite Teaist. So much harm has been done already by the mutual misunderstanding of the New World and the Old, that one need not apologise for contributing his tithe to the furtherance of a better understanding. The beginning of the twentieth century would have been spared the spectacle of sanguinary warfare if Russia had condescended to know Japan better. What dire consequences to humanity lie in the contemptuous ignoring of Eastern problems! European imperialism, which does not disdain to raise the absurd cry of the Yellow Peril, fails to realise that Asia may also awaken to the cruel sense of the White Disaster. You may laugh at us for having "too much tea," but may we not suspect that you of the West have "no tea" in your constitution?

Let us stop the continents from hurling epigrams at each other, and be sadder if not wiser by the mutual gain of half a hemisphere. We have developed along different lines, but there is no reason why one should not supplement the other. You have gained expansion at the cost of restlessness; we have created a harmony which is weak against aggression. Will you believe it?—the East is better off in some respects than the West!

选自 Okakura-Kakuzo, *The Book of Tea*, London and New York: G. P. Putman's Sons, 1906, pp. 6-12.

七、康涅狄格殖民地首部宪法

导读

在康涅狄格早期历史上一共出现过三部被视为宪法的重要文件。最早的一部是 1638—1639 年殖民地初建时订立的《基本法》(Fundamental Orders)，然后是 1662 年由英国王室授予的《特许状》(Charter of the Colony)，最后一部是美国于 1818 年订立的《州宪法》(Constitution of *1818*) 及其修正案。限于篇幅，我们这里只选了最早的一部，即康涅狄格殖民地建立时于 1638 年至 1639 年冬天订立的《基本法》。

1630 年，约翰·温斯洛普（John Winthrop）率领一批清教徒建立了马萨诸塞殖民地。1633 年 9 月 4 日，托马斯·胡克（Thomas Hooker）来到了马萨诸塞，有感于马萨诸塞殖民地的拥挤狭小，同时也是出于马萨诸塞清教领袖们对选举权控制的不满，胡克和他的追随者们向马萨诸塞殖民当局提出了建立新殖民地的申请。虽然遇到很大阻力，但最终获得通过。申请通过后，胡克率领牛顿的居民在康涅狄格河东岸建立了哈特福德，并使之成为康涅狄格殖民地的中心。1639 年 1 月 14 日，哈特福德、威瑟斯菲尔德和温泽三镇的全体自由人（Freemen）齐集哈特福德，通过了这部《基本法》。它被称为康涅狄格的第一部宪法。与马萨诸塞将选举权和被选举权限定于教会成员不同的是，康涅狄格通过这部《基本法》把充分享有政治权利的主体扩大到上述三地的"自由人"。与英国历史上旨在限制王权的《大宪章》不同的是，《基本法》的目标是为三地合并的共同体设计一个能够履行管理职能的政府。因此，有学者评价说它是"历史上第一部构建了政府的成文宪法，标志着美国民主的开端"[1]。

《基本法》规定了大议会的构成以及每年召开的具体时间，总督和地方执法官的选举方式和选民的构成、总督的任期和更替，市镇代表的遴选方式、数量、责任和权利。《基本法》将大议会确定为最高权力机构，具有立法权、征税权、自由人审批权、公共土地处置权以及传讯和惩罚从执法官到普通平民的权力等等。《基本法》通篇未提英国国王，康涅狄格自治特色十分明显。到1662 年康涅狄格终于获得英国王室授予的《特许状》时，该殖民地已经在《基本法》的框架下奠定了稳固的政治基础。

The First Constitution of Connecticut
The Fundamental Orders 1638. 9

Forasmuch as it hath pleased the Almighty God by the wise disposition of his divine providence so to order and dispose of things that we the Inhabitants and Residents of Windsor, Hartford, and Wethersfield are now cohabiting and dwelling in and upon the River of Connectecotte and the lands there unto adjoining; and well knowing where a people are gathered together the word of God requires that to maintain the peace and union of such a people there should be an orderly and decent Government established according to God, to order and dispose of the affairs of the people at all seasons as occasion shall require; do therefore associate and conjoin ourselves to be as one Public State or Commonwealth; and do for ourselves and our Successors and such as shall be adjoined to us at any time hereafter, enter into Combination and Confederation together, to maintain and preserve the liberty and purity of the Gospel of our Lord Jesus which we now profess, as also the discipline of the Churches, which according to the truth

---

[1] John Fiske, *The Beginning of New England or The Puritan Theocracy in Its Relation to Civil and Religious Liberty*, Boston and New York: Houghton, Mifflin and Company, 1891, p. 127.

of the said Gospel is now practiced amongst us; as also in our Civil Affairs to be guided and governed according to such Laws, Rules, Orders, and Decrees as shall be made, ordered, and decreed, as followeth:

1. It is Ordered, sentenced, and decreed, that there shall be yearly two General Assemblies or Courts, the one the second Thursday in April, the other the second Thursday in September following; the first shall be called the Court of Election, wherein shall be yearly chosen from time to time so many Magistrates and other public Officers as shall be found requisite: Whereof one to be chosen Governor for the year ensuing and until another be chosen, and no other Magistrate to be chosen for more than one year; provided always, there be six chosen besides the Governor, which being chosen and sworn according to an Oath recorded for that purpose, shall have power to administer justice according to the Laws here established, and for want thereof, according to the rule of the Word of God; which choice shall be made by all that are admitted freemen and have taken the Oath of Fidelity, and do cohabit within this Jurisdiction (having been admitted in habitants by the major part of the Town wherein they live) [1] or the major part of such as shall be then present.

2. It is Ordered, sentenced, and decreed, that the Election of the aforesaid Magistrates shall be on this manner: every person present and qualified for choice shall bring in (to the persons deputed to receive them) one single paper with the name of him written in it whom he desires to have Governor, and he that hath the greatest number of papers shall be Governor for that year. And the rest of the Magistrates or public Officers to be chosen in this manner: the Secretary for the time being shall first read the names of all that are to be put to choice and then shall severally nominate them distinctly, and every one that would have the person nominated to be chosen shall bring in one single paper written upon, and he that would not have him chosen shall bring in a blank: and every one that hath more written papers than blanks shall be a Magistrate for that year; which papers shall be received and told by one or more that shall be then chosen by the court and sworn to be faithful therein; but in case there should not be six chosen as aforesaid, besides the Governor, out of those which are nominated, then he or they which have the most written papers shall be a Magistrate or Magistrates for the ensuing year, to make up the aforesaid number.

3. It is Ordered, sentenced, and decreed, that the Secretary shall not nominate any person, nor shall any person be chosen newly into the Magistracy, which was not propounded in some General Court before, to be nominated the next Election; and to that end it shall be lawful for each of the Towns aforesaid by their deputies to nominate any two whom they conceive fit to be put to election; and the Court may add so many more as they judge requisite.

4. It is Ordered, sentenced, and decreed, that no person be chosen Governor above once in

---

1 This clause was interlined in a different handwriting, and is of a later date. It was adopted by the General Court of November, 1643.

two years, and that the Governor be always a member of some approved congregation, and formerly of the Magistracy within this Jurisdiction; and all the Magistrates, Freemen of this Commonwealth: and that no Magistrate or other public officer shall execute any part of his or their office before they are severally sworn, which shall be done in the face of the court if they be present, and in case of absence by some deputed for that purpose.

5. It is Ordered, sentenced, and decreed, that to the aforesaid Court of Election the several Towns shall send their deputies, and when the Elections are ended they may proceed in any public service as at other Courts. Also the other General Court in September shall be for making of laws, and any other public occasion, which concerns the good of the Commonwealth.

6. It is Ordered, sentenced, and decreed, that the Governor shall, either by himself or by the secretary, send out summons to the constables of every Town for the calling of these two standing Courts, one month at least before their several times: And also if the Governor and the greatest part of the Magistrates see cause upon any special occasion to call a General Court, they may give order to the Secretary so to do within fourteen days' warning: and if urgent necessity so require, upon a shorter notice, giving sufficient grounds for it to the deputies when they meet, or else be questioned for the same; And if the Governor and major part of Magistrates shall either neglect or refuse to call the two General standing Courts or either of them, as also at other times when the occasions of the Commonwealth require, the Freemen thereof, or the major part of them, shall petition to them so to do; if then it be either denied or neglected, the said Freemen, or the major part of them, shall have power to give order to the Constables of the several Towns to do the same, and so may meet together, and choose to themselves a Moderator, and may proceed to do any act of power which any other General Court may.

7. It is Ordered, sentenced, and decreed, that after there are warrants given out for any of the said General Courts, the Constable or Constables of each Town shall forthwith give notice distinctly to the inhabitants of the same, in some public assembly or by going or sending from house to house, that at a place and time by him or them limited and set, they meet and assemble themselves together to elect and choose certain deputies to be at the General Court then following to agitate the affairs of the Commonwealth; which said deputies shall be chosen by all that are admitted Inhabitants in the several Towns and have taken the oath of fidelity; provided that none be chosen a Deputy for any General Court which is not a Freeman of this Commonwealth.

The aforesaid deputies shall be chosen in manner following: every person that is present and qualified as before expressed, shall bring the names of such, written in several papers, as they desire to have chosen for that employment, and these three or four, more or less, being the number agreed on to be chosen for that time, that have greatest number of papers written for them shall be deputies for that Court; whose names shall be endorsed on the back side of the warrant and returned into the Court, with the constable or constables' hand unto the same.

8. It is Ordered, sentenced, and decreed, that Windsor, Hartford, and Wethersfield shall

have power, each Town, to send four of their Freemen as their deputies to every General Court; and whatsoever other Towns shall be hereafter added to this Jurisdiction, they shall send so many deputies as the Court shall judge meet, a reasonable proportion to the number of Freemen that are in the said Towns being to be at tended therein; which deputies shall have the power of the whole Town to give their votes and allowance to all such laws and orders as may be for the public good, and unto which the said towns are to be bound.

9. It is Ordered and decreed, that the deputies thus chosen shall have power and liberty to appoint a time and a place of meeting together before any General Court, to advise and consult of all such things as may concern the good of the public, as also to examine their own Elections, whether according to the order, and if they or the greatest part of them find any election to be illegal they may seclude such for present from their meeting, and return the same and their reasons to the Court; and if it prove true, the Court may fine the party or parties so intruding, and the Town, if they see cause, and give out a warrant to go to a new election in a legal way, either in part or in whole. Also the said deputies shall have power to fine any that shall be disorderly at their meetings, or for not coming in due time or place according to appointment; and they may return the said fines into the Court if it be refused to be paid, and the Treasurer to take notice of it, and to escheat or levy the same as he does other fines.

10. It is Ordered, sentenced, and decreed, that every General Court, except such as through neglect of the Governor and the greatest part of Magistrates the Freemen themselves do call, shall consist of the Governor, or someone chosen to moderate the Court, and four other Magistrates at least, with the major part of the deputies of the several Towns legally chosen; and in case the Freemen, or major part of them, through neglect or refusal of the Governor and major part of the magistrates, shall call a Court, it shall consist of the major part of Freemen that are present or their deputies, with a Moderator chosen by them: In which said General Courts shall consist the supreme power of the Commonwealth, and they only shall have power to make laws or repeal them, to grant levies, to admit of Freemen, dispose of lands undisposed of, to several Towns or persons, and also shall have power to call either court or Magistrate or any other person whatsoever into question for any misdemeanor, and may for just causes displace or deal otherwise according to the nature of the offence; and also may deal in any other matter that concerns the good of this Commonwealth, except election of Magistrates, which shall be done by the whole body of Freemen.

In which Court the Governor or Moderator shall have power to order the Court, to give liberty of speech, and silence unseasonable and disorderly speakings, to put all things to vote, and in case the vote be equal to have the casting vote. But none of these Courts shall be adjourned or dissolved without the consent of the major part of the Court.

11. It is Ordered, sentenced, and decreed, that when any General Court upon the occasions of the Commonwealth have agreed upon any sum or sums of money to be levied upon the several Towns within this Jurisdiction, that a committee be chosen to set out and appoint what shall be

the proportion of every Town to pay of the said levy, provided the committee be made up of an equal number out of each Town.

14th January, 1638 [N. S., 24th January, 1639], the II Orders above said are voted.

选自 Connecticut Office of the State Comptroller, *The Three Constitutions of Connecticut*, Hartford, Conn.: The Case, Lockwood & Brainard Company, 1901, pp. 11–16.

八、布赖恩《金十字架》演说

导读

《金十字架》演说,是美国民主党总统候选人威廉·詹宁斯·布赖恩在 1896 年芝加哥民主党全国大会上发表的演说。这次演说之所以重要,首先是因为布赖恩的身份。布赖恩是民主党的总统候选人,同时他也是平民党人的精神领袖,因此他代表了当时至少两种政治文化的合流,这在美国历史上是罕有的。其次是布赖恩的演讲风格。布赖恩被认为是美国历史上最擅长公众演讲的总统候选人之一,他的演说词逻辑清楚,文气贯通,有磅礴的气势,《金十字架》就是他的代表作。第三,这篇演讲词的重要性还体现在它发生的历史背景,它借民主党之口,发出了美国历史上平民主义的最强音,提出了一系列对 20 世纪美国影响极为深远的改革提案,但最终布赖恩败给了麦金莱和他背后强大的共和党,后者代表了 19 世纪下半叶美国的正统政治思想。综上可见,这份演讲词是美国历史上一份颇为重要的文献。

阅读这份文献,有以下几点值得注意:

第一是要认识到演讲实际发生时的历史语境。读者可以将自己还原到演讲发生的会场,设想作者或者说演讲者面对的听众是哪些人,他演讲的目的是什么,他应该用什么样的演讲策略来达到自己的目的。带着这些问题,可以在一定程度上更加准确地理解作者的行文及用词,避免盲目阅读,认识不到政治演说词通常具有的那种热情、夸张和具有煽动性的特点,以至于对演讲词中的内容不加批判地照单全收。对待不同性质的文献,首先都应发挥历史想象力,体会文献的语境。

第二是要通篇阅读,抓住作者的逻辑主线和演讲的核心内容。逻辑线索一般紧扣作者的演讲目的,核心内容则是这条线索上的高潮部分。政治演讲一般会从一些轻松的话题谈起,渐渐切入主题,然后到结束前的几段将核心议题郑重提出。就这篇演讲词而言,应当思考"金十字架"的含义,它和作者的核心论题"自由银币主张"是何关系。核心内容部分应一字一句细读,仔细揣摩作者的遣词用句是否有深意。要准确理解文意,为此一项非常重要的前期工作就是要充分掌握背景资料,对文中出现的具体问题要非常熟悉。

第三是要在深度阅读的基础上发现作者在论证其政治观点时动用的理论资

源。政治演说词几乎无一例外地具有这样一个特征,即总是带有鲜明的政治观点,背后是一种或多种政治意识形态的支撑,同时带有确立自己一方观念和意识形态的正确性的意图,目的是在民意面前压倒竞争的一方。就本篇而言,要善于发现作者在哪些地方调用了美国政治文化中哪些有利于自己说理的资源,思考作者对这些资源的使用是否合理,是否具有片面性,最终的论证效果如何。此外,演讲词中也可能出现一些对后世颇有影响的提法或主张,要留意这些提法的历史语境,分析其合理性。

最后还要站在演讲者论敌的角度考虑这篇文献的意义。本文献的演讲者最终输掉了总统选举。那么,这是否意味着作者在文中论述的观点是不足取的?作者使用的理论资源是否站不住脚?如果不是,那么这篇演讲与选举的结果有什么关系?这篇演讲的成功之处体现在哪里?演讲者的敌对方又胜在哪里?可设想作者的敌对方将如何应对其在这篇演讲中抛出的挑战和质疑。

William Jennings Bryan's "Cross of Gold" Speech

July 9, 1896, at the Democratic National Convention, Chicago

Mr. Chairman and Gentlemen of the Convention: I would be presumptuous, indeed, to present myself against the distinguished gentlemen to whom you have listened if this were a mere measuring of abilities; but this is not a contest between persons. The humblest citizen in all the land, when clad in the armor of a righteous cause, is stronger than all the hosts of error. I come to speak to you in defense of a cause as holy as the cause of liberty—the cause of humanity....

Never before in the history of this country has there been witnessed such a contest as that through which we have just passed. Never before in the history of American politics has a great issue been fought out as this issue has been, by the voters of a great party....

With a zeal approaching the zeal which inspired the crusaders who followed Peter the hermit, our silver Democrats[1] went forth from victory unto victory until they are now assembled, not to discuss, not to debate, but to enter up the judgment already rendered by the plain people of this country. In this contest brother has been arrayed against brother, father against son. the warmest ties of love, acquaintance and association have been disregarded; old leaders have been cast aside when they have refused to give expression to the sentiments of those whom they would lead, and new leaders have sprung up to give direction to the cause of truth. Thus has the contest been waged, and we have assembled here under as binding and solemn instructions as were ever imposed upon representatives of the people....

---

1 19世纪末美国的币制为金本位,社会中下层负债者倡导实行双本位制,即允许铸造银币,按一定汇率参与货币流通和结算,以缓解中下层的经济压力。持这一政见的最初是一些平民党人(populists),到1896年支持银币铸造合法化进入民主党的政纲。那些支持铸银合法化的民主党人称为"银派民主党人"(silver Democrats),在该议题上持反对意见的即是后文中的"金派"(gold delegates)。

The gentleman who preceded me (ex-Governor Russell) spoke of the State of Massachusetts; let me assure him that not one present in all this convention entertains the least hostility to the people of the State of Massachusetts, but we stand here representing people who are the equals, before the law, of the greatest citizens in the State of Massachusetts. When you [turning to the gold delegates] come before us and tell us that we are about to disturb your business interests, we reply that you have disturbed our business interests by your course.

We say to you that you have made the definition of a business man too limited in its application. The man who is employed for wages is as much a business man as his employer; the attorney in a country town is as much a business man as the corporation counsel in a great metropolis; the merchant at the cross-roads store is as much a businessman as the merchant of New York; the farmer who goes forth in the morning and toils all day—who begins in the spring and toils all summer—and who by the application of brain and muscle to the natural resources of the country creates wealth, is as much a businessman as the man who goes upon the board of trade and bets upon the price of grain; the miners who go down a thousand feet into the earth, or climb two thousand feet upon the cliffs, and bring forth from their hiding places the precious metals to be poured into the channels of trade are as much business men as the few financial magnates who, in a backroom, corner the money of the world. We come to speak for this broader class of businessmen.

Ah, my friends, we say not one word against those who live upon the Atlantic coast, but the hardy pioneers who have braved all the dangers of the wilderness, who have made the desert to blossom as the rose—the pioneers away out there [pointing to the West], who rear their children near to Nature's heart, where they can mingle their voices with the voices of the birds—out there where they have erected school houses for the education of their young, churches where they praise their Creator, and cemeteries where rest the ashes of their dead—these people, we say, are as deserving of the consideration of our party as any people in this country. It is for these that we speak. We do not come as aggressors. Our war is not a war of conquest; we are fighting in the defense of our homes, our families, and posterity. We have petitioned, and our petitions have been scorned; we have entreated, and our entreaties have been disregarded; we have begged, and they have mocked when our calamity came. We beg no longer; we entreat no more; we petition no more. We defy them.

The gentleman from Wisconsin [Senator Vilas] has said that he fears a Robespierre[1]. My friends, in this land of the free you need not fear that a tyrant will spring up from among the people. What we need is an Andrew Jackson to stand, as Jackson stood, against the encroachments of organized wealth.

They tell us that this platform was made to catch votes. We reply to them that changing conditions make new issues; that the principles upon which Democracy rests are as everlasting

---

1 指担心银币铸造合法化引发革命。

as the hills, but that they must be applied to new conditions as they arise. Conditions have arisen, and we are here to meet those conditions. They tell us that the income tax ought not to be brought in here; that it is a new idea. They criticize us for our criticism of the Supreme Court of the United States. My friends, we have not criticized; we have simply called attention to what you already know. If you want criticisms, read the dissenting opinions of the court. There you will find criticisms. They say that we passed an unconstitutional law; we deny it. The income tax law was not unconstitutional when it was passed; it was not unconstitutional when it went before the Supreme Court for the first time; it did not become unconstitutional until one of the judges changed his mind, and we cannot be expected to know when a judge will change his mind. The income tax is just. It simply intends to put the burdens of government justly upon the backs of the people. I am in favor of an income tax. When I find a man who is not willing to bear his share of the burdens of the government which protects him, I find a man who is unworthy to enjoy the blessings of a government like ours.

They say that we are opposing national bank currency; it is true. If you will read what Thomas Benton said, you will find he said that, in searching history, he could find but one parallel to Andrew Jackson; that was Cicero, who destroyed the conspiracy of Cataline and saved Rome. Benton said that Cicero only did for Rome what Jackson did for us when he destroyed the bank conspiracy and saved America. We say in our platform that we believe that the right to coin and issue money is a function of government. We believe it. We believe that it is a part of sovereignty, and can no more with safety be delegated to private individuals than we could afford to delegate to private individuals the power to make penal statutes or levy taxes. Mr. Jefferson, who was once regarded as good Democratic authority, seems to have differed in opinion from the gentleman who has addressed us on the part of the minority. Those who are opposed to this proposition tell us that the issue of paper money is a function of the bank, and that the Government ought to go out of the banking business. I stand with Jefferson rather than with them, and tell them, as he did, that the issue of money is a function of government, and that the banks ought to go out of the governing business.

They complain about the plank which declares against life tenure in office. They have tried to strain it to mean that which it does not mean. What we oppose by that plank is the life tenure which is being built up in Washington, and which excludes from participation in official benefits the humbler members of society.

Let me call your attention to two or three important things. The gentleman from New York says that he will propose an amendment to the platform providing that the proposed change in our monetary system shall not affect contracts already made. Let me remind you that there is no intention of affecting those contracts which according to present laws are made payable in gold; but if he means to say that we cannot change our monetary system without protecting those who have loaned money before the change was made, I desire to ask him where, in law or in morals, he can find justification for not protecting the debtors when the act of 1873 was passed, if he now insists that we must protect the creditors.

He says he will also propose an amendment which will provide for the suspension of freecoinage if we fail to maintain the parity within a year. We reply that when we advocate apolicy which we believe will be successful, we are not compelled to raise a doubt as to our own sincerity by suggesting what we shall do if we fail. I ask him, if he would apply his logic to us, why he does not apply it to himself. He says he wants this country to try to secure an international agreement. Why does he not tell us what he is going to do if he fails to secure an international agreement? There is more reason for him to do that than there is for us to provide against the failure to maintain the parity. Our opponents have tried for twenty years to secure an international agreement, and those are waiting for it most patiently who do not want it at all.

And now, my friends, let me come to the paramount issue. If they ask us why it is that we say more on the money question than we say upon the tariff question, I reply that, if protection has slain its thousands, the gold standard has slain its tens of thousands. If they ask us why we do not embody in our platform all the things that we believe in, we reply that when we have restored the money of the Constitution all other necessary reforms will be possible; but that until this is done there is no other reform that can be accomplished.

Why is it that within three months such a change has come over the country? Three months ago, when it was confidently asserted that those who believe in the gold standard would frame our platform and nominate our candidates, even the advocates of the gold standard did not think that we could elect a president. And they had good reason for their doubt, because there is scarcely a State here today asking for the gold standard which is not in the absolute control of the Republican party. But note the change. Mr. McKinley was nominated at St. Louis upon a platform which declared for the maintenance of the gold standard until it can be changed into bimetallism by international agreement. Mr. McKinley was the most popular man among the Republicans, and three months ago everybody in the Republican party prophesied his election. How is it today? Why, the man who was once pleased to think that he looked like Napoleon—that man shudders today when he remembers that he was nominated on the anniversary of the battle of Waterloo. Not only that, but as he listens he can hear with ever-increasing distinctness the sound of the waves as they beat upon the lonely shores of St. Helena.

Why this change? Ah, my friends, is not the reason for the change evident to any one who will look at the matter? No private character, however pure, no personal popularity, however great, can protect from the avenging wrath of an indignant people a man who will declare that he is in favor of fastening the gold standard upon this country, or who is willing to surrender the right of self-government and place the legislative control of our affairs in the hands of foreign potentates and powers.

We go forth confident that we shall win. Why? Because upon the paramount issue of this campaign there is not a spot of ground upon which the enemy will dare to challenge battle. If they tell us that the gold standard is a good thing, we shall point to their platform and tell them that their platform pledges the party to get rid of the gold standard and substitute bimetallism. If the gold standard is a good thing, why try to get rid of it? I call your attention to the fact that some of the very people who are in this convention today and who tell us that we ought to declare in favor of international bimetallism—thereby declaring that the gold standard is wrong and that the principle of bimetallism is better—these very people four months ago were open and avowed advocates of the gold standard, and were then telling us that we could not legislate two metals together, even with the aid of all the world. If the gold standard is a good thing, we ought to declare in favor of its retention and not in favor of abandoning it; and if the gold standard is a bad thing why should we wait until other nations are willing to help us to let go? Here is the line of battle, and we care not upon which issue they force the fight; we are prepared to meet them on either issue or on both. If they tell us that the gold standard is the standard of civilization, we reply to them that this, the most enlightened of all the nations of the earth, has never declared for a gold standard and that both the great parties this year are declaring against it. If the gold standard is the standard of civilization, why, my friends, should we not have it? If they come to meet us on that issue we can present the history of our nation. More than that; we can tell them that they will search the pages of history in vain to find a single instance where the common people of any land have ever declared themselves in favor of the gold standard. They can find where the holders of the fixed investments have declared for a gold standard, but not where the masses have.

Mr. Carlisle said in 1878 that this was a struggle between "the idle holders of idle capital" and "the struggling masses, who produce the wealth and pay the taxes of the country"; and, my friends, the question we are to decide is: Upon which side will the Democratic party fight; upon the side of "the idle holders of idle capital" or upon the side of "the struggling masses?" That is the question which the party must answer first, and then it must be answered by each individual hereafter. The sympathies of the Democratic party, as shown by the platform, are on the side of the struggling masses who have ever been the foundation of the Democratic party. There are two ideas of government. There are those who believe that, if you will only legislate to make the well-to-do prosperous, their prosperity will leak through on those below. The Democratic idea, however, has been that if you legislate to make the masses prosperous, their prosperity will find its way up through every class which rests upon them.

You come to us and tell us that the great cities are in favor of the gold standard; we reply that the great cities rest upon our broad and fertile prairies. Burn down your cities and leave our farms, and your cities will spring up again as if by magic; but destroy our farms and the grass will grow in the streets of every city in the country.

My friends, we declare that this nation is able to legislate for its own people on every question, without waiting for the aid or consent of any other nation on earth; and upon that issue we expect to carry every State in the Union. I shall not slander the inhabitants of the fair State of Massachusetts nor the inhabitants of the State of New York by saying that, when they are confronted with the proposition, they will declare that this nation is not able to attend to its own business. It is the issue of 1776 over again. Our ancestors, when but three millions in number, had the courage to declare their politicalindependence of every other nation; shall we, their descendants, when we have grown to seventy millions, declare that we are less independent than our forefathers? No, my friends, that will never be the verdict of our people. Therefore, we care not upon what lines the battle is fought. If they say bimetallism is good, but that we cannot have it until other nations help us, we reply that, instead of having a gold standard because England has, we will restore bimetallism, and then let England have bimetallism because the United States has it. If they dare to come out in the open field and defend the gold standard as a good thing, we will fight them to the uttermost.

Having behind us the producing masses of this nation and the world, supported by the commercial interests, the laboring interests, and the toilers everywhere, we will answer their demand for a gold standard by saying to them: You shall not press down upon the brow of labor this crown of thorns, you shall not crucify mankind upon a cross of gold.

选自 William J. Bryan, *The First Battle: A Story of the Campaign of 1896*, Chicago: W. B. Conkey Company, 1897, pp. 199–206.

推荐阅读

1. Richard Hofstadter, *The Age of Reform*, New York: Vintage Books, 1955.

2. Robert W. Cherny, *A Righteous Cause: The Life of William Jennings Bryan*, Boston: Little, Brown, and Company, 1985.

第五章 国际关系及外交史

一、美西战争与美国外交大辩论

导读

1898 年的美西战争被视为美国对外关系史上的转折点，美国从此由大陆扩张迈向海外扩张，开始以全球性强国的身份走上世界舞台。但美国的这一身份转变并非一蹴而就，美国迈向帝国主义的道路并非毫无阻拦，只是这一阻力并非主要来自西班牙，而是来自国内。在经历了这场"小而辉煌"的战争之后，美国国内围绕伴随战争而来的帝国主义外交，特别是兼并菲律宾问题展开了激烈的辩论，众多的国会成员、政治评论家、工业巨头、教会牧师、社会活动家都参与了这场大辩论。虽然美国参议院在 1899 年 2 月通过了结束美西战争的《巴黎和约》，确认了美国对菲律宾的吞并，但这并未平息争论，争论的主要观点及其思想内涵对此后美国的对外政策仍有深远影响。

下面所选的两份文献分别代表辩论双方的立场。第一份是当时的主要反对力量——反帝国主义联盟于 1899 年通过的一份纲领性文件。它概括了当时反帝国主义理念的主要思想：共和主义、人道主义以及对帝国主义战争可能给美国国内议程带来不利影响的担忧。第二份文件的背景是当时美国已经确认了占领菲律宾的政策，并与菲律宾民族独立运动产生直接冲突，美国国会围绕在菲律宾的军事征服是否要继续展开激烈争辩。来自印第安纳州的共和党国会参议员阿尔伯特·贝弗里奇在辩论中发表的支持战争的长篇演说，获得了共和党议员的广泛赞誉，使得他成为当时最重要的帝国主义者之一。贝弗里奇在演说中宣扬了美国占领菲律宾的重要意义，他以种族主义观点论证了美国对菲军事行动及至战后统治的必要性，并亲自构建了一整套美国在菲律宾殖民统治的政治体系。他还以美国大陆扩张的历史来驳斥反帝国主义者所主张的帝国主义与《独立宣言》及美国宪法相违背的论点，并重申了美国承担对外扩张这一历史重任的必要性。

两份文献需要在对比中阅读。首先需要明确双方所支持和反对的具体观点，仔细分析各自论点背后的理论资源。其次需要注意双方如何攻击对方的立论，并同时为自我辩护。最后需要回答的一个问题是：为何帝国主义者赢得了这场政策辩论，然而反帝国主义者的理念并未彻底消亡？除此之外，两份文献也包含远超具体政策辩论的内容，它们与美国对外关系史上的一些宏大主题有直接联系，如美国如何看待自己与外部世界的关系，通过何种手段来扩大美国影响力才是最合适的，等等。正因如此，可将以这两份文献为代表的此次辩论与美国政府建立初期的汉密尔顿与杰斐逊之争、19世纪中叶围绕美墨战争的争论、第二次世界大战前夕的孤立主义与国际主义的大辩论、20世纪60年代围绕越南战争的争论联系起来，从中思索两份文献在更长历史时段中的意义。

Platform of the American Anti-Imperialist League (1899)

We hold that the policy known as imperialism is hostile to liberty and tends toward militarism, an evil from which it has been our glory to be free. We regret that it has become necessary in the land of Washington and Lincoln to reaffirm that all men, of whatever race or color, are entitled to life, liberty, and the pursuit of happiness. We maintain that governments derive their just powers from the consent of the governed. We insist that the subjugation of any people is "criminal aggression" and open disloyalty to the distinctive principles of our Government.

We earnestly condemn the policy of the present National Administration in the Philippines. It seeks to extinguish the spirit of 1776 in those islands. We deplore the sacrifice of our soldiers and sailors, whose bravery deserves admiration even in an unjust war. We denounce the slaughter of the Filipinos as a needless horror. We protest against the extension of American sovereignty by Spanish methods.

We demand the immediate cessation of the war against liberty, begun by Spain and continued by us. We urge that Congress be promptly convened to announce to the Filipinos our purpose to concede to them the independence for which they have so long fought and which of right is theirs.

The United States have always protested against the doctrine of international law, which permits the subjugation of the weak by the strong. A self-governing state cannot accept sovereignty over an unwilling people. The United States cannot act upon the ancient heresy that might makes right[1].

Imperialists assume that with the destruction of self-government in the Philippines by American hands, all opposition here will cease. This is a grievous error. Much as we abhor the war of "criminal aggression" in the Philippines, greatly as we regret that the blood of the Filipinos is on American hands, we more deeply resent the betrayal of American institutions at home. The real firing line is not in the suburbs of Manila. The foe is of our own household. The attempt of 1861 was to divide the country. That of 1899 is to destroy its fundamental principles and noblest ideals.

Whether the ruthless slaughter of the Filipinos shall end next month or next year is but an incident in a contest that must go on until the Declaration of Independence and the Constitution

---

1　指武力战胜正义。

of the United States are rescued from the hands of their betrayers. Those who dispute about standards of value while the Republic is undermined will be listened to as little as those who would wrangle about the small economies of the household while the house is on fire. The training of a great people for a century, the aspiration for liberty of a vast immigration are forces that will hurl aside those who in the delirium of conquest seek to destroy the character of our institutions.

We deny that the obligation of all citizens to support their Government in times of grave national peril applies to the present situation. If an Administration may with impunity ignore the issues upon which it was chosen, deliberately create a condition of war anywhere on the face of the globe, debauch the civil service for spoils to promote the adventure, organize a truth-suppressing censorship and demand of all citizens a suspension of judgment and their unanimous support while it chooses to continue the fighting, representative government itself is imperiled.

We propose to contribute to the defeat of any person or party that stands forthe forcible subjugation of any people. We shall oppose for reelection [1] all who in the White House or in Congress betray American liberty in pursuit of un-American gains. We still hope that both of our great political parties will support and defend the Declaration of Independence in the closing campaign of the century.

We hold, with Abraham Lincoln, that "no man is good enough to govern another man without that other's consent. When the white man governs himself, that is self-government, but when he governs himself and also governs another man, that is more than self-government—that is despotism [using absolute, unjust authority]." [2] "Our reliance is in the love of liberty which God has planted in us. Our defense is in the spirit which prizes liberty as the heritage of all men in all lands. Those who deny freedom to others deserve it not for themselves, and under a just God cannot long retain it." [3]

We cordially invite the cooperation of all men and women who remain loyal to the Declaration of Independence and the Constitution of the United States.

选自 Frederick Bancroft (ed.), *Speeches, Correspondence, and Political Papers of Carl Schurz*, Vol. 6, New York: G. P. Putnam's Sons, 1913, pp. 77–79.

---

1 1900 年的美国总统大选在帝国主义问题上出现过激烈争执，民主党候选人威廉·詹宁斯·布赖恩坚持反帝国主义立场，与共和党候选人威廉·麦金莱的美西战争政策形成鲜明对比，最终麦金莱获得连任。
2 出自林肯于 1854 年 10 月在伊利诺伊州的演讲，林肯在演讲中对奴隶制进行了抨击。
3 出自林肯于 1858 年 9 月在伊利诺伊州的演讲，林肯在演讲中申明美国的力量在于其自由精神。

第五章　国际关系及外交史

Senator Albert J. Beveridge on U. S. Policy in the Philippines
U. S. Senate, Washington, D. C., January 9, 1900

... Mr. President, the times call for candor. The Philippines are ours forever, "territory belonging to the United States," as the Constitution calls them. And just beyond the Philippines are China's illimitable markets. We will not retreat from either. We will not repudiate our duty in the archipelago. We will not abandon our opportunity in the Orient. We will not renounce our part in the mission of our race, trustee, under God, of the civilization of the world. And we will move forward to our work, not howling out regrets like slaves whipped to their burdens but with gratitude for a task worthy of our strength and thanksgiving to Almighty God that He has marked us as His chosen people, henceforth to lead in the regeneration of the world.

This island empire is the last land left in all the oceans. If it should prove a mistake to abandon it, the blunder once made would be irretrievable. If it proves a mistake to hold it, the error can be corrected when we will. Every other progressive nation stands ready to relieve us.

But to hold it will be no mistake. Our largest trade henceforth must be with Asia. The Pacific is our ocean. More and more Europe will manufacture the most it needs, secure from its colonies the most it consumes. Where shall we turn for consumers of our surplus? Geography answers the question. China is our natural customer. She is nearer to us than to England, Germany, or Russia, the commercial powers of the present and the future. They have moved nearer to China by securing permanent bases on her borders. The Philippines give us a base at the door of all the East.

Lines of navigation from our ports to the Orient and Australia, from the Isthmian Canal[1] to Asia, from all Oriental ports to Australia converge at and separate from the Philippines. They are a self-supporting, dividend-paying fleet, permanently anchored at a spot selected by the strategy of Providence, commanding the Pacific. And the Pacific is the ocean of the commerce of the future. Most future wars will be conflicts for commerce. The power that rules the Pacific, therefore, is the power that rules the world. And, with the Philippines, that power is and will forever be the American Republic.

... To-day we have one of the three great ocean possessions of the globe, located at the most commanding commercial, naval, and military points in the Eastern seas, within hail of India, shoulder to shoulder with China, richer in its own resources than any equal body of land on the entire globe, and peopled by a race which civilization demands shall be improved. Shall we abandon it?...

The military situation, past, present, and prospective, is no reason for abandonment. Our campaign has been as perfect as possible with the force at hand. We have been delayed, first, by

---

1 虽然美国于1904年才开始修筑巴拿马运河，但在这之前美国已有开凿中美洲地峡运河的设想，并在国会下成立了相关委员会。

a failure to comprehend the immensity of our acquisition; and, second, by insufficient force; and, third, by our efforts for peace. In February, after the treaty of peace, General Otis had only 3722 officers and men whom he had a legal right to order into battle. The terms of enlistment of the rest of his troops had expired, and they fought voluntarily and not on legal military compulsion. It was one of the noblest examples of patriotic devotion to duty in the history of the world.

Those who complain do so in ignorance of the real situation. We attempted a great task with insufficient means; we became impatient that it was not finished before it could fairly be commenced; and I pray we may not add that other element of disaster, pausing in the work before it is thoroughly and forever done. That is the gravest mistake we could possibly make, and that is the only danger before us. Our Indian wars would have been shortened, the lives of soldiers and settlers saved, and the Indians themselves benefited had we made continuous and decisive war; and any other kind of war is criminal because ineffective. . . .

. . . This war is like all other wars. It needs to be finished before it is stopped. I am prepared to vote either to make our work thorough or even now to abandon it. A lasting peace can be secured only by overwhelming forces in ceaseless action until universal and absolutely final defeat is inflicted on the enemy. To halt before every armed force, every guerrilla band, opposing us is dispersed or exterminated will prolong hostilities and leave alive the seeds of perpetual insurrection.

. . . It has been charged that our conduct of the war has been cruel. Senators, it has been the reverse. I have been in our hospitals and seen the Filipino wounded as carefully, tenderly cared for as our own. Within our lines they may plow and sow and reap and go about the affairs of peace with absolute liberty. And yet all this kindness was misunderstood, or rather not understood. Senators must remember that we are not dealing with Americans or Europeans. We are dealing with Orientals. We are dealing with Orientals who are Malays. We are dealing with Malays instructed in Spanish methods. They mistake kindness for weakness, forbearance for fear. It could not be otherwise unless you could erase hundreds of years of savagery, other hundreds of years of Orientalism, and still other hundreds of years of Spanish character and custom.

. . . Mr. President, reluctantly and only from a sense of duty am I forced to say that American opposition to the war has been the chief factor in prolonging it. Had Aguinaldo[1] not understood that in America, even in the American Congress, even here in the Senate, he and his cause were supported; had he not known that it was proclaimed on the stump and in the press of a faction in the United States that every shot his misguided followers fired into the breasts of American soldiers was like the volleys fired by Washington's men against the soldiers of King George, his insurrection would have dissolved before it entirely crystallized.

1　埃米利奥·阿奎纳多，菲律宾独立革命领袖。

第五章　国际关系及外交史

... They[1] are not capable of self-government. How could they be? They are not of a self-governing race. They are Orientals, Malays, instructed by Spaniards in the latter's worst estate.

They know nothing of practical government except as they have witnessed the weak, corrupt, cruel, and capricious rule of Spain. What magic will anyone employ to dissolve in their minds and characters those impressions of governors and governed which three centuries of misrule has created? What alchemy will change the Oriental quality of their blood and set the self-governing currents of the American pouring through their Malay veins? How shall they, in the twinkling of an eye, be exalted to the heights of self-governing peoples which required a thousand years for us to reach, Anglo-Saxon though we are?

Let men beware how they employ the term "self-government." It is a sacred term. It is the watchword at the door of the inner temple of liberty, for liberty does not always mean self-government. Self-government is a method of liberty—the highest, simplest, best—and it is acquired only after centuries of study and struggle and experiment and instruction and all the elements of the progress of man. Self-government is no base and common thing to be bestowed on the merely audacious. ...

... In all other islands our government must be simple and strong. It must be a uniform government. Different forms for different islands will produce perpetual disturbance because the people of each island would think that the people of the other islands are more favored than they. In Panay I heard murmurings that we were giving Negros an American constitution. This is a human quality, found even in America, and we must never forget that in dealing with the Filipinos we deal with children. And so our government must be simple and strong. Simple and strong! The meaning of those two words must be written in every line of Philippine legislation, realized in every act of Philippine administration. A Philippine office in our Department of State; an American governor-general in Manila, with power to meet daily emergencies; possibly an advisory council with no power except that of discussing measures with the governor-general, which council would be the germ for future legislatures, a school in practical government; American lieutenant governors in each province, with a like council about him if possible, an American resident in each district and a like council grouped about him. Frequent and unannounced visits of provincial governors to the districts of their province; periodical reports to the governor-general; an American board of visitation to make semiannual trips to the archipelago without power of suggestion or interference to officials or people, but only to report and recommend to the Philippine office of our State Department; a Philippine civil service, with promotion for efficiency; the abolition of duties on exports from the Philippines; the establishment of import duties on a revenue basis, with such discrimination in favor of American imports as will prevent the cheaper goods of other nations from destroying American trade; a complete reform of local taxation on a just and scientific basis, beginning with the establishment

---

1　指菲律宾人。

of a tax on land according to its assessed value; the minting of abundant money for Philippine and Oriental use. The granting of franchises and concessions upon the theory of developing the resources of the archipelago, and therefore not by sale, but upon participation in the profits of the enterprise; the formation of a system of public schools everywhere with compulsory attendance rigidly enforced; the establishment of the English language throughout the Islands, teaching it exclusively in the schools and using it, through interpreters, exclusively in the courts; a simple civil code and a still simpler criminal code, and both common to all the islands except Sulu, Mindanao, and Paluan; American judges for all but smallest offenses; gradual, slow, and careful introduction of the best Filipinos into the working machinery of the government, no promise whatever of the franchise until the people have been prepared for it, all this backed by the necessary force to execute it; this outline of government the situation demands as soon as tranquility is established. [1] . . .

. . . The Declaration of Independence does not forbid us to do our part in the regeneration of the world. If it did, the Declaration would be wrong, just as the Articles of Confederation, drafted by the very same men who signed the Declaration, was found to be wrong. The Declaration has no application to the present situation. It was written by self-governing men for self-governing men.

It was written by men who, for a century and a half, had been experimenting in self-government on this continent, and whose ancestors for hundreds of years before had been gradually developing toward that high and holy estate. The Declaration applies only to people capable of self-government. How dare any man prostitute this expression of the very elect of self-governing peoples to a race of Malay children of barbarism, schooled in Spanish methods and ideas? And you who say the Declaration applies to all men, how dare you deny its application to the American Indian? And if you deny it to the Indian at home, how dare you grant it to the Malay abroad?

The Declaration does not contemplate that all government must have the consent of the governed. It announces that man's "inalienable rights are life, liberty, and the pursuit of happiness; that to secure these rights governments are established among men deriving their just powers from the consent of the governed; that when any form of government becomes destructive of those rights, it is the right of the people to alter or abolish it. " "Life, liberty, and the pursuit of happiness" are the important things; "consent of the governed" is one of the means to those ends.

If "any form of government becomes destructive of those ends, it is the night of the people to alter or abolish it, "says the Declaration. "Any forms"includes all forms. Thus the Declaration itself recognizes other forms of government than those resting on the consent of the governed. The word "consent" itself recognizes other forms, for "consent" means the understanding of the

---

1 注意贝弗里奇在这段中设想的美国在菲律宾治理政策与之后美国在菲殖民统治的联系与区别。

thing to which the "consent" is given; and there are people in the world who do not understand any form of government. . . .

. . . Self-government, when that will best secure these ends, as in the case of people capable of self-government; other appropriate forms when people are not capable of self-government. And so the authors of the Declaration themselves governed the Indian without his consent; the inhabitants of Louisiana[1] without their consent; and ever since the sons of the makers of the Declaration have been governing not by theory but by practice, after the fashion of our governing race, now by one form, now by another, but always for the purpose of securing the great eternal ends of life, liberty, and the pursuit of happiness, not in the savage but in the civilized meaning of those terms. . . .

. . . Mr. President, this question is deeper than any question of party politics; deeper than any question of the isolated policy of our country even; deeper even than any question of constitutional power. It is elemental. It is racial. God has not been preparing the English speaking and Teutonic peoples for a thousand years for nothing but vain and idle self-contemplation and self-admiration. No! He has made us the master organizers of the world to establish system where chaos reigns. He has given us the spirit of progress to overwhelm the forces of reaction throughout the earth. He has made us adepts in government that we may administer government among savage and senile peoples. Were it not for such a force as this the world would relapse into barbarism and night. And of all our race He has marked the American people as His chosen nation to finally lead in the regeneration of the world. This is the divine mission of America, and it holds for us all the profit, all the glory, all the happiness possible to man. We are trustees of the world's progress, guardians of its righteous peace. The judgment of the Master is upon us: "Ye have been faithful over a few things; I will make you ruler over many things."

What shall history say of us? Shall it say that we renounced that holy trust, left the savage to his base condition, the wilderness to the reign of waste, deserted duty, abandoned glory, forget our sordid profit even, because we feared our strength and read the charter of our powers with the doubter's eye and the quibbler's mind? Shall it say that, called by events to captain and command the proudest, ablest, purest race of history in history's noblest work, we declined that great commission? Our fathers would not have had it so. No! They founded no paralytic government, incapable of the simplest acts of administration. They planted no sluggard people, passive while the world's work calls them. They established no reactionary nation. They unfurled no retreating flag.

That flag has never paused in its onward march. Who dares halt it now—now, when history's largest events are carrying it forward; now, when we are at last one people, strong enough for any task, great enough for any glory destiny can bestow? How comes it that our first

---

1　指1803年美国总统托马斯·杰斐逊通过购买的方式从法国获得密西西比河以西的路易斯安那领地。

century closes with the process of consolidating the American people into a unit just accomplished, and quick upon the stroke of that great hour presses upon us our world opportunity, world duty, and world glory, which none but the people welded into an invisible nation can achieve or perform?

　　Blind indeed is he who sees not the hand of God in events so vast, so harmonious, so benign. Reactionary indeed is the mind that perceives not that this vital people is the strongest of the saving forces of the world; that our place, therefore, is at the head of the constructing and redeeming nations of the earth; ...

选自 U. S. Congress (ed.), *Congressional Record: Proceedings and Debates of the 56th Congress*, 1st session, Jan. 9, Washington, D. C. : United States Government Publishing Office, 1900, pp. 704–712.

推荐阅读

1. Robert L. Beisner, *Twelve against Empire: The Anti-Imperialists, 1898–1900*, Chicago: Imprint Publications, 1992.

2. Walter LaFeber, *The American Search for Opportunity, 1865–1913*, Cambridge: Cambridge University Press, 1995.

3. Frank A. Ninkovich, *The United States and Imperialism*, Malden: Blackwell Publishers, 2001.

二、凯南"长电报"

导读

　　冷战时期是人类历史上的一段特殊时期，以美国和苏联为首的两大阵营在政治、外交、军事、经济、文化等方面持续了近半个世纪的对峙。尽管学界对于冷战的起源仍然存在争议，从美国的角度来看，第二次世界大战后期至1947年初美苏关系中一系列事件的接连发生最终导致了冷战对抗由理念变为国家政策，其中乔治·凯南的"长电报"在其中起到了至关重要的作用。1946年2月9日，斯大林在莫斯科选民会议上发表演讲，称世界经济的资本主义体系中包含着危机和军事冲突的因素，资本主义经济的不均衡发展总会导致战争的爆发。斯大林的演讲虽然主要是在总结第二次世界大战中苏联的成就，但其内容及时机选择仍引起美国的疑虑。2月13日，美国国务院要求美国驻苏联大使馆分析斯大林演讲对其未来政策可能产生的影响。美国驻苏大使哈里曼并不在莫斯科，这一重任落在了代办凯南的身上。此时的凯南因其政策意见长期未受采纳已向国务院提交了辞呈，备感挫折又抱恙在身的他根据自己对苏联的理解，于2月22日向华盛顿发回了这封五千余词的"长电报"，将这一非常规的形式视作影响美国政策的最后一次尝试。

凯南在这封电报中分析了斯大林演说中体现出的苏联世界观，认为苏联世界观并非基于对国际形势的客观分析，而是基于战前已经存在的内部需求——俄国传统的不安全感和苏联政权意识形态的结合而形成的。在这一背景下，凯南认为苏联会利用任何官方或非官方的机会来壮大自己的力量，并尽一切可能摧毁美国的国际权威和国内秩序，双方无法实现"永久的和平共存"。正因为苏联"对于理性的逻辑无动于衷，对于力量的逻辑则高度敏感"，凯南认为美国应"拥有足够的力量并表明使用这一力量的意图"才可能使苏联退却。凯南的"长电报"在华盛顿受到广泛阅读和称赞，它适应了当时美国转向对苏强硬的政策需求，"长电报"也被广泛认为是后来杜鲁门政府开始执行的"遏制政策"的奠基性文件之一。凯南因此升任国务院政策设计司的首任主任，参与制定美国对外政策。

凯南在"长电报"中的论述主要体现在三大方面：苏联世界观的起源、苏联对外政策的主要手段及美国的应对策略，行文步步推进，体现出凯南对苏联的观察与思考。在阅读这篇文献时，除深入理解各部分内容及其内在逻辑外，还可从多个视角进行解读。已有学者从心理分析和语言学分析的角度重新解读了凯南对苏联世界观的诊断。除此之外，还可从官僚政治的视角分析为何凯南作为一名中下层外交人员，其报告能够对当时美国的对外政策产生如此巨大的影响，从文化的视角分析凯南对苏联和美国形象的塑造，从国际关系理论的视角分析以凯南"长电报"为代表的美国对苏强硬政策出现的偶然性与必然性。还需将这篇文献嵌入更长时段的冷战史脉络中。凯南关于俄国的知识获取、美国决策高层对"长电报"中不同内容的解读、苏联对凯南分析的回应等，这些都是具体化该文献历史语境的重要角度。凯南在经历了与国务院短暂的蜜月期后很快又成为美国决策层中的边缘人物，后来又成为美国冷战政策的批评者，认为美国公众与政府误解了其遏制理念。"长电报"中凯南的政策建议与此后美国政府实践中的遏制政策之间的区别与联系也是理解这篇文献的重要维度。

861.00/2-2246：Telegram

The Chargé in the Soviet Union (Kennan) to the Secretary of State Secret

Moscow, February 22, 1946—9 p.m.

[Received February 22—3：52 p.m.]

511. Answer to Dept's 284, Feb 3 [13][1] involves questions so intricate, so delicate, so strange to our form of thought, and so important to analysis of our international environment that I cannot compress answers into single brief message without yielding to what I feel would be

---

[1] Not printed; in this telegram the Department informed the Chargé: "We should welcome receiving from you an interpretive analysis of what we may expect in the way of future implementation of these announced policies..." (861.00/2-1246). The policies referred to were those contained in the pre-election speeches of Stalin and his associates.

dangerous degree of over-simplification. I hope, therefore, Dept will bear with me if I submit in answer to this question five parts, subjects of which will be roughly as follows:

(1) Basic features of post-war Soviet outlook.

(2) Background of this outlook.

(3) Its projection in practical policy on official level.

(4) Its projection on unofficial level.

(5) Practical deductions from standpoint of US policy.

I apologize in advance for this burdening of telegraphic channel; but questions involved are of such urgent importance, particularly in view of recent events, that our answers to them, if they deserve attention at all, seem to me to deserve it at once. There follows

Part 1: Basic Features of Post War Soviet Outlook, as Put Forward by Official Propaganda Machine, Are as Follows:

(a) USSR still lives in antagonistic "capitalist encirclement" with which in the long run there can be no permanent peaceful coexistence. As stated by Stalin in 1927 to a delegation of American workers:

"In course of further development of international revolution there will emerge two centers of world significance: a socialist center, drawing to itself the countries which tend toward socialism, and a capitalist center, drawing to itself the countries that incline toward capitalism. Battle between these two centers for command of world economy will decide fate of capitalism and of communism in entire world."

(b) Capitalist world is beset with internal conflicts, inherent in nature of capitalist society. These conflicts are insoluble by means of peaceful compromise. Greatest of them is that between England and US.

(c) Internal conflicts of capitalism inevitably generate wars. Wars thus generated may be of two kinds: intra-capitalist wars between two capitalist states, and wars of intervention against socialist world. Smart capitalists, vainly seeking escape from inner conflicts of capitalism, incline toward latter.[1]

(d) Intervention against USSR, while it would be disastrous to those who undertook it, would cause renewed delay in progress of Soviet socialism and must therefore be forestalled at all costs.

(e) Conflicts between capitalist states, though likewise fraught with danger for USSR, nevertheless hold out great possibilities for advancement of socialist cause, particularly if USSR remains militarily powerful, ideologically monolithic and faithful to its present brilliant leadership.

---

[1] 注意：凯南此处分析与斯大林在选民会议上演讲的联系，实际上凯南认为斯大林的此次讲话并无新意，是苏联政府的一贯理念，凯南只向国务院做出简要总结，但美国国务院对此并不满意，这才导致凯南以长电报的形式系统论述其对苏联政策的理解。

(f) It must be borne in mind that capitalist world is not all bad. In addition to hopelessly reactionary and bourgeois elements, it includes (1) certain wholly enlightened and positive elements united in acceptable communistic parties and (2) certain other elements (now described for tactical reasons as progressive or democratic) whose reactions, aspirations and activities happen to be "objectively" favorable to interests of USSR. These last must be encouraged and utilized for Soviet purposes.

(g) Among negative elements of bourgeois-capitalist society, most dangerous of all are those whom Lenin called false friends of the people, namely moderate-socialist or social-democratic leaders (in other words, non-Communist left-wing). These are more dangerous than out-and-out reactionaries, for latter at least march under their true colors, whereas moderate left-wing leaders confuse people by employing devices of socialism to serve interests of reactionary capital.

So much for premises. To what deductions do they lead from standpoint of Soviet policy? To following:

(a) Everything must be done to advance relative strength of USSR as factor in international society. Conversely, no opportunity must be missed to reduce strength and influence, collectively as well as individually, of capitalist powers.

(b) Soviet efforts, and those of Russia's friends abroad, must be directed toward deepening and exploiting of differences and conflicts between capitalist powers. If these eventually deepen into an "imperialist" war, this war must be turned into revolutionary upheavals within the various capitalist countries.

(c) "Democratic-progressive" elements abroad are to be utilized to maximum to bring pressure to bear on capitalist governments along lines agreeable to Soviet interests.

(d) Relentless battle must be waged against socialist and social-democratic leaders abroad.

Part 2: Background of Outlook

... At bottom of Kremlin's neurotic view of world affairs is traditional and instinctive Russian sense of insecurity. Originally, this was insecurity of a peaceful agricultural people trying to live on vast exposed plain in neighborhood of fierce nomadic peoples. To this was added, as Russia came into contact with economically advanced West, fear of more competent, more powerful, more highly organized societies in that area. But this latter type of insecurity was one which afflicted rather Russian rulers than Russian people; for Russian rulers have invariably sensed that their rule was relatively archaic in form, fragile and artificial in its psychological foundation, unable to stand comparison or contact with political systems of Western countries. For this reason they have always feared foreign penetration, feared direct contact between Western world and their own, feared what would happen if Russians learned truth about world without or if foreigners learned truth about world within. And they have learned to seek security only in patient but deadly struggle for total destruction of rival power, never in compacts and compromises with it.

It was no coincidence that Marxism, which had smouldered ineffectively for half a century in Western Europe, caught hold and blazed for first time in Russia. Only in this land which had never known a friendly neighbor or indeed any tolerant equilibrium of separate powers, either internal or international, could a doctrine thrive which viewed economic conflicts of society as insoluble by peaceful means. After establishment of Bolshevist regime, Marxist dogma, rendered even more truculent and intolerant by Lenin's interpretation, became a perfect vehicle for sense of insecurity with which Bolsheviks, even more than previous Russian rulers, were afflicted. In this dogma, with its basic altruism of purpose, they found justification for their instinctive fear of outside world, for the dictatorship without which they did not know how to rule, for cruelties they did not dare not to inflict, for sacrifices they felt bound to demand. . . .

It should not be thought from above that Soviet party line is necessarily disingenuous and insincere on part of all those who put it forward. Many of them are too ignorant of outside world and mentally too dependent to question [apparent omission] self-hypnotism, and who have no difficulty making themselves believe what they find it comforting and convenient to believe. Finally we have the unsolved mystery as to who, if anyone, in this great land actually receives accurate and unbiased information about outside world. In atmosphere of oriental secretiveness and conspiracy which pervades this Government, possibilities for distorting or poisoning sources and currents of information are infinite. The very disrespect of Russians for objective truth—indeed, their disbelief in its existence—leads them to view all stated facts as instruments for furtherance of one ulterior purpose or another. There is good reason to suspect that this Government is actually a conspiracy within a conspiracy; and I for one am reluctant to believe that Stalin himself receives anything like an objective picture of outside world. Here there is ample scope for the type of subtle intrigue at which Russians are past masters. Inability of foreign governments to place their case squarely before Russian policy makers—extent to which they are delivered up in their relations with Russia to good graces of obscure and unknown advisers whom they never see and cannot influence—this to my mind is most disquieting feature of diplomacy in Moscow, and one which Western statesmen would do well to keep in mind if they would understand nature of difficulties encountered here.

Part 3: Projection of Soviet Outlook in Practical Policy on Official Level

We have now seen nature and background of Soviet program. What may we expect by way of its practical implementation?

Soviet policy, as Department implies in its query under reference, is conducted on two planes: (1) official plane represented by actions undertaken officially in name of Soviet Government; and (2) subterranean plane of actions undertaken by agencies for which Soviet Government does not admit responsibility. .

. . . On official plane we must look for following:

(a) Internal policy devoted to increasing in every way strength and prestige of Soviet state: intensive military-industrialization; maximum development of armed forces; great displays to impress outsiders; continued secretiveness about internal matters, designed to conceal weaknesses and to keep opponents in dark.

(b) Wherever it is considered timely and promising, efforts will be made to advance official limits of Soviet power. For the moment, these efforts are restricted to certain neighboring points conceived of here as being of immediate strategic necessity, such as Northern Iran, Turkey, possibly Bornholm[1]. However, other points may at any time come into question, if and as concealed Soviet political power is extended to new areas. Thus a "friendly" Persian Government might be asked to grant Russia a port on Persian Gulf. Should Spain fall under Communist control, question of Soviet base at Gibraltar Strait might be activated. But such claims will appear on official level only when unofficial preparation is complete. . . .

Part 4: Following May Be Said as to What We May Expect by Way of Implementation of Basic Soviet Policies on Unofficial, or Subterranean Plane, i. e. on Plane for Which Soviet Government Accepts no Responsibility

Agencies utilized for promulgation of policies on this plane are following:

1. Inner central core of Communist Parties in other countries. While many of persons who compose this category may also appear and act in unrelated public capacities, they are in reality working closely together as an underground operating directorate of world communism, a concealed Comintern tightly coordinated and directed by Moscow. It is important to remember that this inner core is actually working on underground lines, despite legality of parties with which it is associated.

2. Rank and file of Communist Parties. Note distinction is drawn between these and persons defined in paragraph 1. This distinction has become much sharper in recent years. Whereas formerly foreign Communist Parties represented a curious (and from Moscow's standpoint often inconvenient) mixture of conspiracy and legitimate activity, now the conspiratorial element has been neatly concentrated in inner circle and ordered underground, while rank and file—no longer even taken into confidence about realities of movement—are thrust forward as bona fide internal partisans of certain political tendencies within their respective countries, genuinely innocent of conspiratorial connection with foreign states. Only in certain countries where communists are numerically strong do they now regularly appear and act as a body. As a rule they are used to penetrate, and to influence or dominate, as case may be, other organizations less likely to be suspected of being tools of Soviet Government, with a view to accomplishing their purposes through [apparent omission] organizations, rather than by direct action as a separate political party. . . .

---

1 丹麦的伯恩霍尔姆岛位于波罗的海，苏联军队曾于第二次世界大战后期登陆该岛，进攻占领此处的德国军队。后苏联军队虽撤退，但要求丹麦政府不得使外国军队驻扎于此岛。

(f) In general, all Soviet efforts on unofficial international plane will be negative and destructive in character, designed to tear down sources of strength beyond reach of Soviet control. This is only in line with basic Soviet instinct that there can be no compromise with rival power and that constructive work can start only when Communist power is dominant. But behind all this will be applied insistent, unceasing pressure for penetration and command of key positions in administration and especially in police apparatus of foreign countries. The Soviet regime is a police regime par excellence, reared in the dim half world of Tsarist police intrigue, accustomed to think primarily in terms of police power. This should never be lost sight of in gauging Soviet motives.

Part 5: [Practical Deductions From Standpoint of US Policy]

In summary, we have here a political force committed fanatically to the belief that with US there can be no permanent modus vivendi, that it is desirable and necessary that the internal harmony of our society be disrupted, our traditional way of life be destroyed, the international authority of our state be broken, if Soviet power is to be secure. This political force has complete power of disposition over energies of one of world's greatest peoples and resources of world's richest national territory, and is borne along by deep and powerful currents of Russian nationalism. In addition, it has an elaborate and far flung apparatus for exertion of its influence in other countries, an apparatus of amazing flexibility and versatility, managed by people whose experience and skill in underground methods are presumably without parallel in history. Finally, it is seemingly inaccessible to considerations of reality in its basic reactions. For it, the vast fund of objective fact about human society is not, as with us, the measure against which outlook is constantly being tested and re-formed, but a grab bag from which individual items are selected arbitrarily and tendenciously to bolster an outlook already preconceived. This is admittedly not a pleasant picture. Problem of how to cope with this force in [is] undoubtedly greatest task our diplomacy has ever faced and probably greatest it will ever have to face. It should be point of departure from which our political general staff work at present juncture should proceed. It should be approached with same thoroughness and care as solution of major strategic problem in war, and if necessary, with no smaller outlay in planning effort. I cannot attempt to suggest all answers here. But I would like to record my conviction that problem is within our power to solve—and that without recourse to any general military conflict. And in support of this conviction there are certain observations of a more encouraging nature I should like to make:

(1) Soviet power, unlike that of Hitlerite Germany, is neither schematic nor adventuristic. It does not work by fixed plans. It does not take unnecessary risks. Impervious to logic of reason, and it is highly sensitive to logic of force. For this reason it can easily withdraw—and usually does—when strong resistance is encountered at any point. Thus, if the adversary has sufficient force and makes clear his readiness to use it, he rarely has to do so. If situations are properly handled there need be no prestige-

engaging showdowns.

(2) Gauged against Western World as a whole, Soviets are still by far the weaker force. Thus, their success will really depend on degree of cohesion, firmness and vigor which Western World can muster. And this is factor which is within our power to influence.

(3) Success of Soviet system, as form of internal power, is not yet finally proven. It has yet to be demonstrated that it can survive supreme test of successive transfer of power from one individual or group to another. Lenin's death was first such transfer, and its effects wracked Soviet state for 15 years. After Stalin's death or retirement will be second. But even this will not be final test. Soviet internal system will now be subjected, by virtue of recent territorial expansions, to series of additional strains which once proved severe tax on Tsardom. We here are convinced that never since termination of civil war have mass of Russian people been emotionally farther removed from doctrines of Communist Party than they are today. In Russia, party has now become a great and—for the moment—highly successful apparatus of dictatorial administration, but it has ceased to be a source of emotional inspiration. Thus, internal soundness and permanence of movement need not yet be regarded as assured.

(4) All Soviet propaganda beyond Soviet security sphere is basically negative and destructive. It should therefore be relatively easy to combat it by any intelligent and really constructive program.

For these reasons I think we may approach calmly and with good heart problem of how to deal with Russia. As to how this approach should be made, I only wish to advance, by way of conclusion, following comments:

(1) Our first step must be to apprehend, and recognize for what it is, the nature of the movement with which we are dealing. We must study it with same courage, detachment, objectivity, and same determination not to be emotionally provoked or unseated by it, with which doctor studies unruly and unreasonable individual.

(2) We must see that our public is educated to realities of Russian situation. I cannot over-emphasize importance of this. Press cannot do this alone. It must be done mainly by Government, which is necessarily more experienced and better informed on practical problems involved. In this we need not be deterred by [ugliness?] of picture. I am convinced that there would be far less hysterical anti-Sovietism in our country today if realities of this situation were better understood by our people. There is nothing as dangerous or as terrifying as the unknown. It may also be argued that to reveal more information on our difficulties with Russia would reflect unfavorably on Russian-American relations. I feel that if there is any real risk here involved, it is one which we should have courage to face, and sooner the better. But I cannot see what we would be risking. Our stake in this country, even coming on heels of tremendous demonstrations of our friendship for Russian people, is remarkably small. We have here no investments

to guard, no actual trade to lose, virtually no citizens to protect, few cultural contacts to preserve. Our only stake lies in what we hope rather than what we have; and I am convinced we have better chance of realizing those hopes if our public is enlightened and if our dealings with Russians are placed entirely on realistic and matter-of-fact basis.

(3) Much depends on health and vigor of our own society. World communism is like malignant parasite which feeds only on diseased tissue. This is point at which domestic and foreign policies meet. Every courageous and incisive measure to solve internal problems of our own society, to improve self-confidence, discipline, morale and community spirit of our own people, is a diplomatic victory over Moscow worth a thousand diplomatic notes and joint communiqués. If we cannot abandon fatalism and indifference in face of deficiencies of our own society, Moscow will profit—Moscow cannot help profiting by them in its foreign policies.

(4) We must formulate and put forward for other nations a much more positive and constructive picture of sort of world we would like to see than we have put forward in past. It is not enough to urge people to develop political processes similar to our own. Many foreign peoples, in Europe at least, are tired and frightened by experiences of past, and are less interested in abstract freedom than in security. They are seeking guidance rather than responsibilities. We should be better able than Russians to give them this. And unless we do, Russians certainly will.

(5) Finally we must have courage and self-confidence to cling to our own methods and conceptions of human society. After all, the greatest danger that can befall us in coping with this problem of Soviet communism, is that we shall allow ourselves to become like those with whom we are coping.

KENNAN

选自 U. S. Department of State (ed.), *Foreign Relations of the United States, 1946*, Volume VI: Eastern Europe; The Soviet Union, Washington, D. C.: United States Government Printing Office, 1969, pp. 696-709.

推荐阅读

1. John Lewis Gaddis, George F. Kennan, *An American Life*, New York: Penguin, 2011.

2. Melvyn P. Leffler, *A Preponderance of Power: National Security, the Truman Administration, and the Cold War*, Stanford: Stanford University Press, 1992.

三、NSC 13/2 号文件

导读

NSC 13/2 是美国国家安全委员会（National Security Council, NSC）在 1948 年 10 月 9 日正式通过的一份政策性文件，起草人是号称"冷战之父"的乔治·凯南（George F. Kennan）。这份文件的出台标志着美国对日本占领政策的重大战略性转变。

1947 年 3 月杜鲁门总统的国会咨文揭开美苏冷战大幕后，美国对外政策即面临全面调整。为强化决策，7 月美国通过《国家安全法案》，建立了国家安全委员会、国防部、中央情报局等。国家安全委员会此后成为美国政府的重要决策机构，尤其在杜鲁门政府时期，冷战相关重大决策的出台均经国家安全委员会反复讨论，很多重要决策文件都被冠以 NSC。

NSC 13 系列文件是冷战早期国家安全委员会讨论决定的重要的对日政策文件。当时美国对日政策所面临的困境是，1947 年 3 月冷战开始时有关缔结对日和约的问题已按既定方针提上日程，国务院同年夏天在华盛顿召集远东委员会各国开了对日和约准备会议，此次会议虽因中苏美英四大国间的重大分歧而未果，但美国自身也没有准备好相应对策。此时美国准备的对日和约还遵循《波茨坦公告》的对日惩罚压制路线，规定中有防止日本重新崛起成为美国威胁的内容，远在东京的对日占领盟军总司令（Supreme Commander for the Allied Powers, SCAP）麦克阿瑟也还在执行民主化非军事化的占领改革方针。1948 年 2 月底 3 月初，为使对日政策尽快服务于冷战遏制的新目标，美国国务院政策设计组（Policy Planning Staff, PPS）组长凯南专程访日与麦克阿瑟协调。回国后，凯南起草了一份新的对日政策文件，即 PPS 28，该文件成为后来美国国家安全委员会 NSC 13 系列文件的原型。

NSC 13/2 是经各方讨论修改后的产物，融汇国务院、军方以及麦克阿瑟等各方意见。具体包含对日政策中四方面的问题，即和约谈判的时间与程序、安全事务、管理体制以及占领政策。其中明确指出：由于国际形势的深刻变化，美国此时应暂缓对日和约，并集中关注占领结束后对日本人的控制；对日和约本身应尽可能简洁，应该是一般性和非惩罚性的；暂不决定和约缔结后美国对日本安全保障的立场，具体留待和约交涉时视国际形势以及日本国内的安定程度而定；占领改革政策应符合新的占领目的，美国不再强制日本政府进一步改革；放宽整肃政策，以及到缔结对日和约前美国占领政策的中心是复兴日本的经济；等等。相对于《波茨坦公告》规定的民主化非军事化的对日占领改造目标，上述内容体现了美国冷战后对日占领政策的根本转变。

作为公文书，NSC 13/2 的文字表述简洁明确，其阅读难度主要在于文中的一些不常见的词汇、表述，以及一些结构相对复杂的句子。

以下列举部分阅读时须留意的词汇和表述，以帮助理解。生僻词与用法，如：nonpunitive（非惩罚性）、envisage（设想、预想）、stoppage（停止、中止）、bar（排除、去除）、screen（检查、筛查）、provision（供应品；储备；规定、条款）等。固定用法，如：tactical and non-tactical force（战术部队与非战术部队）、the regime of control（管理体制）、property rights（财产权）、restitution（赔偿）、the Japanese authorities（日本当局、日本政府）、rights and powers（权利与权力）、the Purge（整肃、清洗；褫夺公职）、interested agencies and departments of the United States Government（美国政府相关机构）、internal and external trade（内外贸易）、Censorship（审查制度）、post-censorship（邮件审查）、counter-intelligence（谍报活动）、medium and long-wave broadcasts（中波与长波广播）、by virtue of（因为，由于）。专有名词和专门表述，如：peace treaty（和约）、peace conference（和平会议、和会）、the Allied Powers（盟国，即第二次世界大战时反法西斯盟国）、Far Eastern Commission（远东委员会）、Allied Council（盟国对日理事会）、the Ryukyu Islands（琉球群岛）、Okinawa（冲绳）、Yokosuka base（横须贺基地）、Supreme Commander for the Allied Power（盟国最高司令官，即 SCAP）、the State（即 the State Department，美国国务院）、Army Department（陆军部）。

较长的句子，要注意辨析句式，分析句子结构。例如：

1. The United States Navy should shape its policy in the development of the Yokosuka base in such a way as to favor the retention on a commercial basis in the post-treaty period of as many as possible of the facilities it now enjoys there. 意思是：美国海军制定其关于横须贺基地的政策，应有利于在对日和约之后亦能尽可能多地保留其目前在彼处享有之便益。(6. Naval Base)

2. As for reform measures already taken or in process of preparation by the Japanese authorities, SCAP should be advised to relax pressure steadily but unobtrusively on the Japanese Government in connection with these reforms and should intervene only if the Japanese authorities revoke or compromise the fundamentals of the reforms as they proceed in their own way with the process of implementation and adjustment. 意思是：对于日本政府已采取或正准备实行的改革措施，应建议 SCAP 悄悄稳步缓和对日本政府的压力，除非日本当局以其自身方式进行改革，实施调整，废除或违背了改革的根本原则，SCAP 方应介入其中。(12. Internal Political and Economic Changes)

3. . . . certain others who have been barred or who are subject to being barred from public life on the basis of positions occupied should be allowed to have their cases re-examined solely on the basis of personal actions; . . . 意思是：除因其职位而被从公共生活中排除者或成为排除对象者外，其他人应被允许仅基于其个人行为重新审查其事案。(13. The Purge)

4. It should be sought through a combination of United States aid program envisaging shipments and/or credits on a declining scale over a number of years, and by a vigorous and concerted effort by all interested agencies and departments of the

United States Government to cut away existing obstacles to the revival of Japanese foreign trade, with provision for Japanese merchant shipping, and to facilitate restoration and development of Japan's exports. 意思是：该目标（指上文提到的经济复兴目标）的实现应与美国的援助计划相结合，该计划设想了数年规模渐减的物资供应和信用，还应通过美国政府所有相关机构与部门积极协调努力，扫除目前障碍，复兴日本对外贸易，并与日本商船队的规定一道，有利于日本对外贸易的恢复与发展。(15. Economic Recovery)

NSC 13/2

REPORT BY THE NATIONAL SECURITY COUNCIL
ON
RECOMMENDATIONS WITH RESPECT TO UNITED STATES POLICY TOWARD JAPAN [1]

THE PEACE TREATY

1. Timing and Procedure. In view of the differences which have developed among the interested countries regarding the procedure and substance of a Japanese peace treaty and in view of the serious international situation created by the Soviet Union's policy of aggressive Communist expansion, this Government should not press for a treaty of peace at this time. It should remain prepared to proceed with the negotiations, under some generally acceptable voting procedure, if the Allied Powers can agree among themselves on such a procedure. We should, before actually entering into a peace conference, seek through the diplomatic channel the concurrence of a majority of the participating countries in the principal points of content we desire to have in such a treaty. Meanwhile, we should concentrate our attention on the preparation of the Japanese for the eventual removal of the regime of control.

2. The Nature of the Treaty. It should be our aim to have the treaty, when finally negotiated, as brief, as general, and as nonpunitive as possible. To this end we should try to clear away during this intervening period as many as possible of the matters which might otherwise be expected to enter into the treaty of peace. Our aim should be to reduce as far as possible the number of questions to be treated in the peace treaty. This applies particularly to such matters as property rights, restitution, etc. Our policy for the coming period should be shaped specifically with this in mind.

SECURITY MATTERS

3. The Pre-Treaty Arrangements. Every effort, consistent with the proper performance of the occupational mission as envisaged in this policy paper and with military security and morale, should be made to reduce to a minimum the psychological impact of the presence of

---

1　此处标题排列格式依原文件。

occupational forces on the Japanese population. The numbers of tactical, and especially non-tactical, forces should be minimized. In determining the location of occupation forces, their employment, and support from the Japanese economy in the pre-treaty period, full weight should be given to the foregoing.

4. The Post-Treaty Arrangements. United States tactical forces should be retained in Japan until the entrance into effect of a peace treaty. A final U. S. position concerning the post-treaty arrangements for Japanese military security should not be formulated until the peace negotiations are upon us. It should then be formulated in the light of the prevailing international situation and of the degree of internal stability achieved in Japan.

5. The Ryukyu Islands. (Recommendations on this subject are to be submitted separately.)

6. Naval Bases. The United States Navy should shape its policy in the development of the Yokosuka base in such a way as to favor the retention on a commercial basis in the post-treaty period of as many as possible of the facilities it now enjoys there. Meanwhile, it should proceed to develop the possibilities of Okinawa as a naval base, on the assumption that we will remain in control there on a long-term basis. This policy does not preclude the retention of a naval base as such at; Yokosuka if, at the time of finalizing the U. S. position concerning the post-treaty arrangements for Japanese military security, the prevailing international situation makes such action desirable and if it is consistent with U. S. political objectives.

7. The Japanese Police Establishment. The Japanese Police establishment, including the coastal patrol, should be strengthened by the re-enforcing and re-equipping of the present forces, and by expanding the present centrally directed police organization.

THE REGIME OF CONTROL

8. Supreme Commander for the Allied Powers. This Government should not at this time propose or consent to any major change in the regime of control. SCAP should accordingly be formally maintained in all its existing rights and powers. However, responsibility should be placed to a steadily increasing degree in the hands of the Japanese Government. To this end the view of the United States Government should be communicated to SCAP that the scope of its operations should be reduced as rapidly as possible, with a corresponding reduction in personnel, to a point where its mission will consist largely of general supervisory observation of the activities of the Japanese Government and of contact with the latter at high levels on questions of broad governmental policy.

9. Far Eastern Commission. (Recommendations on this subject are to be submitted separately.)

10. Allied Council. The Allied Council should be continued, with its functions unchanged.

OCCUPATIONAL POLICY

11. Relations with the Japanese Government. (See paragraph 8 above.)

12. Internal Political and Economic Changes. Henceforth emphasis should be given to Japanese assimilation of the reform programs. To this end, while SCAP should not stand in the way of reform measures initiated by the Japanese if he finds them consistent with the overall objectives of the occupation, he should be advised not to press upon the Japanese Government any further reform legislation. As for reform measures already taken or in process of preparation by the Japanese authorities, SCAP should be advised to relax pressure steadily but unobtrusively on the Japanese Government in connection with these reforms and should intervene only if the Japanese authorities revoke or compromise the fundamentals of the reforms as they proceed in their own way with the process of implementation and adjustment. If exigencies of the situation permit, SCAP should consult with the U. S. Government before intervention in the event the Japanese should resort to action of such serious import. Definite background guidance embodying the above principles and indicating the United States Government's view as to the nature and extent of the adjustment to be permitted should be provided SCAP in the case of certain reforms.

13. The Purge. Since the purpose of the purge has been largely accomplished, the U. S. now should advise SCAP to inform the Japanese Government informally that no further extension of the purge is contemplated and that the purge should be modified along the following lines: (1) Categories of persons who have been purged or who are subject to the purge by virtue of their having held relatively harmless positions should be made re-eligible for governmental, business and public media positions; (2) certain others who have been barred or who are subject to being barred from public life on the basis of positions occupied should be allowed to have their cases re-examined solely on the basis of personal actions; and (3) a minimum age limit should be fixed, under which no screening for public office would be required.

14. Occupation Costs. The occupational costs borne by the Japanese Government should continue to be reduced to the maximum extent consonant with the policy objectives of the pre-treaty period as envisaged in this paper.

15. Economic Recovery. Second only to U. S. security interests, economic recovery should be made the primary objective of United States policy in Japan for the coming period. It should be sought through a combination of United States aid program envisaging shipments and/or credits on a declining scale over a number of years, and by a vigorous and concerted effort by all interested agencies and departments of the United States Government to cut away existing obstacles to the revival of Japanese foreign trade, with provision for Japanese merchant shipping, and to facilitate restoration and development of Japan's exports. In developing Japan's internal and external trade and industry, private enterprise should be encouraged. Recommendations concerning the implementation of the above points, formulated in the light of Japan's economic relationship with other Far Eastern countries, should be worked out between the State and Army Departments after consultation with the other interested departments and agencies of the Government. We should make it clear to the Japanese Government that the success of the recovery program will in large part depend on Japanese efforts to raise production and to maintain high export levels through hard work, a minimum of work-stoppages, internal austerity measures and the stern combatting of inflationary trends including efforts to achieve a balanced internal budget as rapidly as possible.

16. Property Matters. SCAP should be advised to expedite the restoration or final disposal of property of United Nations members and their nationals in such a way that the process will be substantially completed by July 1, 1949. It should be the objective of United States policy to have all property matters straightened out as soon as possible and certainly well in advance of a treaty of peace in order that they may not hamper treaty negotiations.

17. Information and Education.

a. Censorship. Censorship of literary materials entering Japan should be conducted with the minimum of delay and pre-censorship of the Japanese press should cease. This should not operate, however, to prevent SCAP from exercising a broad post-censorship supervision and from engaging in counter-intelligence spot-checking of the mails.

b. Radio. The United States Government should immediately undertake a regular program of medium- and long-wave broadcasts to Japan from a suitably located transmitter station possibly on Okinawa. These programs should be carefully prepared with a view to developing an understanding and appreciation of American ideas and at the same time to maintaining as wide a Japanese radio audience as possible.

c. Interchange of Persons. The interchange between Japan and the United States of scholars, teachers, lecturers, scientists and technicians should be strongly encouraged. SCAP should continue the policy of permitting approved Japanese to go abroad for cultural as well as economic purposes.

18. War Crime Trials. The trial of Class A suspects is completed and decision of the court is awaited. We should continue and push to an early conclusion the screening of all "B" and "C" suspects with a view to releasing those whose cases we do not intend to prosecute. Trials of the others should be instituted and concluded at the earliest possible date.

19. Control of Japanese Economic War Potential. Production in, importation into, and use within Japan of goods and economic services for bona fide peaceful purposes should be permitted without limitation, except:

a. Japan's economic war potential should be controlled by restrictions on allowable stockpiling of designated strategic raw materials in Japan.

b. Japan's industrial disarmament should be limited to the prohibition of the manufacture of weapons of war and civil aircraft and the minimum of temporary restrictions on industrial production which can be advocated in the light of commitments already made by the United States regarding the reduction of the industrial war potential.

20. Japanese Reparations. (Recommendations on this subject are to be submitted separately.)

选自 United States Department of State (ed.), *Foreign Relations of the United States, 1948*, Vol. VI: The Far East and Australasia, Washington, D. C. : U. S. Government Printing Office, 1948, 858-862.

第六章　史学理论与史学史

一、弗兰西斯·培根的史学思想

导读

弗兰西斯·培根（Francis Bacon，1561—1626）在自然哲学和科学方法领域是西欧从传统社会迈向近代这一转型时期的巨人。他的学术贡献是多方面的。他论述法律、国家和宗教，评述当代政治，思考社会和伦理问题，对近代哲学思想和科学方法有杰出贡献。同时，他还是英国近代早期著名的历史家。培根有宏大的学术抱负，曾计划分六个部分来写一部巨著《伟大的复兴》（*Instauratio Magna*）：第一部分分析人类知识现状，第二部分阐述一种新的科学方法，第三部分汇集实验和研究数据，第四部分解释他的新科学工作方法，第五部分提出一些暂定的结论，最后一部分综述用他的新方法所获得的知识。《学术的进展》（*The Advancement of Learning*，1605）和《新工具》（*Novum Organum*，1620）就是他这一宏大计划的头两个部分。培根最终没有完成他的宏大计划，但我们可以看到他的复兴科学计划主要围绕两个中心主题：一个是对自然的认识，另一个是对人自身的认识。他认为自然科学应该以自然史为基础，而人的科学则应该以人类历史为基础。因此，作为文艺复兴之子，培根重视对既存知识的整理；作为欧洲近代学术的奠基人，他提出了研究自然和人的崭新方法。培根对历史学术的贡献主要表现在两个方面：一是历史理论，二是具体的历史写作。培根虽然没有关于历史学理论的专门论著，但他散见于各种著作中的历史理论依然阐述了深刻的史学观点，闪现着思想的光辉。下面的材料选自《学术的进展》第二卷的第一节和第二节，这两节集中论述了培根关于历史分类和历史理论问题的观点，是研究其史学思想的重要文献，也是我们了解近代早期西欧史学向近代迈进的重要材料。

阅读材料第一节共有六段文字，分量不大，文字也不艰深，内容非常集中，就是论述历史的分类。文中培根遵循传统，按照研究主题对全部历史进行了分类，将其分为自然史、政治史、宗教史、学术史等。从表面上看，培根的历史分类没什么新意，然而他在通常三种历史之外加上学术史这一类别，尤其是他对学术的论述展现出卓越的创新精神，体现出开创一种全新的人类知识史的意图。培根认为，真正的学术史应该从古代开始写，追溯学术及其各流派的起源，记述它们的产生和传统，它们的治学机构和管理方法；还要记述它们的兴衰存亡，褒贬毁誉，传承流布，并分析其原因，确定其地点。除此之外，学术史应把全世界各时代所有其他与知识学术相关的事件载入史册。培根的学术研究远远超越了传统人文主义者的文献研究的范畴，他把各时代的文献看作是思想和智慧的载体，研究它们是要考察各时代思想学术的观点、风格和方法，由此洞悉各时代的学术精神。写作这样的学术史不是为了满足热爱学术者的好奇心，而是为了一个更严肃、更重要的目的——使学者在运用学术和管理学术时更睿智。因此，他的学术史要通过梳理学术发展历史来为欧洲学术重新定向，这是他改造欧洲学术，促进学术复兴的宏大计划的基础。

阅读材料的第二节有十四个自然段，在这一节中培根继续他的历史分类，首先把政治史按完成的程度分成三种，即纪事杂录（memorial）、完美历史（perfect history）和古物逸史（antiquities）。在三种政治史中，培根非常重视完备公正的历史，即所谓完美历史。他认为，根据记录或声称记录的对象的不同，完美历史又可分为三种，即记录时间的编年史（chronicles）、记录人物生平的传记（lives）和记录事件的纪事（narrations）。三种完美历史各有所长，编年史最为完备，最为精致。这一节中除了他关于"完美历史"的论述值得关注外，还有两点是培根在史学史上有影响的地方。其一，培根似乎原封不动地接受了传统人文主义者关于历史的分期，实际上他是将人文主义者的历史分期从学术文化史推广到了政治史。他认为，在人类整个历史长河中，希腊、罗马是上帝选定的世界各国在军事、学术、道德、政体、法律等方面的榜样。这两个国家于是被置于时间序列的中部，比它们古老的历史有一个共同的名称，叫古代史（antiquities），它们之后的历史可以称为近代史（modern history），他称自己所处的时代为当代（these times），所以就有一个"中间时代"把他自己的时代与古代榜样分隔开来了。培根虽然没有使用"中世纪"一词，但他将欧洲历史分为三个时期的做法有助于西方史学传统历史分期方法的最后成型。其二，他向英国国王建议，倡导写作英国历史，特别是英国当代历史："既然大不列颠岛从今以后联合成为一个君主国，那么它过去时代的历史也应该作为一个整体来叙述……如果写作一部完整的英国史工程太浩大而难以完成，那么可以选择英国历史中一段不长的时期作为叙述对象，比如从红、白玫瑰两个家族的联合到英格兰与苏格兰两个王国的联合这一辉煌的时代。"培根的这一提议说明他充分认识到写作英国民族国家历史的急迫性，英国的民族身份和民族国家认同需要通过写作民族历史来界定和加强。

另外，我们在阅读培根的著作时，要逐渐适应近代早期英国学者的那种行文风格。这是一个崇古之风盛行的时代，也是英国民族文学语言发展的重要时期，文人的散文写作都受到古代散文作家和古典修辞学的影响，来自古希腊、罗马历史和圣经故事典故的必不可少，像莎士比亚剧作中那种形象的比喻也不会少。培根是大学问家，散文写作高手，他的学术著作中充满格言警句和形象的比喻，读来是一种享受，同时也会有一定的难度。

The Advancement of Learning

I Triple Distribution of Human Learning: and First of Natural History.

1. The parts of human learning have reference to the three parts of man's understanding, which is the seat of learning: history to his memory, poesy to his imagination, and philosophy to his reason. Divine learning receiveth the same distribution; for, the spirit of manis the same, though the revelation of oracle and sense be diverse. So as theology consisteth also of history of the Church; of parables, which is divine poesy; and of holy doctrine or precept. For as for that part which seemeth supernumerary, which is prophecy, it is but divine history, which hath that prerogative over human, as the narration may be before the fact as well as after.

2. History is natural, civil, ecclesiastical, and literary; whereof the first three I allow as extant, the fourth I note as deficient. For no man hath propounded to himself the general state of learning to be described and represented from age to age, as many have done the works of Nature, and the state, civil and ecclesiastical; without which the history of the world seemeth to me to be as the statue of Polyphemus[1] with his eye out, that part being wanting which doth most show the spirit and life of the person. And yet I am not ignorant that in divers particular sciences, as of the jurisconsults, the mathematicians, the rhetoricians, the philosophers, there are set down some small memorials of the schools, authors, and books; and so likewise some barren relations touching the invention of arts or usages. But a just story of learning, containing the antiquities and originals of knowledges and their sects, their inventions, their traditions, their diverse administrations and managings, their flourishings, their oppositions, decays, depressions, oblivions, removes, with the causes and occasions of them, and all other events concerning learning, throughout the ages of the world, I may truly affirm to be wanting; the use and end of which work I do not so much design for curiosity or satisfaction of those that are the lovers of learning, but chiefly for a more serious and grave purpose, which is this in few words, that it will make learned men wise in the use and administration of learning. For it is not Saint Augustine's nor Saint Ambrose's works that will make so wise a divine as ecclesiastical history thoroughly read and observed, and the same reason is of learning.

3. History of Nature is of three sorts; of Nature in course, of Natureerring or varying, and of Nature altered or wrought; that is, history of creatures, history of marvels, and history of arts. The first of these, no doubt, is extant, and that in good perfection; the two latter are handled so weakly and unprofitably, as I am moved to note them as deficient. For I find no sufficient or competent collection of the works of Nature which have a digression and deflexion from the ordinary course of generations, productions, and motions; whether they be singularities of place and region, or the strange events of time and chance, or the effects of yet unknown properties, or the instances of exception to general kinds. It is true I find a number ofbooks of fabulous

---

1 波吕斐摩斯，希腊神话中的独眼巨人。

experiments and secrets, and frivolous impostures for pleasure and strangeness; but a substantial and severe collection of the heteroclites or irregulars of Nature, well examined and described, I find not, specially not with due rejection of fables and popular errors. For as things now are, if an untruth in Nature be once on foot, what by reason of the neglect of examination, and countenance of antiquity, and what by reason of the use of the opinion in similitudes and ornaments of speech, it is never called down.

4. The use of this work, honored with a precedent in Aristotle, is nothing less than to give contentment to the appetite of curious and vain wits, as the manner of Mirabilaries is to do; but for two reasons, both of great weight: the one to correct the partiality of axioms and opinions, which are commonly framed only upon common and familiar examples; the other because from the wonders of Nature is the nearest intelligence and passage towards the wonders of art, for it is no more but by following and, as it were, hounding Nature in her wanderings, to be able to lead her afterwards to the same place again. Neither am I of opinion, in this history of marvels, that superstitious narrations of sorceries, witchcrafts, dreams, divinations, and the like, where there is an assurance and clear evidence of the fact, be altogether excluded. For it is not yet known in what cases and how far effects attributed to superstition do participate of natural causes; and, therefore, howsoever the practice of such things is to be condemned, yet from the speculation and consideration of them light may be taken, not only for the discerning of the offences, but for the further disclosing of Nature. Neither ought a man to make scruple of entering into these things for inquisition of truth, as your Majesty [1] hath showed in your own example, who, with the two clear eyes of religion and natural philosophy, have looked deeply and wisely into these shadows, and yet proved yourself to be of the nature of the sun, which passeth through pollutions and itself remains as pure as before. But this I hold fit, that these narrations, which have mixture with superstition, be sorted by themselves, and not to be mingled with the narrations which are merely and sincerely natural. But as for the narrations touching the prodigies and miracles of religions, they are either not true or not natural; and, therefore, impertinent for the story of Nature.

5. For history of Nature, wrought or mechanical, I find some collections made of agriculture, and likewise of manual arts; but commonly with a rejection of experiments familiar and vulgar; for it is esteemed a kind of dishonor unto learning to descend to inquiry or meditation upon matters mechanical, except they be such as may be thought secrets, rarities, and special subtleties; which humour of vain and supercilious arrogancy is justly derided in Plato, where he brings in Hippias, a vaunting sophist, disputing with Socrates, a true and unfeigned inquisitor of truth; where, the subject being touching beauty, Socrates, after his wandering manner of inductions, put first an example of a fair virgin, and then of a fair horse, and then of a fair pot well glazed, whereat Hippias was offended, and said, "More than for courtesy's sake, he

---

[1] 指国王詹姆士一世,他登基为国王以前是一位学者,研究魔鬼、女巫等问题,写有三卷本的相关专著。

did think much to dispute with any that did allege such base and sordid instances."Whereunto Socrates answereth, "You have reason, and it becomes you well, being a man so trim in your vestments,"&c., and so goeth on in an irony. But the truth is, they be not the highest instances that give the securest information, as may be well expressed in the tale so common of the philosopher that, while he gazed upwards to the stars, fell into the water;[1] for if he had looked down he might have seen the stars in the water, but looking aloft he could not see the water in the stars. So it cometh often to pass that mean and small things discover great, better than great can discover the small; and therefore Aristotle noteth well, "That the nature of everything is best seen in his smallest portions." And for that cause he inquireth the nature of a commonwealth, first in a family, and the simple conjugations of man and wife, parent and child, master and servant, which are in every cottage. Even so likewise the nature of this great city of the world, and the policy thereof, must be first sought in mean concordances and small portions. So we see how that secret of Nature, of the turning of iron touched with the loadstone towards the north, was found out in needles of iron, not in bars of iron.

6. But if my judgment be of any weight, the use of history mechanical is of all others the most radical and fundamental towards natural philosophy; such natural philosophy as shall not vanish in the fume of subtle, sublime, or delectable speculation, but such as shall be operative to the endowment and benefit of man's life. For it will not only minister and suggest for the present many ingenious practices in all trades, by a connection and transferring of the observations of one art to the use of another, when the experiences of several mysteries shall fall under the consideration of one man's mind; but further, it will give a more true and real illuminationconcerning causes and axioms than is hitherto attained. For like as a passages and variations of nature cannot appear so fully in the liberty of nature as in the trials and vexations of art. man's disposition is never well known till he be crossed, nor Proteus[2] ever changed shapes till he was straitened and held fast; so the passages and variations of nature cannot appear so fully in the liberty of nature as in the trials and vexations of art.

II Of Civil History.

1. For civil history, it is of three kinds; not unfitly to be compared with the three kinds of pictures or images. For of pictures or images, we see, some are unfinished, some are perfect, and some are defaced. So of histories we may find three kinds: memorials, perfect histories, and antiquities; for memorials are history unfinished, or the first or rough drafts of history; and antiquities are history defaced, or some remnants of history which have casually escaped the shipwreck of time.

2. Memorials, or preparatory history, are of two sorts; whereof theone may be termed commentaries, and the other registers. Commentaries are they which set down a continuance of

---

1 典出古希腊哲学家泰勒斯（约前 624—约前 546）。
2 普罗透斯，古希腊神话中波塞冬属下的一位海神，是一位会多种变化的老人。

the naked events and actions, without the motives or designs, the counsels, the speeches, the pretexts, the occasions, and other passages of action. For this is the true nature of a commentary (though Cæsar, in modesty mixed with greatness, did for his pleasure apply the name of a commentary to the best history of the world). Registers are collections of public acts, as decrees of council, judicial proceedings, declarations and letters of estate, orations, and the like, without a perfect continuance or contexture of the thread of the narration.

3. Antiquities, or remnants of history, are, as was said, Tanquam tabula naufragii (像破船板): when industrious persons, by an exact and scrupulous diligence and observation, out of monuments, names, words, proverbs, traditions, private records and evidences, fragments of stories, passages of books that concern not story, and the like, do save and recover somewhat from the deluge of time.

In these kinds of unperfect histories I do assign no deficience, for they are Tanquam imperfecte mista (如同不完备的东西的混合); and therefore any deficience in them is but their nature. As for the corruptions and moths of history, which are epitomes, the use of them deserveth to bebanished, as all men of sound judgment have confessed, as those that have fretted and corroded the sound bodies of many excellent histories, and wrought them into base and unprofitable dregs.

4. History, which may be called just and perfect history, is of three kinds, according to the object which it propoundeth, or pretendeth to represent: for it either representeth a time, or a person, or an action. The first we call chronicles, the second lives, and the third narrations or relations. Of these, although the first be the most complete and absolute kind of history, and hath most estimation and glory, yet the second excelleth it in profit and use, and the third in verity and sincerity. For history of times representeth the magnitude of actions, and the public faces and deportments of persons, and passeth over in silence the smaller passages and motions of men and matters. But such being the workmanship of God, as He doth hang the greatest weight upon the smallest wires, maxima è minimis suspendens, it comes therefore to pass, that such histories do rather set forth the pomp of business than the true and inward resorts thereof. But lives, if they be well written, propounding to themselves a person to represent, in whom actions, both greater and smaller, public and private, have a commixture, must of necessity contain a more true, native, and lively representation. So again narrations and relations of actions, as the war of Peloponnesus, the expedition of Cyrus Minor, the conspiracy of Catiline[1], cannot but be more purely and exactly true than histories of times, because they may choose an argument comprehensible within the notice and instructions of the writer: whereas he that undertaketh the story of a time, specially of any length, cannot but meet with many blanks and spaces, which he must be forced to fill up out of his own wit and conjecture.

1　喀提林（前108—前62），罗马共和国贵族，因竞选执政官失败而密谋叛乱，遭执政官西塞罗镇压，于公元前62年战死。

5. For the history of times, I mean of civil history, the providence of God hath made the distribution. For it hath pleased God to ordain and illustrate two exemplar states of the world for arms, learning, moral virtue, policy, and laws; the state of Græcia and the state of Rome; the histories whereof occupying the middle part of time, have more ancient to them histories which may by one common name be termed the antiquities of the world; and after them, histories which may be likewise called by the name of modern history.

6. Now to speak of the deficiences. As to the heathen antiquities of the world, it is in vain to note them for deficient. Deficient they are no doubt, consisting most of fables and fragments; but the deficience cannot be holpen; for antiquity is like fame, Caput inter nubila condit[1], her head is muffled from our sight. For the history of the exemplar states, it is extant in good perfection. Not but I could wish there were a perfect course of history for Græcia, from Theseus to Philopoemen (what time the affairs of Græcia drowned and extinguished in the affairs of Rome), and for Rome from Romulus to Justinianus, who may be truly said to be Ultimus Romanorum (最后一个罗马人). In which sequences of story the text of Thucydides and Xenophon in the one, and the texts of Livius, Polybius, Sallustius, Cæsar, Appianus, Tacitus, Herodianus in the other, to be kept entire, without any diminution at all, and only to be supplied and continued. But this is a matter of magnificence, rather to be commended than required; and we speak now of parts of learning supplemental, and not of supererogation.

7. But for modern histories, whereof there are some few very worthy, but the greater part beneath mediocrity, leaving the care of foreign stories to foreign states, because I will not be curiosus in alienarepublica (外国), I cannot fail to represent to your Majesty the unworthiness of the history of England in the main continuance thereof, and the partiality and obliquity of that of Scotland in the latest and largest author[2] that I have seen: supposing that it would be honor for your Majesty, and a work very memorable, if this island of Great Britain, as it is now joined in monarchy for the ages to come, so were joined in one history for the times passed, after the manner of the sacred history, which draweth down the story of the ten tribes and of the two tribes as twins together. And if it shall seem that the greatness of this work may make it less exactly performed, there is an excellent period of a much smaller compass of time, as to the story of England; that is to say, from the uniting of the Roses to the uniting of the kingdoms; a portion of time wherein, to my understanding, there hath been the rarest varieties that in like number of successions of any hereditary monarchy hath been known. For it beginneth with the mixed adoption of a crown by arms and title; an entry by battle, an establishment by marriage; and therefore times answerable, like waters after a tempest, full of working and swelling, though without extremity of storm; but well passed through by the wisdom of the pilot, being one of the most sufficient kings of all the number. Then followeth the reign of a king, whose actions,

---

1 语出维吉尔诗，意为"把头脑藏于云雾中"，喻不明不白，看不清楚。
2 指史家布坎南（George Buchanan, 1506—1582）。

howsoever conducted, had much intermixture with the affairs of Europe, balancing and inclining them variably; in whose time also began that great alteration in the state ecclesiastical, an action which seldom cometh upon the stage. Then the reign of a minor; then an offer of a usurpation, though it was but as febris ephemera[1]. Then the reign of a queen matched with a foreigner; then of a queen that lived solitary and unmarried, and yet her government so masculine, as it had greater impression and operation upon the states abroad than it any ways received from thence. And now last, this most happy and glorious event, that this island of Britain, divided from all the world, should be united in itself, and that oracle of rest given to Eneas（埃涅阿斯）, antiquam exquirite matrem[2], should now be performed and fulfilled upon the nations of England and Scotland, being now reunited in the ancient mother name of Britain, as a full period of all instability and peregrinations. So that as it cometh to pass in massive bodies, that they have certain trepidations and waverings before they fix and settle, so it seemeth that by the providence of God this monarchy, before it was to settle in your majesty and your generations, (in which, I hope, it is now established for ever,) had these prelusive changes and varieties.

8. For lives, I do find strange that these times have so little esteemed the virtues of the times, as that the writings of lives should be no more frequent. For although there be not many sovereign princes or absolute commanders, and that states are most collected into monarchies, yet are there many worthy personages that deserve better than dispersed report or barren eulogies. For herein the invention of one of the late poets is proper[3], and doth well enrich the ancient fiction. For he feigneth that at the end of the thread or web of every man's life there was a little medal containing the person's name, and that Time waited upon the shears, and as soon as the thread was cut caught the medals, and carried them to the river of Lathe; and about the bank there were many birds flying up and down, that would get the medals and carry them in their beak a little while, and then let them fall into the river. Only there were a few swans, which if they got a name would carry it to a temple where it was consecrate. And although many men, more mortal in their affections than in their bodies, do esteem desire of name and memory but as a vanity and ventosity, "Animi nil magnæ laudis egentes;"[4] which opinion cometh from that root, Non prius laudes contempsimus, quam laudanda facere desivimus[5]: yet that will not alter Solomon's judgment, Memoria justicum laudibus, at impiorum nomen putrescet: the one flourisheth, the other either consumeth to present oblivion, or turneth to an ill odour. And therefore in that style or addition, which is and hath been long well received and brought in use, Felicis memoriæ, piæ memoriæ, bonæ memoriæ,[6] we do acknowledge that which Cicero

---

1 "febris ephemera", 拉丁语, 意为"热症"。
2 语出维吉尔诗, 意为"寻找你的母亲"。
3 指意大利诗人阿里奥斯托 (1474—1533)。
4 拉丁语, 意为"不在乎名声的人"。
5 拉丁格言, 意为"他们不能再做出什么值得人称赞的事情, 才来鄙弃世人的称赞"。
6 拉丁语, 意为"幸运、虔诚、美好的名声"。

saith, borrowing it from Demosthenes, that Bona fama propria possessio defunctorum [1]; which possession I cannot but note that in our times it lieth much waste, and that therein there is a deficience.

9. For narrations and relations of particular actions, there were also to be wished a greater diligence therein; for there is no great action but hath some good pen which attends it. And because it is an ability not common to write a good history, as may well appear by the small number of them; yet if particularity of actions memorable were but tolerably reported as they pass, the compiling of a complete history of times might be the better expected, when a writer should arise that were fit for it: for the collection of such relations might be as a nursery garden, whereby to plant a fair and stately garden when time should serve.

10. There is yet another partition of history which Cornelius Tacitus maketh, which is not to be forgotten, specially with that application which he accoupleth it withal, annals and journals: appropriating to the former matters of estate, and to the latter acts and accidents of a meaner nature. For giving but a touch of certain magnificentbuildings, he addeth, Cum ex dignitate populi Romani repertum sit, res illustres annalibus talia diurnis urbis actis mandare. [2] So as there is a kind of contemplative heraldry, as well as civil.

And as nothing doth derogate from the dignity of a state more than confusion of degrees, so it doth not a little imbase the authority of a history to intermingle matters of triumph, or matters of ceremony, or matters of novelty, with matters of state. But the use of a journal hath not only been in the history of time, but likewise in the history of persons, and chiefly of actions; for princes in ancient time had, upon point of honor and policy both, journals kept, what passed day by day. For we see the chronicle which was read before Ahasuerus [3], when he could not take rest, contained matter of affairs, indeed, but such as had passed in his own time and very lately before. But the journal of Alexander's house expressed every small particularity, even concerning his person and court; and it is yet a use well received in enterprises memorable, as expeditions of war, navigations, and the like, to keep diaries of that which passeth continually.

11. I cannot likewise be ignorant of a form of writing which some grave and wise men have used, containing a scattered history of those actions which they have thought worthy of memory, with politic discourse and observation thereupon: not incorporate into the history, but separately, and as the more principal in their intention; which kind of ruminated history I think more fit to place amongst books of policy, whereof we shall hereafter speak, than amongst books of history. For it is the true office of history to represent the events themselves together with the counsels, and to leave the observations and conclusions thereupon to the liberty and faculty of every man's judgment. But mixtures are things irregular, whereof no man can define.

1　拉丁格言，意为"好名声是死者的正当财富"。
2　罗马历史家塔西陀语，意为"罗马人应该让历史只记叙那些丰功伟业，细小事情则由日志来载录，这样才配得上罗马人的尊严"。
3　《圣经》中的波斯国王亚哈随鲁。

12. So also is there another kind of history manifoldly mixed, and that is history of cosmography: being compounded of natural history, in respect of the regions themselves; of history civil, in respect of the habitations, regiments, and manners of the people; and the mathematics, in respect of the climates and configurations towards the heavens: which part of learning of all others in this latter time hath obtained most proficience. For it may be truly affirmed to the honor of these times, and in a virtuous emulation with antiquity, that this great building of the world had never through lights made in it, till the age of us and our fathers. For although they had knowledge of the Antipodes,

"Nosque ubi primus equis Oriens afflavit anhelis,
Illic sera rubens accendit lumina Vesper," [1]

yet that might be by demonstration, and not in fact; and if by travel, it requireth the voyage but of half the globe. But to circle the earth, as the heavenly bodies do, was not done nor enterprised till these later times: and therefore these times may justly bear in their word, not only plus ultra (再远一点), in precedence of the ancient non ultra (不要再远), and imitabile fulmen (效仿雷电), in precedence of the ancient non imitabile fulmen (不要效仿雷电),

"Demens qui nimbos et non imitabile fulmen," [2] &c.

but likewise imitabile cælum; in respect of the many memorable voyages after the manner of heaven about the globe of the earth.

13. And this proficience in navigation and discoveries may plant also an expectation of the further proficience and augmentation of all sciences; because it may seem they are ordained by God to be coevals, that is, to meet in one age. For so the prophet Daniel speaking of the latter times, foretelleth Plurimi pertransibunt, et multiplex erit scientia: as if the openness and through passage of the world and the increase of knowledge were appointed to be in the same ages; as we see it is already performed in great part: the learning of these later times not much giving place to the former two periods or returns of learning, the one of the Grecians, the other of the Romans.

选自 Francis Bacon, *The Two Books of Francis Bacon: Of the Proficience and Advancement of Learning, Divine and Human*, London: Parker, Son, and Bourn, West Strand, 1863, pp. 68–78.

二、博林布鲁克论历史

导读

博林布鲁克（Henry St. John, Lord Viscount Bolingbroke, 1678–1751）是 18 世纪英国著名的政治家，博学多才，其著述涉及政治、哲学、历史等多个

---

1 语出维吉尔诗，意为"这边清晨旭日东升，那边暮色长庚点灯"。
2 语出维吉尔诗，意为"白痴才效仿雷电"。

领域。18世纪20年代开始,博林布鲁克、蒲伯、斯威夫特等以《匠人》杂志为阵地,展开对沃波尔政府的全面攻击。沃波尔方面则以《伦敦杂志》等报纸杂志为阵地,在D.笛福等人的带领下进行反击。于是双方爆发了一场旷日持久的政治论战。当1730年博林布鲁克开始从历史的角度对沃波尔政府展开批判的时候,沃波尔阵营同样进行了相应的反驳,由此有了英国历史上这场著名的"历史大论战"。正是他们与沃波尔政府的政治论战激发了博林布鲁克对历史问题的思考,所以他以与法国和英国友人的通信的形式,较为系统地阐述了自己的历史观点。后来,这些书信汇编成《历史研究书简》(1738)一书,单独出版。博林布鲁克的这部著作可以说是源远流长的"历史艺术"著作的余绪。在文艺复兴时期,迪奥尼索斯和琉善(Lucian,125—180)是这类著作的古典榜样。作为复兴古典学术的结果,与琉善的《怎样写历史》类似的历史手册首先产生于意大利,16世纪成为一种公认的人文主义文类,随后不久就传播到了其他国家。这类著作最初被称为历史的艺术(artes historicae),书名一般叫《怎样写历史》《历史的观念》《历史的艺术》,或者叫《历史研究》。它们最初主要论述历史的文学和修辞方法,逐渐发展成为对历史的实用性的论述,不过直到18世纪,其中许多著作依然表现出对修辞问题,即逻辑顺序、内容安排和风格等问题的关注。博林布鲁克的《历史研究书简》包括八封书信,论及历史研究的目的、方法、益处和用处,以及历史编写和历史分期等问题,将历史实用性的论题与他的时代的政治、哲学观点混合在一起。他关于历史问题的思考的重要性不在于其创新性,而在于他的观点反映了那个时代历史观点的微妙变化,是以伦理和政治垂训为目的,实用的传统事例史的衰落,以及"历史是生活的导师"这一格言开始消解的最好例证。

我们选择《历史研究书简》中第三封书信的上半部分作为阅读材料,是因为它继续第一封信的话题,集中论述了研究历史的作用。从中我们能清楚地看到,到18世纪初期,随着怀疑论思潮进一步发展,传统历史艺术所教导的那一套分类、摘录和使用历史事例的方法完全过时了。博林布鲁克在其中对脱离语境的历史事例的有用性表示怀疑。实际上,他对迪奥尼索斯的"历史是用事例教导的哲学"的说法,以及把历史看作是教育事例的宝库的古典观点是认可的,不过他的认可是带有批判性前提的:不具备个人经验,这类事例知识是学究的财产,在最好的情况下是死知识,在最糟的情况下会误导人,积极的生活与沉思的生活必须相互渗透。博林布鲁克特别批判了马基雅维利的方法,表现出对圭怡尔迪尼的认同。他还猛烈抨击了让·波丹历史理论著作中所谈到的做历史阅读笔记的方法,他指出:"我怀疑波丹的这种'方法'是在教我们一种同样糟糕的方式,它会使我们没时间去行动,或者使我们力不胜任。从历史著作中去搜集、摘抄大量的著名格言和事实可以使一个人像波丹那样言谈或写作,但绝不能使他成为一个更优秀的人,也不能使他如一位有用的公民那样去促进他所属社会的安全、和平和福利,或者使它更伟大。"

博林布鲁克的许多著作都产生于党派论战中,所以其行文较为流畅,富于激情，虽说不上深刻，但有洞见。总之，下面的选文不会有太大的阅读难度，又能激起大家阅读原著的兴趣。

Letters on the Study and Use of History
LETTER 3: Of the Study of History

  Were these letters to fall into the hands of some ingenious persons who adorn the age we live in, your lordship's correspondent would be joked upon for his project of improving men in virtue and wisdom by the study of history. The general characters of men, it would be said, are determined by their natural constitutions, as their particular actions are by immediate objects. Many very conversant in history would be cited, who have proved ill men, or bad politicians; and a long roll would be produced of others, who have arrived at a great pitch of private, and public virtue, without any assistance of this kind. Something has been said already to anticipate this objection; but, since I have heard several persons affirm such propositions with great confidence, a loud laugh, or a silent sneer at the pedants who presumed to think otherwise; I will spend a few paragraphs, with your lordship's leave, to show that such affirmations, for to affirm amongst these fine men is to reason, either prove too much, or prove nothing.

  If our general characters were determined absolutely, as they are certainly influenced, by our constitutions, and if our particular actions were so by immediate objects; all instruction by precept, as well as example, and all endeavors to form the moral character by education, would be unnecessary. Even the little care that is taken, and surely it is impossible to take less, in the training up our youth, would be too much. But the truth is widely different from this representation of it; for, what is vice, and what is virtue? I speak of them in a large and philosophical sense. The former is, I think, no more than the excess, abuse, and misapplication of appetites, desires, and passions, natural and innocent, nay useful and necessary. The latter consists in the moderation and government, in the use and application of these appetites, desires, and passions, according to the rules of reason, and therefore often in opposition to their own blind impulse.

  What now is education? That part, that principle and most neglected part of it, I mean, which tends to form the moral character? It is, I think, an institution designed to lead men from their tender years, by precept and example, by argument and authority, to the practice, and to the habit of practising these rules. The stronger our appetites, desires, and passions are, the harder indeed is the task of education: but when these efforts of education are proportioned to this strength, although our keenest appetites and desires, and our ruling passions cannot be reduced to a quiet and uniform submission, yet, are not their excesses assuaged? Are not their abuses and misapplications, in some degree, diverted or checked? Though the pilot cannot lay the storm, cannot he carry the ship, by his art, better through it, and often prevent the wreck that would always happen, without him? If Alexander who loved wine, and was naturally choleric, had been bred under the severity of Roman discipline, it is probable he would neither have made a bonfire of Persepolis for his whore, nor have killed his friend. If Scipio, who was naturally given to women, for which anecdote we have, if I mistake not, the authority of Polybius, as well as some verses of Naevius preserved by A. Gellius, had been educated by Olympius at the court of Philip, it is improbable that he would have restored the beautiful Spaniard. In short, if the renowned Socrates had not corrected nature by art, this first apostle of the gentiles had been a very profligate fellow, by his own confession; for he was inclined to all the vices Zopyrus imputed to him, as they say, on the observation of his physiognomy.

With him, therefore, who denies the effects of education, it would be in vain to dispute; and with him who admits them, there can be dispute, concerning that share which I ascribe to the study of history, in forming our moral characters, and making us better men. The very persons who pretend that inclinations cannot be restrained, nor habits corrected, against our natural bent, would be the first perhaps to prove, in certain cases, the contrary. A fortune at court, or the favors of a lady, have prevailed on many to conceal, and they could not conceal without restraining, which is one step towards correcting, the vices they were by nature addicted to the most. Shall we imagine now, that the beauty of virtue and the deformity of vice, the charms of a bright and lasting reputation, the terror of being delivered over as criminals to all posterity, the real benefit arising from a conscientiousdischarge of the duty we owe to others, which benefit fortune can neither hinder nor take away, and the reasonableness of conforming ourselves to the designs of God manifested in the constitution of the human nature; shall we imagine, I say, that all these are not able to acquire the same power over those who are continually called upon to a contemplation of them, and they who apply themselves to the study of history are so called upon, as other motives, mean and sordid in comparison of these, can usurp on other men?

2. That the study of history, far from making us wiser, and more useful citizens, as well as better men, may be of no advantage whatsoever; that it may serve to render us mere antiquaries and scholars; or that it may help to make us forward coxcombs, and prating pedants, I have already allowed. But this is not the fault of history: and to convince us that it is not, we need only contrast the true use of history with the use that is made of it by such men as these. We ought always to keep in mind, that history is philosophy teaching by examples how to conduct ourselves in all the situations of private and public life; that therefore we must apply ourselves to it in a philosophical spirit and manner; that we must rise from particular to general knowledge, and that we must fit ourselves for the society and business of mankind by accustoming our minds to reflect and meditate on the characters we find described, and the course of events we find related there. Particular examples may be of use sometimes in particular cases; but the application of them is dangerous. It must be done with the utmost circumspection, or it will be seldom done with success. And yet one would think that this was the principal use of the study of history, by what has been written on the subject. I know not whether Machiavel himself is quite free from defect on this account: he seems to carry the use and application of particular

examples sometimes too far. Marius and Catulus passed the Alps, met, and defeated the Cimbri beyond the frontiers of Italy. Is it safe to conclude from hence, that whenever one people is invaded by another, the invaded ought to meet and fight the invaders at a distance from their frontiers? Machiavel's countryman, Guicciardin, was aware of the danger that might arise from such an application of examples. Peter of Medicis had involved himself in great difficulties, when those wars and calamities began which Lewis Sforza first drew and entailed on Italy, by flattering the ambition of Charles the Eighth in order to gratify his own, and calling the French into that country. Peter owed his distress to his folly in departing from the general tenor of conduct his father Laurence had held, and hoped to relieve himself by imitating his father's example in one particular instance. At a time when the wars with the pope and king of Naples had reduced Laurence to circumstances of great danger, he took the resolution of going to Ferdinand, and of treating in person with that prince. The resolution appears in history imprudent and almost desperate: were we informed of the secret reasons on which this great man acted, it would appear very possible a wise and safe measure. It succeeded, and Laurence brought back with him public peace, and private security. As soon as the French troops entered the dominions of Florence, Peter was struck with a panic terror, went to Charles the Eighth, put the port of Leghorn, the fortresses of Pisa, and all the keys of the country, into this prince's hands; whereby he disarmed the Florentine commonwealth, and ruined himself. he was deprived of his authority, and driven out of the city, by the just indignation of the magistrates, and people: and in the treaty which they made afterwards with the king of France, it was stipulated, that Peter should not remain within an hundred miles of the state, nor his brothers within the same distance of the city of Florence. On this occasion Guicciardin observes, how dangerous it is to govern ourselves by particular examples; since to have the same success, we must have the same prudence, and the same fortune; and since the example must not only answer the case before us in general, but in every minute circumstance. This is the sense of that admirable historian, and these are his words——"é senza dubio molta pericoloso il governarsi con gl'esempi, se non concorrono, non solo in generale, ma in tutti i particulari, le medesime ragioni; se le cose non sono regolate con la medesima prudenza, et se oltre a tutti li altri fondamenti, non, v'ha la parte sua la medesima fortuna."[1] An observation that Boileau makes, and a rule he lays down in speaking of translations, will properly find their place here, and serve to explain still better what I would establish. "To translate servilely into modern language an ancient author phrase by phrase, and word by word, is preposterous: nothing can be more unlike the original than such a copy. It is not to show, it is to disguise the author: and he who has known him only in this dress, would not know him in his own. A good writer, instead of taking this inglorious and unprofitable task upon him, will jouster contre l'original, rather imitate than translate, and rather

---

[1] 语出意大利史家圭恰尔迪尼，大意是：如果不是原因相同，不仅是在总体上相同，而且甚至在细节上也相同，如果事情不是由同样的才智来支配，那么，人们要用事例来指导自己的行动，那是一件非常危险的事情。

emulate than imitate; he will transfuse the sense and spirit of the original into his own work, and will endeavor to write as the ancient author would have written, had he written in the same language. " Now, to improve by examples is to improve by imitation. We must catch the spirit, if we can, and conform ourselves to the reason of them; but we must not affect to translate servilely into our conduct, if your lordship will allow me the expression, the particular conduct of those good and great men, whose images history sets before us. Codrus and the Decii devoted themselves to death: one, because an oracle had foretold that the army whose general was killed would be victorious; the others in compliance with a superstition that bore great analogy to a ceremony practised in the old Egyptian church, and added afterwards, as many others of the same origin were, to the ritual of the Israelites. These are examples of great magnanimity, to be sure, and of magnanimity employed in the most worthy cause. In the early days of the Athenian and Roman government, when the credit of oracles and all kinds of superstition prevailed, when heaven was piously thought to delight in blood, and even human blood was shed under wild notions of atonement, propitiation, purgation, expiation, and satisfaction; they who set such examples as these, acted an heroical and a rational part too. But if a general should act the same part now, and, in order to secure his victory, get killed as fast as he could, he might pass for a hero, but, I am sure, he would pass for a madman. Even these examples, however, are of use: they excite us at least to venture our lives freely in the service of our country, by proposing to our imitation men who devoted themselves to certain death in the service of theirs. They show us what a turn of imagination can operate, and how the greatest trifle, nay the greatest absurdity, dressed up in the solemn airs of religion, can carry ardor and confidence, or the contrary sentiments, into the breasts of thousands.

There are certain general principles, and rules of life and conduct, which always must be true, because they are conformable to the invariable nature of things. He who studies history as he would study philosophy, will soon distinguish and collect them, and by doing so will soon form to himself a general system of ethics and politics on the surest foundations, on the trial of these principles and rules in all ages, and on the confirmation of them by universal experience. I said he will distinguish them; for once more I must say, that as to particular modes of actions, and measures of conduct, which the customs of different countries, the manners of different ages, and the circumstances of different conjunctures, have appropriated, as it were; it is always ridiculous, or imprudent and dangerous to employ them. But this is not all. By contemplating the vast variety of particularcharacters and events; by examining the strange combination of causes, different, remote, and seemingly opposite, that often concur in producing one effect; and the surprising fertility of one single and uniform cause in the producing of a multitude of effects, as different, remote, and seemingly as opposite; by tracing carefully, as carefully as if the subject he considers were of personal and immediate concern to him, all the minute and sometimes scarce perceivablecircumstances, either in the characters of actors, or in the course of actions, that history enables him to trace, and according to which the success of affairs, even the greatest, is mostly determined; by these, and such methods as these, for I might descend into a much greater detail, a man of parts may improve the study of history to its proper and principal use; he may sharpen the penetration, fix the attention of his mind, and strengthen his judgment; he may acquire the faculty and the habit of discerning quicker, and looking farther; and of exerting that flexibility, and steadiness, which are necessary to be joined in the conduct of all affairs that depend on the concurrence or opposition of other men.

Mr. Locke, I think, recommends the study of geometry even to those who have no design of being geometricians: and he gives a reason for it, that may be applies to the present case. Such persons may forget every problem that has been proposed, and every solution that they or others have given; but the habit of pursuing long trains of ideas will remain with them, and they will pierce through the mazes of sophism, and discover a latent truth, where persons who have not this habit will never find it.

In this manner the study of history will prepare us for action and observation. History is the ancient author: experience is the modern language. We form our taste on the first, we translate the sense and reason, we transfuse the spirit and force; but we imitate only the particular graces of the original; we imitate them according to the idiom of our own tongue, that is, we substitute often equivalents in the lieu of them, and are far from affecting to copy them servilely. To conclude, as experience is conversant about the present, and the present enables us to guess at the future; so history is conversant about the past, and by knowing the things that have been, we become better able to judge of the things that are.

This use, my lord, which I make the proper and principal use of the study of history, is not insisted on by those who have written concerning the method to be followed in this study: and since we propose different ends, we must of course take different ways. Few of their treatises have fallen into my hands: one, the method of Bodin, a man famous in his time, I remember to have read. I took it up with much expectation many years ago; I went through it, and remained extremely disappointed. He might have given almost any other title to his book as properly as that which stands before it. There are not many pages in it that relate any more to his subject than a tedious fifth chapter, wherein he accounts for the characters of nations according to their positions on the globe, and according to the influence of the stars; and assures his reader that nothing can be more necessary than such a disquisition; "ad universam historiarum cognitionem, et incorruptum earum judicium."[1] In his method, we are to take first a general view of universal history, and chronology, in short abstracts, and then to study all particular histories and systems. Seneca speaks of men who spend their whole lives in learning how to act in life, "dum vitae instrumenta conquirunt."[2] I doubt that this method of Bodin would conduct us in the same, or as bad a way; would leave us no time for action, or would make us unfit for it.

---

1 语出法国思想家让·波丹的《易于理解历史的方法》,意为"关于普遍史的知识以及对它的公正判断"。
2 语出罗马哲学家塞涅卡的书信,意为"积累生活的方法"。

A huge common-place book, wherein all the remarkable sayings and facts that we find in history are to be registered, may enable a man to talk or write like Bodin, but will never make him a better man, nor enable him to promote, like an useful citizen, the security, the peace, the welfare, or the grandeur of the community to which he belongs. I shall proceed therefore to speak of a method that leads to such purposes as these directly and certainly, without any regard to the methods that have been prescribed by others.

I think then we must be on our guard against this very affectation of learning, and this very wantonness of curiosity, which the examples and precepts we commonly meet with are calculated to flatter and indulge. We must neither dwell too long in the dark, nor wander about till we lose our way in the light. We are too apt to carry systems of philosophy beyond all our ideas, and systems of history beyond all our memorials. The philosopher begins with reason, and ends with imagination. The historian inverts this order: he begins without memorials, and he sometimes ends with them. This silly custom is so prevalent among men of letters who apply themselves to the study of history, and lias so much prejudice and so much authority on the side of it, that your lordship must give me leave to speak a little more particularly and plainly than I have done, in favor of common sense against an absurdity which is almost sanctified.

选自 Henry St. John Bolingbroke, *Letters on the Study and Use of History*, Basil: J. J. Tourneisen, 1791, pp. 43–58.

三、布洛赫《历史学家的技艺》节选

导读

下面的内容选自布洛赫《历史学家的技艺》(写作于 1941 年至 1942 年)第一章的第二节"历史与人类"和第三节"历史的时间"。《历史学家的技艺》是布洛赫对历史学整体性质的反思。有学者指出，正是布洛赫参军从事抵抗德国侵略的经历，使得以前只是在书本、统计册上见到的农民、工人，成为战场上有血有肉的形象在他的眼前飘浮，这让布洛赫做出了人（尤其是作为复数的人类）才是历史的精髓的判断。因此，这部著作和所选篇章与布洛赫的其他著作具有很强的对观性，在和布洛赫其他著作（如《法国农村史》《封建社会》）强调整体和抽象分析的对比中，可以看到命运、机遇、惊奇和不可预见性受到了重视，历史学由今知古、由古知今的反思性得到宣扬。布洛赫的这一思想转变显露出其所秉承的年鉴史观之外的一面，对于历史现实的理解和史学的当下因素在《历史学家的技艺》这部著作中得到了重视。在"历史与人类"中，布洛赫主要阐述了历史学必须贴近人们的生活，远离抽象的过去，以现实变化和问题为契机思考历史的观点，这需要一种不同于自然科学的人文方法论的支撑，即所谓历史学的特殊性质和交叉学科诉求问题。"历史的时间"中，布洛赫拒斥了机械时间观，他认为历史时间的定位必须置于历史对象变化发展的背景中才能得到理解。这节是上一节"历史与人类"的观点的自然延伸。

选文部分大多涉及关于历史时间的思考，因此，一方面需要对使布洛赫深受启发的以柏格森为代表的绵延时间观有所了解。历史时间在布洛赫看来不是可以随意切割安排的抽象时间（那是编年史的工作），而是一个连续统一体，处于不断变化之中。因此，我们对于历史事件的联系与比较都是从这一前提出发的。另一方面，也可以将选文与布罗代尔的《历史与社会科学：长时段》（1958）一文进行对比，体会所谓年鉴学派内部的代表人物对于历史时间及其对历史研究作用的分歧。布洛赫史学的当下性特征正与这种时间观念密不可分。

这部分行文较为口语化和随意，很难理出一条逻辑清晰的线索。布洛赫往往在陈述完自己对某个问题的看法后，紧接着就刚才提到的某个概念和观点进行引申和评论，因此整体上的脉络较难把握。此外，布洛赫还经常引用自然科学方面的研究作为例子，如果对此没有初步了解的话，阅读起来会比较困难。布洛赫强调的历史学的人文性和历史时间的独特性，为其后来宣扬历史学的理解功能和求真、实用并重的目标打下了理论基础，所以对选文意义的真正领会必须在通读全书后才能实现。这一整体是无法切割孤立的，或许在阅读了全书特别是最后一章后，我们能够对选文有新的认识。

History and Men

It is sometimes said: "History is the science of the past." To me, this is badly put.

For, to begin with, the very idea that the past as such can be the object of science is ridiculous. How, without preliminary distillation, can one make of phenomena, having no other common character than that of being not contemporary with us, the matter of rational knowledge? On the reverse side of the medal, can one imagine a complete science of the universe in its present state?

Doubtless, in the origins of historiography, the old annalists were scarcely embarrassed by these scruples. They narrated pell-mell events whose only connection was that they had happened about the same time: eclipses, hailstorms, and the sudden appearance of astonishing meteors along with battles and the deaths of kings and heroes. But into these early reminiscences of humanity, as garbled as the observations of a small child, a sustained effort of analysis has gradually introduced the necessary classification. It is true that our language, fundamentally conservative, freely retains the name of history for any study of a change taking place in time. The custom is harmless, for it deceives no one. In that sense, there is a history of the solar system, because the stars which compose it have not always been as we now see them. It belongs to the province of astronomy. There is a history of volcanic eruptions which is, I am sure, of most lively interest as regards the composition of the earth. It does not concern the history of historians.

Or, at least, it does so only in so far as its observations chance to coincide with the specific preoccupations of our history. How, then, is the division of labor determined in practice? To understand this, a single example will be worth more than a thousand words.

In the tenth century a. d., a deep gulf, the Zwin[1], indented the Flemish coast. It was later blocked up with sand. To what department of knowledge does the study of this phenomenon belong? At first sight, anyone would suggest geology. The action of alluvial deposit, the operation of ocean currents, or, perhaps, changes in sea level: was not geology invented and put on earth to deal with just such as these? Of course. But at close range, the matter is not quite so simple. Is there not first a question of investigating the origin of the transformation? Immediately, the geologist is forced to ask questions which are no longer strictly within his jurisdiction. For there is no doubt that the silting of the gulf was at least assisted by dyke construction, changing the direction of the channel, and drainage—all activities of man, founded in collective needs and made possible only by a certain social structure. At the other end of the chain there is a new problem: the consequences. At a little distance from the end of the gulf, and communicating with it by a short river passage, rose a town. This was Bruges. By the waters of the Zwin it imported or exported the greatest part of the merchandise which made of it, relatively speaking, the London or New York of that day. Then came, every day more apparent, the advance of the sand. As the water receded, Bruges vainly extended its docks and harbor further toward the mouth of the river. Little by little, its quays fell asleep. To be sure, this was not the sole cause of its decline. (Does the physical ever affect the social, unless its operations have been prepared, abetted, and given scope by other factors which themselves have already derived from man?) But this was certainly at least one of the most efficacious of the links in the causal chain.

Now, the act of a society remodeling the soil upon which it lives in accordance with its needs is, as any one recognizes instinctively, an eminently "historical" event. It is the same with the vicissitudes of a powerful seat of trade. Hence, in an example entirely characteristic of the topography of learning, we see, on the one hand, an area of overlap, where the union of two disciplines is shown to be indispensable to any attempt at explanation; on the other, a point of transition, where when a phenomenon has been described with the sole exception that its consequences remain undetermined, it is, in some definitive way, yielded up by one discipline to another. What is it that seems to dictate the intervention of history? It is the appearance of the human element.

1　茨温湾，位于荷兰与比利时交界处的弗莱芒海岸，后因淤塞导致了布鲁日等城市地位的衰落。

Long ago, indeed, our great forebears, such as Michelet or Fustel de Coulanges[1], taught us to recognize that the object of history is, by nature, man. Let us say rather, men. Far more than the singular, favoring abstraction, the plural which is the grammatical form of relativity is fitting for the science of change. Behind the features of landscape, behind tools or machinery, behind what appear to be the most formalized written documents, and behind institutions, which seem almost entirely detached from their founders, there are men, and it is men that history seeks to grasp.[2] Failing that, it will be at best but an exercise in erudition. The good historian is like the giant of the fairy tale. He knows that wherever he catches the scent of human flesh, there his quarry lies.

From the character of history as the knowledge of men derives its peculiar situation as regards the problem of expression. Is it "science" or "art"? About 1800, our great-grandfathers delighted in solemn debates on this question. Later, about 1890, saturated with the aura of a rather primitive positivism, the methodologists were indignant that the public should attach an excessive importance to what they called "form" in historical works. Art versus science, form versus matter: the history of scholarship abounds with such fine debates!

There is no less beauty in a precise equation than in a felicitous phrase, but each science has its appropriate aesthetics of language. Human actions are essentially very delicate phenomena, many aspects of which elude mathematical measurement. Properly to translate them into words and, hence, to fathom them rightly (for can one perfectly understand what he does not know how to express?), great delicacy of language and precise shadings of verbal tone are necessary. Where calculation is impossible we are obliged to employ suggestion. Between the expression of physical and of human realities there is as much difference as between the task of a drill operator and that of a lutemaker[3]: both work down to the last millimeter, but the driller uses precision tools, while the lutemaker is guided primarily by his sensitivity to sound and touch. It would be unwise either for the driller to adopt the empirical methods of the lutemaker or for the lutemaker to imitate the deiller. Will anyone deny that one may not feel with words as well as with fingers?

Historical Time

We have called history "the science of men." That is still far too vague. It is necessary to add: "of men in time." The historian does not think of the human in the abstract. His thoughts

---

1　米什莱（Jules Michelet, 1798—1874），法国历史学家，代表作有《法国史》《法国大革命史》等，并且他是维柯《新科学》的译者和重新发现者。库朗热（Fustel de Coulanges, 1830—1899），法国历史学家，代表作有《古代城邦》《古代法国政治制度史》等。米什莱在1829年巴黎高等师范学校的课程中表示："关注个体的人就是哲学，研究社会的人就是历史。"库朗热在1862年的讲座中进一步认为："历史不是有关过去发生的各类事件的累积，而是关于人类社会的科学。"

2　费弗尔也认为历史学对象不是单数的人，而是人类社会和有组织的群体。

3　鲁特琴制琴师。鲁特琴是中世纪到巴洛克时期欧洲的一类古乐器的总称，是文艺复兴时期欧洲最风靡的家庭独奏乐器。

breathe freely the air of the climate of time.

To be sure, it is difficult to imagine that any of the sciences could treat time as a mere abstraction. Yet, for a great number of those who, for their own purposes, chop it up into arbitrarily homogeneous segments, time is nothing more than a measurement. In contrast, historical time [1] is a concrete and living reality with an irreversible onward rush. It is the very plasma in which events are immersed, and the field within which they become intelligible. The number of seconds, years, or centuries required for a radioactive substance to change into other substances is a fundamental datum for the atomic scientist. But the idea any particular one of these metamorphoses had occurred a thousand years ago, or yesterday, or today, or that another such is bound to occur tomorrow—all of which would unquestionably interest the geologist, because geology is, in its way, a historical discipline—leaves the physicist perfectly unmoved. In his turn, no historian would be satisfied to state that Cæsar devoted eight years to the conquest of Gaul, or that it took fifteen years for Luther to change from the orthodox novice of Erfurt into the reformer of Wittenberg. It is of far greater importance to him to assign the conquest of Gaul its exact chronological place amid the vicissitudes of European societies; and, without in the least denying the eternal aspect of such spiritual crises as Brother Martin's, he will feel that he has given a true picture of it only when he has plotted its precise moment upon the life charts of both the man who was its hero and the civilization which was its climate.

Now, this real time is, in essence, a continuum. It is also perpetual change. The great problems of historical inquiry derive from the antitheses of these two attributes. There is one problem especially, which raises the very raison d'être [2] of our studies. Let us assume two consecutive periods taken out of the uninterrupted sequence of the ages. To what extent does the connection which the flow of time sets between them predominate, or fail to predominate, over the differences born out of that same flow? Should the knowledge of the earlier period be considered indispensable or superfluous for the understanding of the later?

选自 Marc Bloch, *The Historian's Craft*, translated by Peter Putnam, New York: Vintage Books, 1953, pp. 22–29.

---

1 这里布洛赫所主张的是法国哲学家柏格森在《时间与自由意志》一书中阐述的绵延时间观，反对传统机械时间观。

2 "raison d'être"，法语，意为"存在理由"。

四、克罗齐《历史作为自由的故事》

导读

《历史作为自由的故事》初版于1938年,意大利文版原标题可译为"作为思想与行动的历史",它是克罗齐20世纪二三十年代的论文的结集,按照内在逻辑的联系由作者本人对其加以编排。它可以看作是1915年出版的《历史学的理论与历史》的续篇,克罗齐在其中深化发展了他的历史观和史学理论。当时欧洲法西斯主义日益猖獗的国际现实深深地刺激了克罗齐,在这本书中,他特别高扬历史是自由的历史这一主张,认为自由既是历史进程的解释原则,又是人类追求的道德理想。这一特色使得这本书在出版后大受好评,很快便被译成了各种文字加以传播。下面的内容选自这本书的第一章第十二节"作为自由历史的历史",该节小标题被英文版用以冠名全书,足以说明其思想上的代表性。克罗齐通过对黑格尔自由观的扬弃,逐步阐发了自己的自由历史的观念。他认为,自由与生活是不可分割的一体两面,自由作为一种理想应当是内在孕育在生活与历史之中的。克罗齐用诗意的语言,简要回顾了自由在欧洲大陆的处境与历史发展,道出了历史的本质是一部自由与不自由相互角力的戏剧,不能从脱离现实与历史的角度思考历史。

选文部分一开始就是克罗齐对黑格尔历史观的批判,因此对于黑格尔《世界历史哲学讲演录》主要观点的了解和进一步比较是解读选文的必要出发点。克罗齐反对黑格尔及其相关历史学家对于历史是自由的历史的误读。这些历史学家认为自由的历史是评判历史发展阶段(以空间作为例子便是"东方—古典—日耳曼"这一世界发展的序列)的产物,或者说是衡量不同种类历史(原始的、反思的、哲学的)的依据。而克罗齐则认为我们应该从自由是历史的创造者和历史主题本身这一角度进行重新评价。他在选文中所叙述的自由在欧洲历史上的遭遇,即在每个年代都有积极和消极的部分,显然和他所反对的自由历史发展的谱系迥异,具有很鲜明的时代特色和克氏风格。另外,克罗齐在这本书中强调的历史的整体性也是我们理解选文的一把钥匙,它与前一部论文集所宣扬的历史的当下性具有逻辑上的内在联系。

克罗齐的自由观是他哲学、历史作品的重要主题,尤其是在其后期的著作中,这一观念的重要性得到了不断提升,该书便是这方面的一个代表。要理解选文的重要意义,就需要对克罗齐生平尤其是思想发展的脉络有一个大致的掌握。他对墨索里尼统治以及法西斯政府的态度变化在行文中时有显露,其理论表达以一种夹叙夹议的方式展现在读者面前。这是阅读时要注意的一个方面,必须时刻提醒自己鉴别这两种不同的表达层,并体会它们是如何很好地结合在一起的。另一方面,我们还可以参考克罗齐的其他历史著作,如同样以自由观念贯穿全书的《十九世纪欧洲史》《那不勒斯史》等,以便更全面、直观地对其史学思想背景有所认知。

History as the History of Liberty

Hegel's famous statement that history is the history of liberty [1] was repeated without being altogether understood and then spread throughout Europe by Cousin [2], Michelet and other French writers. But Hegel and his disciples used it with the significance which we have criticized above, of a history of the first birth of liberty, of its growth, of its maturity and of its stable permanence in the definite era in which it is incapable of further development. (The formula was: Orient, Classic World, Germanic World = one free, some free, all free.) The statement is adduced in this place with a different intention and content, not in order to assign to history the task of creating a liberty which did not exist in the past but will exist in the future, but to maintain that liberty is the eternal creator of history and itself the subject of every history. As such it is on the one hand the explanatory principle of the course of history, and on the other the moral ideal of humanity.

Jubilant announcements, resigned admissions or desperate lamentations that liberty has now deserted the world are frequently heard nowadays; the ideal of liberty is said to have set on the horizon of history, in a sunset without promise of sunrise. Those who talk or write or print this deserve the pardon pronounced by Jesus, for they know not what they say. If they knew or reflected they would be aware that to assert that liberty is dead is the same as saying that life is dead, that its mainspring is broken. And as for the ideal, they would be greatly embarrassed if invited to state the ideal which has taken, or ever could take, the place of the ideal of liberty. Then they would find that there is no other like it, none which makes the heart of man, in his human quality, so beat, none other which responds better to the very law of life which is history; and that this calls for an ideal in which liberty is accepted and respected and so placed as to produce ever greater achievements.

Certainly when we meet the legions of those who think or speak differently with these self-evident propositions, we are conscious that they may well be of the kind to raise laughter or derision about philosophers who seem to have tumbled on the earth from another world ignorant of what reality is, blind and deaf to its voice, to its cries, and to its hard features. Even if we omit to consider contemporary events and conditions in many countries, owing to which a liberal order which seemed to be the great and lasting achievement of the nineteenth century [3] has crumbled, while in other countries the desire for this collapse is spreading, all history still gives evidence of an unquiet, uncertain and disordered liberty with brief intervals of unrest, rare and lightning moments of a happiness perceived rather than possessed, mere pauses in the tumult of

---

1 具体可对照黑格尔《世界历史哲学讲演录》导论"人的自由的理念"部分。
2 库赞（Victor Cousin，1792—1867），法国哲学家、历史学家和教育家。他曾在青年时代追随黑格尔，1828 年起在巴黎大学开设哲学史导论课程，大力引介和传播黑格尔的哲学思想和历史观念。他和基内、米什莱等成为 19 世纪德国史学和历史哲学对法国产生影响的中间人。
3 这是克罗齐《十九世纪欧洲史》的主旨。

oppressions, barbarian invasions, plunderings, secular and ecclesiastical tyrannies, wars between peoples, persecutions, exiles and gallows. With this prospect in view the statement that history is the history of liberty sounds like irony or, if it is seriously maintained, like stupidity.

But philosophy is not there just to be overwhelmed by the kind of reality which is apprehended by unbalanced and confused imaginings. Thus philosophy, when it inquires and interprets, knowing well that the man who enslaves another wakes in him awareness of himself and enlivens him to seek for liberty, observes with serenity how periods of increased or reduced liberty follow upon each other and how a liberal order, the more it is established and undisputed, the more surely decays into habit, and thereby its vigilant self-awareness and readiness for defence is weakened, which opens the way for a "recourse," as Vico termed it, to all of those things which seemed to have vanished from the world, and which themselves, in their turn, open a new "course."[1] Philosophy considers, for example, the democracies and the republics like those of Greece in the fourth century, or of Rome in the first, in which liberty was still preserved in the institutional forms but no longer in the soul or the customs of the people, and then lost even those forms, much as a man who has not known how to help himself but has in vain for a time received ministrations of good advice is finally abandoned to the hard school of life. Or philosophy looks at Italy, exhausted and defeated, entombed by barbarians in all her pompous Imperial array, rising again, as the poet said, "in her Tyrrhenian and Adriatic republics"[2] like an agile sailor. Or philosophy contemplates the absolute monarchs who beat down the liberty of the barons and the clergy once they had become privileged, and superimposed on all men their own form of government, exercised by their own bureaucracy, and sustained by their own army, thus preparing a far greater and more useful participation of the people in political liberty. A Napoleon destroys a merely apparent and nominal liberty, he removes its appearance and its name, levels down the peoples under his rule and leaves those same people with a thirst for liberty and a new awareness of what it really was and a keenness to set up, as they did shortly afterwards in all Europe, institutions of liberty. Even in the darkest and crassest times liberty trembles in the lines of poets and affirms itself in the pages of thinkers and bums, solitary and magnificent, in some men who cannot be assimilated by the world around them, as Vittorio Alfieri[3] discovered in the eighteenth century grand-ducal Siena, where he found a friend, "freest of spirits," born "in hard prison," and abiding there "like a sleeping lion," for whom he wrote the dialogue in his Virtue Unrecognized. Yes, to the eye of philosophy, whether the age is propitious or unfavourable, liberty appears as abiding purely and invincibly and consciously only in a few spirits; but these alone are those which count historically, just as great philosophers, great poets, great men and every kind of great work have

---

1 可参考维柯《新科学》有关"诗性的政治"部分。
2 指的是意大利北部诸城市共和国。
3 阿尔菲艾里(1749—1803),意大利作家、剧作家。

a real message only to the few, even though crowds may acclaim and deify them, ever ready to abandon them in order noisily to acclaim other idols and to exercise, under whatever slogan or flag, a natural disposition for courtisanship and servility. And on account of this, and through experience and meditation, the philosopher thinks and tells himself that if in liberal times one enjoys the welcome illusion of belonging to a great company, while in illiberal times one has the opposite and unwelcome illusion of being alone or almost alone, die first optimistic view was surely illusory, but maybe the second pessimistic view was illusory also. He sees this and he sees so many other things and he draws the conclusion that if history is not an idyll, neither is it "a tragedy of horrors" but a drama in which all the actions, all the actors, and all the members of the chorus are, in the Aristotelian sense, "middling"[1], guilty-non-guilty, a mixture of good and bad, yet ruled always by a governing thought which is good and to which evil ends by acting as a stimulus and that this achievement is the work of liberty which always strives to re-establish and always does reestablish the social and political conditions of a more intense liberty. If anyone needs persuading that liberty cannot exist differently from the way it has lived and always will live in history, a perilous and fighting life, let him for a moment consider a world of liberty without obstacles, without menaces and without oppressions of any kind; immediately he will look away from this picture with horror as being something worse than death, an infinite boredom.[2]

Having said this, what is then the anguish that men feel for liberty that has been lost, the invocations, the lost hopes, the words of love and anger which come from the hearts of men in certain moments and in certain ages of history? We have already said it in examining a similar case: these are not philosophical nor historical truths, nor are they errors or dreams; they are movements of moral conscience; they are history in the making.

选自 Benedetto Croce, *History as the Story of Liberty*, translated by Sylvia Sprigge, London: George Allen and Unwin Ltd., pp. 59-62.

五、比尔德《书写历史作为一种信仰行为》

导读

下面的内容选自1933年12月28日比尔德在美国历史协会就职典礼上的演讲，作者对美国历史学当时面临的危机状况进行了概括与反思。比尔德在文中以克罗齐的相关思想为切入点，批驳了历史学必须以自然科学为师的种种论点。他认为历史学具有一种整体性，它超越了神学、科学和文学等其他知识形

---

1 可参照亚里士多德《诗学》第2章。
2 对克罗齐而言，抽象的自由和自由世界不是他寻求的目标，自由在历史中的痕迹是值得历史学家捕捉的最高价值。

式所具有的界限，前述学科的意义只有在历史和历史学的背景下才能得到充分展示。然而，在近现代历史学独立发展的进程中，史学家往往错误地借用物理学的机械决定论和生物学的有机论来解释历史运动过程，比尔德对此一一举例并且加以批驳。他认为，历史学的科学性不能建筑在这些类比之上，而且历史学家们日益感受到了来自相对主义的威胁。越来越多的史学家体认到历史学选择史料、组织叙述和建立关联方面的主观因素无法避免，每个人心中的客观性和精确性的定义大相径庭。比尔德呼吁历史学家们不可逃避这场发生于历史科学内部的危机，沉溺于过去那种客观科学史学的梦想中。他提出必须重视研究客观现实尤其是经济现实对于历史的影响，辨明科学方法的性质与限度，破除它们能够完全把握历史学整体的幻象。最后，他提出了历史作为混乱的历史、循环的历史和进步的历史这三种模式，它们对于主观选择组织历史事件的行为具有普遍的规范价值，是一种由信仰决定的行为。

20世纪30年代，美国历史学界掀起了一场有关相对主义史学的讨论，它远承特纳、鲁滨孙的边疆史学和新史学变革，矛头指向以亚当斯以及更早的班克罗夫特等人为代表的所谓客观科学史学。选文可以和1931年贝克尔的《人人都是自己的历史学家》、1935年史密斯坚持所谓"高贵的梦想"的客观史学辩护，还有后来比尔德以同样标题的回应文章构成一个思想史上的连续体，以考察当时各具代表性的历史学家对于历史学家写作中的主观性、知识确证的中立性等诸多重要理论问题的反思。这些问题在历史学寻求自身作为标准运作学科的规范的过程中浮现，成为诸多历史学者不得不回应的代表学术史思潮的要点。

比尔德对于相对性具有一种两面态度，一方面他认为相对性在历史学家的工作中难以避免，另一方面他并不否认历史学作为一种整体性科学的可能，正是这一可能使得相对性本身就相对化了。这种观念在选文中作为一条潜伏的线索时有体现，而在1935年10月《那高贵的梦想》一文中表现得更加明确，比尔德给出了有关相对主义本身也会过时的诸条理由。因此，我们在阅读中，除了明显的对于客观科学史学的批判，这点也是需要加以重视和分辨的。

Written History as an Act of Faith

History has been called a science, an art, an illustration of theology, a phase of philosophy, a branch of literature. It is none of these things, nor all of them combined. On the contrary, science, art, theology, and literature are themselves merely phases of history as past actuality and their particular forms at given periods and places are to be explained, if explained at all, by history as knowledge and thought. The philosopher, possessing little or no acquaintance with history, sometimes pretends to expound the inner secret of history, but the historian turns upon him and expounds the secret of the philosopher, as far as it may be expounded at all, by placing him in relation to the movement of ideas and interests in which he stands or floats, by giving to his scheme of thought its appropriate relativity. So it is with systems of science, art, theology, and literature. All the light on these subjects that can be discovered by the human mind comes from history as past actuality.

What, then, is this manifestation of omniscience called history? It is, as Croce says, contemporary thought about the past.[1] History as past actuality includes, to be sure, all that has been done, felt, and thought by human beings on this planet since humanity began its long career. History as record embraces the monuments, documents, and symbols which provide such knowledge as we have or can find respecting past actuality. But it is history as thought, not as actuality, record, or specific knowledge, that is really meant when the term history is used in its widest and most general significance. It is thought about past actuality, instructed and delimited by history as record and knowledge—record and knowledge authenticated by criticism and ordered with the help of the scientific method. This is the final, positive, inescapable definition. It contains all the exactness that is possible and all the bewildering problems inherent in the nature of thought and the relation of the thinker to the thing thought about.

Although this definition of history may appear, at first glance, distressing to those who have been writing lightly about "the science of history" and "the scientific method" in historical research and construction, it is in fact in accordance with the most profound contemporary thought about history, represented by Croce, Riezler, Karl Mannheim, Mueller-Armack, and Heussi[2], for example. It is in keeping also with the obvious and commonplace. Has it not been said for a century or more that each historian who writes history is a product of his age, and that his work reflects the spirit of the times, of a nation, race, group, class, or section? No contemporary student of history really believes that Bossuet, Gibbon, Mommsen, or Bancroft could be duplicated to-day. Every student of history knows that his colleagues have been influenced in their selection and ordering of materials by their biases, prejudices, beliefs, affections, general upbringing, and experience, particularly social and economic; and if he has a sense of propriety, to say nothing of humor, he applies the canon to himself, leaving no exceptions to the rule. The pallor of waning time, if not of death, rests upon the latest volume of history, fresh from the roaring press.

Why do we believe this to be true? The answer is that every written history—of a village, town, county, state, nation, race, group, class, idea, or the wide world—is a selection and arrangement of facts, of recorded fragments of past actuality. And the selection and arrangement of facts—a combined and complex intellectual operation—is an act of choice, conviction, and interpretation respecting values, is an act of thought. Facts, multitudinous and beyond calculation, are known, but they do not select themselves or force themselves automatically into any fixed scheme of arrangement in the mind of the historian. They are selected and ordered by

---

1 出自克罗齐《历史学的理论与历史》第一节"历史与编年史"。
2 克罗齐、里兹勒、曼海姆、阿马克、豪伊西等人都是当时讨论历史主义思潮的代表人物。

him as he thinks. True enough, where the records pertaining to a small segment of history are few and presumably all known, the historian may produce a fragment having an aspect of completeness as, for example, some pieces by Fustel de Coulanges [1]; but the completeness is one of documentation, not of history. True enough also, many historians are pleased to say of their writings that their facts are selected and ordered only with reference to inner necessities, but none who takes this position will allow the same exactitude and certainty to the works of others except when the predilections of the latter conform to his own pattern.

Contemporary thought about history, therefore, repudiates the conception dominant among the schoolmen during the latter part of the nineteenth century and the opening years of the twentieth century—the conception that it is possible to describe the past as it actually was, somewhat as the engineer describes a single machine. The formula itself was a passing phase of thought about the past. Its author, Ranke, a German conservative, writing after the storm and stress of the French Revolution, was weary of history written for, or permeated by, the purposes of revolutionary propaganda. He wanted peace. The ruling classes in Germany, with which he was affiliated, having secured a breathing spell in the settlement of 1815 [2], wanted peace to consolidate their position. Written history that was cold, factual, and apparently undisturbed by the passions of the time served best the cause of those who did not want to be disturbed. Later the formula was fitted into the great conception of natural science—cold neutrality over against the materials and forces of the physical world. Truths of nature, ran the theory, are to be discovered by maintaining the most severe objectivity; therefore the truth of history may be revealed by the same spirit and method. The reasoning seemed perfect to those for whom it was satisfactory. But the movement of ideas and interests continued, and bondage to conservative and scientific thought was broken by criticism and events. As Croce and Heussi have demonstrated, so-called neutral or scientific history reached a crisis [3] in its thought before the twentieth century had advanced far on the way.

This crisis in historical thought sprang from internal criticism—from conflicts of thought within historiography itself—and from the movement of history as actuality; for historians are always engaged, more or less, in thinking about their own work and are disturbed, like their fellow citizens, by crises and revolutions occurring in the world about them. As an outcome of this crisis in historiography, the assumption that the actuality of history is identical with or closely akin to that of the physical world, and the assumption that any historian can be a disembodied spirit as coldly neutral to human affairs as the engineer to an automobile have both been challenged and rejected. Thus, owing to internal criticism and the movement of external events, the Ranke formula of history has been discarded and laid away in the museum of

---

1 库朗热在《古代城邦》中强调运用一手文献和客观视角的重要性。
2 指1814年至1815年维也纳会议和之后形成的维也纳体系。
3 以特勒尔奇的《历史主义及其问题》(1922)、豪伊西的《历史主义的危机》(1932)为典型。

antiquities. It has ceased to satisfy the human spirit in its historical needs. Once more, historians recognize formally the obvious, long known informally, namely, that any written history inevitably reflects the thought of the author in his time and cultural setting.

That this crisis in thought presents a digressing dilemma to many historians is beyond question. It is almost a confession of inexpiable sin to admit in academic circles that one is not a man of science working in a scientific manner with things open to deterministic and inexorable treatment, to admit that one is more or less a guesser in this vale of tears. But the only escape from the dust and storm of the present conflict, and from the hazards of taking thought, now before the historian, is silence or refuge in some minute particularity of history as actuality. He may edit documents, although there are perils in the choice of documents to be edited, and in any case the choice of documents will bear some reference to an interpretation of values and importance—subjective considerations. To avoid this difficulty, the historian may confine his attention to some very remote and microscopic area of time and place, such as the price of cotton in Alabama between 1850 and 1860, or the length of wigs in the reign of Charles II., on the pleasing but false assumption that he is really describing an isolated particularity as it actually was, an isolated area having no wide-reaching ramifications of relations. But even then the historian would be a strange creature if he never asked himself why he regarded these matters as worthy of his labor and love, or why society provides a living for him during his excursions and explorations.

The other alternative before the student of history as immense actuality is to face boldly, in the spirit of Cato's[1] soliloquy, the wreck of matter and the crush of worlds—the dissolution of that solid assurance which rested on the formula bequeathed by Ranke[2] and embroidered by a thousand hands during the intervening years. And when he confronts without avoidance contemporary thought about the nature of written history, what commands does he hear?

The supreme command is that he must cast off his servitude to the assumptions of natural science and return to his own subject matter—to history as actuality. The hour for this final declaration of independence has arrived: the contingency is here and thought resolves it. Natural science is only one small subdivision of history as actuality with which history as thought is concerned. Its dominance in the thought of the Western World for a brief period can be explained, if at all, by history; perhaps in part by reference to the great conflict that raged between the theologians and scientists after the dawn of the sixteenth century—an intellectual conflict associated with the economic conflict between landed aristocracies, lay and clerical, on the one side, and the rising bourgeois on the other.

The intellectual formulas borrowed from natural science, which have cramped and distorted

---

1 这里指的是老加图（前234—前149），古罗马第一个拉丁文作家，著有《农业志》《创始记》等。
2 指"wie es eigentlich gewesen"这句格言，意为"如实书写历史"，出自兰克《罗曼与日耳曼诸民族史1494—1514》的序言。

the operations of history as thought, have taken two forms: physical and biological. The first of these rests upon what may be called, for convenience, the assumption of causation: everything that happens in the world of human affairs is determined by antecedent occurrences, and events of history are the illustrations or data of laws to be discovered, laws such as are found in hydraulics. It is true that no historian has ever been able to array the fullness of history as actuality in any such deterministic order; Karl Marx has gone further than any other. But under the hypothesis that it is possible, historians have been arranging events in neat little chains of causation which explain, to their satisfaction, why succeeding events happen; and they have attributed any shortcomings in result to the inadequacy of their known data, not to the falsity of the assumption on which they have been operating. Undiscouraged by their inability to bring all history within a single law, such as the law of gravitation, they have gone on working in the belief that the Newtonian trick will be turned some time, if the scientific method is applied long and rigorously enough and facts are heaped up high enough, as the succeeding grists of doctors of philosophy are ground out by the universities, turned loose on "research projects", and amply supplied by funds.

Growing rightly suspicious of this procedure in physico-historiography, a number of historians, still bent on servitude to natural science, turned from physics to biology. The difficulties and failures involved in all efforts to arrange the occurrences of history in a neat system of historical mechanics were evident to them. But on the other side, the achievements of the Darwinians were impressive. If the totality of history could not be brought into a deterministic system without doing violence to historical knowledge, perhaps the biological analogy of the organism could be applied. And this was done, apparently without any realization of the fact that thinking by analogy is a form of primitive animism. So under the biological analogy, history was conceived as a succession of cultural organisms rising, growing, competing, and declining. To this fantastic morphological assumption Spengler[1] chained his powerful mind. Thus freed from self-imposed slavery to physics, the historian passed to self-imposed subservience to biology. Painfully aware of the perplexities encountered as long as he stuck to his own business, the historian sought escape by employing the method and thought of others whose operations he did not understand and could not control, on the simple, almost childlike, faith that the biologic, if not the physicist, really knew what he was about and could furnish the clue to the mystery.

But the shadow of the organismic conception of history had scarcely fallen on the turbulent actuality of history when it was scrutinized by historians who were thinking in terms of their own subject as distinguished from the terms of a mere subdivision of history. By an inescapable

---

1 斯宾格勒在1918年出版的《西方的没落》中运用历史形态学方法，对世界八大文化以生物学中的青春期、成长期、成熟期和衰败期区分法加以论述。

demonstration Kurt Riezler[1] has made it clear that the organismic theory of history is really the old determinism of physics covered with murky words. The rise, growth, competition, and decline of cultural organisms is meaningless unless fitted into some overarching hypothesis—either the hypothesis of the divine drama or the hypothesis of causation in the deterministic sense. Is each cultural organism in history, each national or racial culture, an isolated particularity governed by its own mystical or physical laws? Knowledge of history as actuality forbids any such conclusion. If, in sheer desperation, the historian clings to the biological analogy, which school is he to follow—the mechanistic or the vitalistic? In either case he is caught in the deterministic sequence, if he thinks long enough and hard enough.

Hence the fate of the scientific school of historiography turns finally upon the applicability of the deterministic sequence to the totality of history as actuality. Natural science in a strict sense, as distinguished from mere knowledge of facts, can discover system and law only where occurrences are in reality arranged objectively in deterministic sequences. It can describe these sequences and draw from them laws, so-called. From a given number of the occurrences in any such sequence, science can predict what will happen when the remainder appear.

With respect to certain areas of human occurrences, something akin to deterministic sequences is found by the historian, but the perdurance of any sequence depends upon the perdurance in time of surrounding circumstances which cannot be brought within any scheme of deterministic relevancies. Certainly all the occurrences of history as actuality cannot be so ordered; most of them are unknown and owing to the paucity of records must forever remain unknown.

If a science of history were achieved, it would, like the science of celestial mechanics, make possible the calculable prediction of the future in history. It would bring the totally of historical occurrences within a single field and reveal the unfolding future to its last end, including all the apparent choices made and to be made. It would be omniscience. The creator of it would possess the attributes ascribed by the theologians to God. The future once revealed, humanity would have nothing to do except to await its doom.

To state the case is to dispose of it. The occurrences of history—the unfolding of ideas and interests in time-motion—are not identical in nature with the data of physics, and hence in their totality they are beyond the reach of that necessary instrument of natural science—mathematics—which cannot assign meaningful values to the imponderables, immeasurables, and contingencies of history as actuality.

Having broken the tyranny of physics and biology, contemporary thought in historiography turns its engines of verification upon the formula of historical relativity—the formula that makes

---

[1] 里兹勒（1882—1955），德国哲学家、政治家、记者。在第一次世界大战时曾任首相霍尔维格的首席顾问，他的日记与笔记的出版在后来的"费舍尔争论"中扮演了重要角色。

all written history merely relative to time and circumstance, a passing shadow, an illusion.[1] Contemporary criticism shows that the apostle of relativity is destined to be destroyed by the child of his own brain. If all historical conceptions are merely relative to passing events, to transitory phases of ideas and interests, then the conception of relativity is itself relative. When absolutes in history are rejected the absolutism of relativity is also rejected. So we must inquire: To what spirit of the times, to the ideas and interests of what class, group, nation, race, or region does the conception of relativity correspond? As the actuality of history moves forward into the future, the conception of relativity will also pass, as previous conceptions and interpretations of events have passed. Hence, according to the very doctrine of relativity, the skeptic of relativity will disappear in due course, beneath the ever-tossing waves of changing relativities. If he does not suffer this fate soon, the apostle of relativity will surely be executed by his own logic. Every conception of history, he says, is relative to time and circumstances. But by his own reasoning he is then compelled to ask: To what are these particular times and circumstances relative? And he must go on with receding sets of times and circumstances until he confronts an absolute: the totality of history as actuality which embraces all times and circumstances and all relativities.

Contemporary historical thought is, accordingly, returning upon itself and its subject matter. The historian is casting off his servitude to physics and biology, as he formerly cast off the shackles of theology and its metaphysics. He likewise sees the doctrine of relativity crumble in the cold light of historical knowledge. When he accepts none of the assumptions made by theology, physics, and biology, as applied to history, when he passes out from under the fleeting shadow of relativity, he confronts the absolute in his field—the absolute totality of all historical occurrences past, present, and becoming to the end of all things. Then he finds it necessary to bring the occurrences of history as actuality under one or another of three broad conceptions.

The first is that history as total actuality is chaos, perhaps with little islands of congruous relativities floating on the surface, and that the human mind cannot bring them objectively into any all-embracing order or subjectively into any consistent system. The second is that history as actuality is a part of some order of nature and revolves in cycles eternally—spring, summer, autumn, and winter, democracy, aristocracy, and monarchy, or their variants, as imagined by Spengler. The third is that history as actuality is moving in some direction away from the low level of primitive beginnings, on an upward gradient toward a more ideal order—as imagined by Condorcet, Adam Smith, Karl Marx, or Herbert Spencer.[2]

Abundant evidence can be marshaled, has been marshaled, in support of each of these conceptions of history as actuality, but all the available evidence will not fit any one of them. The hypothesis of chaos admits of no ordering at all; hence those who operate under it cannot

---

1 可参考贝克尔1931年12月29日就任美国历史学会主席的演说《人人都是他自己的历史学家》。
2 可分别参考孔多塞的《人类精神进步史表纲要》、斯密的《国富论》、马克思与恩格斯的《德意志意识形态》、斯宾塞的《社会静力学》。

write history, although they may comment on history. The second admits of an ordering of events only by arbitrarily leaving out of account all the contradictions in the evidence. The third admits of an ordering of events, also by leaving contradictions out of consideration. The historian who writes history, therefore, consciously or unconsciously performs an act of faith, as to order and movement, for certainty as to order and movement is denied to him by knowledge of the actuality with which he is concerned. He is thus in the position of a statesman dealing with public affairs; in writing he acts and in acting he makes choices, large or small, timid or bold, with respect to some conception of the nature of things. And the degree of his influence and immortality will depend upon the length and correctness of his forecast—upon the verdict of history yet to come. His faith is at bottom a conviction that something true can be known about the movement of history and his conviction is a subjective decision, not a purely objective discovery.

But members of the passing generation will ask: Has our work done in the scientific spirit been useless? Must we abandon the scientific method? The answer is an emphatic negative. During the past fifty years historical scholarship, carried on with judicial calm, has wrought achievements of value beyond calculation. Particular phases of history once dark and confused have been illuminated by research, authentication, scrutiny, and the ordering of immediate relevancies. Nor is the empirical or scientific method to be abandoned. It is the only method that can be employed in obtaining accurate knowledge of historical facts, personalities, situations, and movements. It alone can disclose conditions that made possible what happened. It has a value in itself—a value high in the hierarchy of values indispensable to the life of a democracy. The inquiring spirit of science, using the scientific method, is the chief safeguard against the tyranny of authority, bureaucracy, and brute power. It can reveal by investigation necessities and possibilities in any social scene and also offerings with respect to desirabilities to be achieved within the limits of the possible.

The scientific method is, therefore, a precious and indispensable instrument of the human mind; without it society would sink down into primitive animism and barbarism. It is when this method, a child of the human brain, is exalted into a master and a tyrant that historical thought must enter a caveat. So the historian is bound by his craft to recognize the nature and limitations of the scientific method and to dispel the illusion that it can produce a science of history embracing the fullness of history, or of any large phase, as past actuality.

This means no abandonment of the tireless inquiry into objective realities, especially economic realities and relations; not enough emphasis has been laid upon the conditioning and determining influences of biological and economic necessities or upon researches designed to disclose them in their deepest and widest ramifications. This means no abandonment of the inquiry into the forms and development of ideas as conditioning and determining influences; not enough emphasis has been laid on this phase of history by American scholars.

But the upshot to which this argument is directed is more fundamental than any aspect of historical method.

It is that any selection and arrangement of facts pertaining to any large area of history, either local or world, race or class, is controlled inexorably by the frame of reference in the mind of the selector and arranger. This frame of reference includes things deemed necessary, things deemed possible, and things deemed desirable. It may be large, informed by deep knowledge, and illuminated by wide experience; or it may be small, uninformed, and unilluminated. It may be a grand conception of history or a mere aggregation of confusions. But it is there in the mind, inexorably. To borrow from Croce, when grand philosophy is ostentatiously put out at the front door of the mind, then narrow, class, provincial, and regional prejudices come in at the back door and dominate, perhaps only half-consciously, the thinking of the historian.

The supreme issue before the historian now is the determination of his attitude to the disclosures of contemporary thought. He may deliberately evade them for reasons pertaining to personal, economic, and intellectual comfort, thus joining the innumerable throng of those who might have been but were not. Or he may proceed to examine his own frame of reference, clarify it, enlarge it by acquiring knowledge of greater areas of thought and events, and give it consistency of structure by a deliberate conjecture respecting the nature or direction of the vast movements of ideas and interests called world history.

This operation will cause discomfort to individual historians but all, according to the vows of their office, are under obligation to perform it, as Henry Adams[1] warned the members of this Association in his letter of 1894. And as Adams then said, it will have to be carried out under the scrutiny of four great tribunals for the suppression of unwelcome knowledge and opinion: the church, the state, property, and labor. Does the world move and, if so, in what direction? If he believes that the world does not move, the historian must offer the pessimism of chaos to the inquiring spirit of mankind. If it does move, does it move backward toward some old arrangement, let us say, of 1928, 1896, 1815, 1789, or 1295? Or does it move forward to some other arrangement which can be only dimly divined—a capitalist dictatorship, a proletarian dictatorship, or a collectivist democracy? The last of these is my own guess, founded on a study of long trends and on a faith in the indomitable spirit of mankind. In any case, if the historian cannot know or explain history as actuality, he helps to make history, petty or grand.

To sum up contemporary thought in historiography, any written history involves the selection of a topic and an arbitrary delimitation of its borders—cutting off connections with the universal. Within the borders arbitrarily established, there is a selection and organization of facts by the processes of thought. This selection and organization—a single act—will be controlled by the historian's frame of reference composed of things deemed necessary and of things deemed desirable. The frame may be a narrow class, sectional, national, or group conception of history, clear and frank or confused and half conscious, or it may be a large, generous conception,

---

1 指1894年美国历史协会主席就职演说《历史趋势》，当时亚当斯本人并未到场，仅为缺席宣读。

clarified by association with the great spirits of all ages. Whatever its nature the frame is inexorably there, in the mind. And in the frame only three broad conceptions of all history as actuality are possible. History is chaos and every attempt to interpret it otherwise is an illusion. History moves around in a kind of cycle. History moves in a line, straight or spiral, and in some direction. The historian may seek to escape these issues by silence or by a confession of avoidance or he may face them boldly, aware of the intellectual and moral perils inherent in any decision—in his act of faith.

选自 Charles A. Beard, "Written History as an Act of Faith", *The American Historical Review*, Vol. 39, No. 2, 1934, pp. 219-231.

六、特勒尔奇《历史主义及其问题》节选

导读

下面的内容选自特勒尔奇《历史主义及其问题》(1922) 第一章第一节"历史学的当代危机"。该书体现了特勒尔奇晚年对历史哲学问题的反思，他看到了神学在现代性冲击下，原有超自然主义教义根基的动摇，提出用历史的方法重新论证信仰，并提出"统一的文化价值"——文化综合这一伟大理想。尽管这些超前的见识遭到了当时学者们的反对，但特勒尔奇的历史主义思想不断被后人挖掘，以应对种种两难处境，即如何面对多元化和历史性，而不陷入相对主义的深渊，如何接受基督教的历史性质而不屈从于相对主义，如何在不诉诸超自然的形而上学的情况下确认基督教的超越性主张，以及如何更充分地实现基督教对普遍正义的承诺而又不强加一种文化的价值观念。在"历史学的当代危机"中，作者指出，当今 (1922) 历史学的危机是历史思维的危机，而不是历史研究的危机。随着19世纪自然科学发展高峰的到来，历史学走向科学化，与此同时，历史学本身的合法性遭到质疑。历史科学现在所采用的方法是通过计划周密的工作组织来抵御专业化危机。但作者认为，历史学的研究客体不同于自然科学，因此，不应盲目追随自然科学，而应有自己的研究方法。

选文部分一开始就指出当今 (1922) 历史学的危机是历史思维的危机。因为随着历史学的科学化，现代历史研究在技术方面取得了较大成就，但历史学仍然存在危机——历史学本身的合法性遭到质疑。面对质疑，回到原始状态并没有用，只能继续规范历史研究，走向历史学的科学化，而历史学现在所采用的方法也是通过计划周密的工作组织来抵御专业化危机。但作者认为，历史学的研究客体不同于自然科学，因此，不应盲目追随自然科学，而应有自己的研究方法。此外，19世纪中期，随着历史学由普遍历史走向多元化，历史价值观念也发生了变化，开始出现研究某地区、某时段、某方面历史的倾向，马克

思、尼采等学者为此寻找新出路，这一切对中产阶级的价值观产生了冲击。因此，历史学和世界观之间的普遍联系需要重新进行表述，作者认为有必要重新解释历史哲学的意义和本质。

特勒尔奇的历史主义是他历史哲学思想的精髓所在。想要理解选文，不仅需要一定的史学理论、哲学功底，还要对特勒尔奇的思想有一定的了解，包括他的神学、宗教哲学、社会伦理学背景。他的历史主义理论带有明显的宗教色彩，如果对此没有初步的了解的话，阅读起来会比较困难。此外，特勒尔奇计划用历史学方法重塑神学，且十分关注历史主义问题以及人的形而上学和实践需要，这一点需要我们注意，以便更全面地认识其史学思想。

When today one often hears of a crisis in the science of history, what is meant is less crisis in the historical investigation of expert historians, than a crisis in historical thinking of people in general. Since a long time both have drifted rather far apart. Critical editions and work on the sources, art of combining facts by comparing and valueing the material, supplementing the material and bringing it to life by means of a historical and cultural psychology exemplifying the general principles of a period by various examples: all these have become methods and techniques of an almost exact science, accurately to be learned and every time accurately to be criticized by experts. Applying this technique to the most different periods which gradually become smaller and easier to view, and repeating the same task over and over again while shifting the means of solution or by giving a new meaning or by criticizing the predecessor's accuracy, brings to light a huge multitude of historical investigations which, from time to time, have to be put together, collected and so to speak codified in large textsbooks. To this have to be added the resources of the different languages and philollgies, of palaeography and diplomatics, of the study of libraries and archives, of travel and direct perception through the eye, as well as the geographical, juristical, economical and other assistant sciences without which an explanation of the sources and a clear picture of them would not be possible.[1]

In all this, crisis and change is not possible as long as history values truth, scientifical exactness and a accuracy congenial to that of the natural sciences. It is not possible as long as one does not seek excitement of imagination and emotion by more or less suggestive novels and dictatorial arguments on certain theses and interests. With great effort historical science since

---

[1] 原文注释提到了以下著述：伯伦汉（Ernst Bernheim）的《史学方法论》（1908）、朗格卢瓦（Charles-Victor Langlois）与瑟诺博司（Charles Seignobos）的《历史研究导论》（1898）、弗里曼（E. A. Freeman）的《历史研究法》（1886）、贝佐尔德（Friedrich V. Bezold）的《历史方法论的发展史》（1914）、贝内德托·克罗齐的《历史学的理论和历史》（1915）、莫里茨·里特尔（Moritz Ritter）的《历史科学的发展》（1919）、爱德华·菲特（Eduard Fueter）的《近代史学史》（1911）、乔治·皮博迪·古奇的《十九世纪历史学与历史学家》（1913）、威廉·鲍尔的《历史研究导论》（1921）、瓦赫勒的《德意志文学文化复兴中的历史研究与技艺史》（1812—1820）、韦格勒（F. X. Wegele）的《德国史学史》（1885）等。

the Maurins[1] and the great philologically trained historians of the 19th century, has risen to this height, and its performance have become admirably broad, full and accurate. Of all this nothing can be abandoned without abandoning the height of scientifical culture itself, the assuredness, clearness, communicability of handicraft without which even the highest and noblest art and mastery is not possible. Naturally, it is possible that we have come to a point where the task has become at the same time refined and extensive to such degree that it goes beyond our strength and that a great science, possible to be curbed in the beginning, grows beyond us and, like a great torso, remains lying. Similarly, in the graphic arts, tradition and mastery of crafts in the centuries from late middle age to the French revolution was torn off and broken, making room for a more personal experimenting and looking on or for the demand of the market and of the journalists. But in its own circle historical work dose not yet show such fatigue and break-up. Danger of specializing, though, not to be avoided by any extensive and intensive science which works out the thoughts of its originally more uniform founders, naturally has grown stronger. But against it stands the will to concentration and the planned-out organization of work. Universities and associations of historians, influential teachers in their seminars and classes may distribute the problems and bring together the workers. Masters in creative art may work on the cast and mould it, thus prepared, and show the way to new distributions of labor, a method, by the way, employed by historical science of today. Mommsen[2] for instance was master in both directions. It is not at all impossible to build out this system farther and farther, the casual and plan-less writing of books will become rarer, their compilation will be left entirely to the masters, while the students will work on the details. The factories of theses and textbooks may be closed; there still remains to the talented and industrious student lots of work and of the happiness in investigating and exploring. Science will become more impersonal, which is, indeed, its character. Originality of design and view will become rarer, results will have to be awaited with more patience. This, however, is inseparable from the maturity and cultivation of a science, as may be seen in the natural sciences.

It is not here that the crisis lies. For all this can not be different and these methods have not yet come to an end. It may be difficult to digest all this knowledge and still be master of the enlarged material. But the ccaze of writing and producing books in the last decades was in itself entirely superfluous. If the "ahistorical" youth of today—as far as it really is "ahistorical"—despairs of the huge meal through which it has to eat its way, we can well understand this despair to be the first horror of the beginner. But, at the same time, it is the fate of all mature cultures growing odd and combing many assumptions. If you trust yourself to the right leaders and have only a little instinct for the essential, you may win through in spite of everything. A

---

1 指圣摩尔派，17至18世纪博学时代依托于法国圣摩尔修道院的学术团体，以语文学和历史学方法考订古代文献为己任，代表人物有马比昂和蒙福孔，代表著作是《古代遗物说明》《希腊古文字学》。
2 蒙森（Theodor Mommsen，1817—1903），德国著名历史学家、古典学家，著有《罗马史》（5卷，1854—1885），主持部分《拉丁铭文大全》（16卷，1867—1959）编纂工作。

certain economy and organization of strength, a throwing-out of the obsolets and an abandoning of that notorious universal knowledge in literature may and should be added to this. The destruction of historical culture and historical knowledge, on the other hand, can be understood only as a determination to go back to barbarism, and it can be done only if all the other spheres of life also return to barbarism. But this last can not be done merely by wishing it and deciding upon it. Rousseau, disgusted with an artificial culture,[1] yet could not bring back barbarism. Getting barbarized, viewed by many as threatening apparition or as attractive salvation, is not the determination of youth choking under the burden of books; it is the result of a general world's crisis. Getting barbarized is not a joyful release to strength and vigour; it is the dismal and long drawn out end of antiquated cultures. We may sift our bundle and change it to the other shoulder, but we must carry it on. We cannot just throw it away, for all the possession and tools of our life are in it. We of the older generation felt and experienced the same when we are young, and we, too, had to find and finally did find our way through. Only with us, all this took place on the quiet, whereas today it takes place in the public, and if it seems more interesting, yet the results will be the same.

If, then, a real crisis is not to be looked for in the field of historical investigation—which latter to destroy would be mental suicide—a crisis certainly is to be found in the general philosophical foundations and elements of historical thinking, in the conception of historical values which influence our reconstruction of historical continuity. In Germany, historical science since ca 1850 turned away from the great and extensive picture of universal history, as Ranke still saw it, and partly broke up into specialized research of different regions and periods, partly, since Bismarck's foundation of the German empire, it treated European history from the political, diplomatic and military angle exclusively. The idea of historical values has, in fact, since a long time undergone a change. Against such dispersal and evacuation of the historical picture there arose a great longing to treat the force and aims of historical life as a whole and let historical values penetrate each other so as to form a spiritual and creative whole. Not only this; the historical values themselves have again begun to move and ail at renewed selection, comprehension and formation. On one side, Karl Marx and those congenial to him consumed the whole conventional picture of history and taught new methods and new aims. The effect of this was and still is immense, even if just now his historical constructions are seen to be fragile. On the other side, with no less effect, Friedrich Nietzsche destroyed former values and taught a new psychology of understanding European history. This psychology may be one sided and even dangerous; it certainly had immense consequences. Then came French pessimism and criticism of culture of the aesthetes. Followed by the counter-attack of Bergson and of French youth. In

---

1 指的是卢梭的《论科学与艺术》(1750)。

Italy, Croce made new tracks for history. In England, H. G. Wells[1] in his *Outline of History* shook the Englishman's historical conscience. The weaker but still effective influence of the recovering arts of history and of religion upset the conventional protestant liberal Prussian or atheistic-nationalistic-imperialistic idea of history or threw a new light on the relations between classical, gothic and modern times, employing art in a large measure as a key to the spiritual qualities of a period. All this strikes upon the conventional valuation of a middle, grown feeble and decadent without realizing it and not in a position to attract youth.

And then came the dreadful test for all historical theories, which arising in times of peaces and progress, extended their system of values as a matter of course into the progress of the future. World war and revolutions became forceful historical examples. Our theories and constructions are not protected anymore by an assimilating order which restores the inoffensiveness of the most audacious and blasphemous theories. They now stand in midst the turmoil of world's reorganization where words can be tested according to their usefulness and where that which seemed or really was of importance before, has become empty talk. Here the earth shakes beneath our feet and we are surrounded by the most different possibilities of future being, specially in German and Russia, where world war meant total change.

This indeed is a crisis in historical thought, and it is only natural that it should be felt the strongest by the younger generation which suffered more under the effect of new thoughts and fetes than their elders, who, in the first place, will have to shape their own fate out of this chaos. To youth, this means a theoretical and practical problem at the same and one of such tremendous force that one can understand if, for the most part, they keep away from these problems; only the lively, the agile, the enthusiastic, the philosophically excitable are caught by its whole force. It would be erroneous to believe that the older generation dose not fully realise the same. But the new does not concern them as such as it does the younger. It is youth, therefore, who should speak and act in order to bring about: if not a solution of the crisis itself, yet tempestuous demands for new solutions.

My own idea about the solution of the crisis can be formulated only as a result from this book. In the beginning, it only matters to appreciate the crisis as such and to differentiate thoroughly between the state of technical-historical investigation and historical-philosophical thinking. The crisis is to be mostly found in the latter, and only to a small degree in the first. That means that the critical mood should not pass unnoticed from the latter to the former. In the former, too, there is decay and conventionalism, but, in general, this science is sound. In the latter, on the other hand, the whole experience of life is changing and tending towards fullness and wholeness which indeed seems indispensable to us. Here new creations must arise out of a

---

[1] 韦尔斯（Herbert George Wells，1866—1946），英国著名小说家、政治家。1920年出版的《世界史纲》是他对第一次世界大战后欧洲命运的反思，由此出发，他认为"通史不是国别史的累加，而需要一种不同的思维方式与眼光"。

superior experience of life. But we do not want to destroy our science, to despise and to slander it. The present time destroyed so much, that more destruction in this field might become doubly dangerous. Seriousness and matter-of-factness, thoroughness and honesty of German science will always be one of the pillars of our spiritual position in the world and expression of our being.[1]

The crisis then is to be found in the philosophical elements and reference of history, in that which may be called its connection with and its importance for our "Weltanschauung". The relation there is a mutual one: importance of history for "Weltanschauung" and importance of Weltanschauung for history. If we look for a name for this group of problems, we can only call them problems of philosophy of history, similarly to the analogous problems of natural science which are called philosophy of nature. The meaning of both words has been fixed already for certain solutions of problems, the one for Schelling's philosophy of history and its descendants, the other for Hegel's philosophy of history and its relatives[2], and is therefore suspicious to many. But if we do not want to be deprived of the most indispensable words, we must not leave those two words to those past solutions of problems. For those solutions of problems meant only one solution among many and they are not possible any more in this manner. The problem of philosophy of nature does not concern us here. Regarding philosophy of history we may say at once that the word today cannot anymore be understood to mean systematization and deduction of history. Word and problem of philosophy of history today mean general relations between history and Weltanschauung, as we have said before, and philosophical assumptions and results of history. Its problem is to find anew the right of formation and mutual order of these problems demanded by the moment.

This has been a problem to be formulated anew by each more important change of generation since the time of Aufklärung[3], mainly interested as it was in natural sciences and quick solutions of a useful and practical manner, gave way to historical thinking and historical consciousness. Since the great international counter-attack against French revolution and since the parallel, although different, spiritual revolution of German classical philosophy and poetry, it has been a problem of all modern science in every country. Beside natural science and its philosophy interpretation it has been carried into effect and it has been a burning question wherever conventional education to historical self-reflection has somehow been abolished. That means that the problem always been less acute in England than on the European continent where people again and again became excited politically, socially and philosophically, specially

---

1 此处注释中作者推荐了自己的论文《科学的革命》(*Die Revolution der Wissenschaft*, 1922)、马克斯·皮卡德 (Max Picard) 的《最后的人》(*Der Letzte Mensch*, 1921),以及鲁道夫·潘维兹 (Rudolf Pannwitz) 的《欧洲文化中的危机》(*Die Krisis in der Europäischen Kultur*, 1917)。
2 这里分别意指"历史对于世界观""世界观对于历史"的重要性。关于世界观理论,可参考狄尔泰的《哲学的本质》(1907) 这篇文章。
3 关于"启蒙"的含义,可参考康德的《答复这个问题:"什么是启蒙运动?"》这篇文章。

in Germany where hard times have been continual.

If you look at it this way, the problem really means a fundamental question of modern spiritual life, i. e. the problem of socalled historism itself, i. e. the problem of the advantage and disadvantage which arise out of the principle of historizing our knowledge and thinking, to the formation of a personal spiritual life and to the creation of new political and social states of life. Historizing of thoughts, in the 18th century, followed slowly upon its naturalizing or, better, its mathematizing and arose, forced by practical wants, together with modern state and its task of understanding and justifying itself. It grew up high with romanticism and influenced the principles of modern thinking, captivating even, in the shape of the general conception of development, our image of nature. Historizing became the leading force of Weltanschauungen, which followed the dogmatism of Aufklärung and of the French revolution. Therefore we have today a tremendous historical-empirical investigation, embedded into the biology of living things on our planet and striving from the beginning for philosophical illumination by great historical-philosophical systems. In the beginning, as long as it concerned the enthusiasm which we have from history, and as long as history meant liberation of the mathematical-technical notion of nature, history without doubt intensified and animated spiritual life in all regions. It also made really to understand art and literature, and it accompanied the formation of national states with its pathos. Afterwards, its growing heap of material became a burden, the impression of changing and contradictory possibilities of construction and the disputes of the critics of sources made us sceptical, the renewed approach of history towards natural science had a determining and hostile effect on greatness and heroism, the connection between history's great syntheses and monuments of art handed it over to the relativism of the aesthetes, and the severe matter-of-factness of its professional studies of sources handed it over to the specialists. What was liberation and rise in the beginning became burden and confusion.

This is the reason why philosophy, almost or quite dead since 1848, as soon as it came back to life, turned at first to discussions with mechanistical naturalism, then to those with history. Forgotten and slandered philosophy of history came to life again and progressed rapidly, assisted by the catastrophe of the world war. Today we may speak of a strong reawakening of philosophy of history. We expect it to answer our questions from the beginning. This answer, indeed, can not be given by single aphorisms or more or less subtle ideas on the subject. It can only be found by a systematic philosophical conquest of the essence of history and of the inquiry into its spiritual aims and contents.

Next, we shall have to paraphrase meaning and nature of philosophy of history itself as it is today in this situation and in its needs. Only after that we shall be able to ask new questions and to answer them. First, we need a survey of its nature and of what it can do.

选自 Ernst Troeltsch, *Historism and Its Problems*, translated by Gerda Hartmann, Tuebingen, 1922, pp. 1-8.

第七章 跨学科与新范式

一、儿童史专题：洛克论儿童教育

导读

约翰·洛克（John Locke，1632—1704）生活在17世纪的英国，是哲学家、医生、经济学家、政治理论家、心理学家和注经（圣经）学者。在写作了大量关于理解人类、政府、经济和宽容等主题的文章后，他于1693年出版了极具影响力的《教育片论》（又译《教育漫话》）一书。

该书缘于爱德华·克拉克爵士为教育其子女向洛克寻求建议时所形成的系列信札。其中一些有关教育的思想在1693年集合成册，以《教育片论》为名发表。此后在修订《人类理解论》时，被收入其中并成为《人类理解论》一书的重要组成部分。此后，仅《教育片论》英文单行本就有二十多种版本，并且译本众多，被英语世界之外广泛接受。而在洛克身后，与他同时代的思想家、作家，如斯威夫特、戈德史密斯和理查森等人都对他的教育理论展开了大规模讨论。今天，洛克已被公认为"英国现代教育之父"及世界上最具实际影响力的教育思想家之一。

洛克的教育理论，既挑战了当时关于儿童心理的共识，也挑战了当时的标准教育实践。不过，仅把这些思想当作其对现代教育理论的重大贡献，局限了我们对洛克贡献的理解。正如1996年露丝·格兰特和内森·塔可夫在其新编辑版本《教育片论》和《理解行为论》序言中所写的那样：要理解洛克的政治和哲学思想，不能略过其有关教育和理解行为的观点，这两样搭建起了《人类理解论》和洛克有关政治论断之间最好的桥梁。因此，洛克的教育思想是他哲学认识论的一部分，是关于道德和政治的全面反思。

洛克所提倡的教育，被称为"自由教育"。这种教育使人们能够独立思考，能够参与自我管理并参与国家事务，即能够有效决定自己的生活，而其观念中蕴含着理性、自由和道德之间的联系。在洛克看来，个体良好自治所必需的条件即理性，不偏袒、宽容、不被激情所控、能够质疑权威，就能形成公正的判断和行动。因此，人们有责任培养理性，以避免激情、偏袒等道德缺陷。而公正是对他人权利的尊重，文明、慷慨、勤奋、节俭、勇气、诚实，以及质疑偏见、权威和个人私利等都是自由社会公民所需要的品质，教育的目的是培养有用的、有道德的、通情达理的"人"。洛克的教育理念源于他对智力活动的系统观察和他对人类思维活动的理解，在他看来，唯有通过教育才能培养心智,这种教育事业关乎人类道德和政治。

如何实现这一目标呢?

洛克建议要从具体的日常实践入手。阅读《教育片论》,我们会惊讶地发现,洛克教育理论的方法从"吃、喝、拉、撒、睡"这些人们通常认为不起眼的日常小事着手。实际上,洛克认为这是在建立健康的习惯,不但为物质性身体本身的健康,也为一种良好的自律方式,因此"习惯化"是一种强有力的教育方法。如果可以养成习惯,儿童几乎可以养成任何行为。

洛克式教育强调实践和榜样。他虽然鼓励家长的温柔与耐心,记得"把他们当作孩子",摒弃规则和戒律,但在体罚等问题上,他仍然是17世纪的洛克。对于固执、叛逆、随心所欲、任性的孩子,他说"你就必须打",必须抑制才可停止。他也提醒为人父母者,不要让孩子感到恐惧,因为"教导颤抖的心灵就像在颤抖的纸上写字",他敦促父母花时间陪伴他们的孩子,根据他们的性格和癖好调整教育方式,培养健全的身体和性格。

《教育片论》内容丰富,从身体健康到心智培养,从文明习惯到政治自由,种种论述都从"日常实践"出发,这跟17世纪知识世俗化这一特征紧密相连,如巴特菲尔德所描述:17世纪下半叶"思想在每一个可能的领域里都同时发生了巨大的世俗化"。洛克的经验主义哲学是这一现象的代表。

要理解洛克的教育思想,必须将《教育片论》与《人类理解论》中的其他文章联系起来,尤其是有关语言的部分。洛克教育理论通常被简单化约为"白板"论,即认为人的大脑从出生起便是一张"白纸",此后通过对外界信息的吸收、储存从而转化为"观念",最终形成人们对外部世界的经验认知及政治道德观。在这一系列的观念生成过程中,人自身的五种感官能力起了重要作用,因此,经由简单信息塑造的复杂思想其实是环境的产物,人是从经验中习得知识、塑造思想的。这一论断打破了柏拉图以来的古希腊哲学认为人出生就具有"先天观念"的认识,而这一观念的产生与他对语言的持续思考联系紧密。

洛克致力于人类对语言的理解,认为语言在获得知识方面具有相当重要的作用。他在对语言的讨论中逐渐认识到并不是所有的语词都与思想有关,他根据文章第二卷中所建立的思想范畴来区分词语,在第三卷中从单词的用法开始集中关注词语和思想的关系。在洛克看来,如果人们滥用词语,我们将无法通过获得更清晰和明确的想法来提高自身的知识和理解。

在阅读洛克的作品时,我们还需意识到洛克自身所处的时代,他自己所使用的语言依然属于早期现代英语。早期现代英语与现代英语仍有区别,比如,早期现代英语在名词复数、名词主格等方面的特点。另要注意冠词省略及任意转换词性等惯用法。

Some Thoughts Concerning Education

Section 1

A sound mind in a sound body, is a short, but full description of a happy state in this world. He that has these two, has little more to wish for; and he that wants either of them, will be but little the better for any thing else. Mens happiness or misery is most part of their own making. He, whose mind directs not wisely, will never take the right way, and he, whose body is crazy and feeble, will never be able to advance in it. I confess, there are some men's constitutions of body and mind so vigorous, and well fram'd by nature, that they need not much assistance from others: but by the strength of their natural genius, they are, from their cradles, carried towards what is excellent; and by the privilege of their happy constitutions, are able to do wonders. But examples of this kind are but few; and I think I may say, that of all the men we meet with, nine parts of ten are what they are, good or evil, useful or not, by their education. 'Tis that which makes the great difference in mankind. The little, or almost insensible impressions on our tender infancies, have very important and lasting consequences: And there 'tis, as in the fountains of some rivers, where a gentle application of the hand turns the flexible waters into channels, that make them take quite contrary courses; and by this little direction given them at first in the source, they receive different tendencies, and arrive at last very remote and distant places.

Section 2

I imagine the minds of children as easily turned this or that way, as water itself: And though this be the principal part, and our main care should be about the inside, yet the clay-cottage is not to be neglected. I shall therefore begin with the case, and consider first the health of the body: as that which perhaps you may rather expect from that study I have been thought more peculiarly to have apply'd myself to; and that also which will be soonest dispatched, as lying, if I guess not amiss, in a very little compass.

Section 3

How necessary health is to our business and happiness; and how requisite a strong constitution, able to endure hardships and fatigue, is to one that will make any figure in the world, is too obvious to need any proof.

Section 4

The consideration I shall here have of health, shall be, not what a physician ought to do with a sick and crazy child; but what the parents without the help of physick should do for the preservation and improvement of an healthy, or at least not sickly constitution in their children. And this perhaps might be all dispatched in this one short rule, viz. That gentlemen should use their children as the honest farmers and substantial yeomen do theirs. But because the mothers possibly may think this a little too hard, and the fathers too short, I shall explain myself more particularly; only laying down this as a general and certain observation for the women to consider, viz. That most children's constitutions are either spoiled, or at tenderness least harmed by cockering and tenderness.

Section 5

The first thing to be taken care of, is, that children be not too warmly clad or cover'd, winter or summer. Warmth. The face when we are born, is no less tender than any other part of the body. 'Tis use alone hardens it, and makes it more able to endure the cold. And therefore the Scythian[1] philosopher gave a very significant answer to the Athenian, who wondered how he could go naked in frost and snow. "How," said the Scythian, "can you endure your face expos'd to the sharp winter air?" "My face is us'd to it," said the Athenian. "Think me all face," reply'd the Scythian. Our bodies will endure any thing, that from the beginning they are accustomed to.

An eminent instance of this, though in the contrary excess of heat, being to our present purpose, to shew what use can do, I shall set down in the author's word's as I meet with it in a late ingenious voyage.

"The heats, says he are more violent in Malta, than in any part of Europe: They exceed those of Rome itself, and are perfectly stifling; and so much the more, because there are seldom any cooling breezes here. This makes the common people as black as Gypsies: But yet the peasants defy the sun; they work on in the hottest part of the day, without intermission, or sheltering themselves from his scorching rays. This has convinc'd me, that nature can bring itself to many things, which seem impossible, provided we accustom ourselves from our infancy. The Malteses do so, who harden the bodies of their children, and reconcile them to the heat, by making them go stark naked, without shirt, drawers, or any thing on their heads, from their cradles, till they are ten years old."

Give me leave therefore to advise you, not to fence too carefully against the cold of this our climate. There are those in England, who wear the same clothes winter and summer, and that without any inconvenience, or more sense of cold than others find. But if the mother will needs have an allowance for frost and snow, for fear of harm, and the father, for fear of censure, be sure let not his winter clothing be too warm: And amongst other things, remember, that when nature has so well covered his head with hair, and strengthened it with a year or two's age, that he can run about by day without a cap, it is best that by night a child should also ly without one; there being nothing that more exposes to headaches, colds, catarrhs, coughs, and several other diseases, than keeping the head warm.

Section 6

I have said he here, because the principal aim of my discourse, is, how a young gentleman should be brought up from his infancy, which, in all things will not so perfectly suit the

---

1 斯基泰人，又译"西古提人"，《教育漫话》译者徐大建译为"锡西厄人"。生活在公元前8世纪至公元前3世纪以黑海北岸为中心的欧洲东南部地区。

education of Daughters; though where the difference of sex requires different treatment, 'twill be no hard matter to distinguish.

Section 7

I will also advise his feet to be washed every day in cold water, and to have his shoes so thin, that they might leak and let in water, whenever he comes near it. Here, I fear I shall have the mistress and maids too against me. One will think it too filthy, and the other perhaps too much pains, to make clean his stockings. But yet truth will have it, that his health is much more worth, than all such considerations, and ten times as much more. And he that considers how mischievous and mortal a thing taking wet in the feet is, to those who have been bred nicely, will wish he had, with the poor people's children, gone bare-foot, who, by that means, come to be so reconciled by custom to wet in their feet, that they take no more cold or harm by it, than if they were wet in their hands. And what is it, I pray, that makes this great difference between the hands and the feet in others, but only custom? I doubt not but if a man from his cradle had been always used to go barefoot, whilst his hands were constantly wrapt up in warm mittins, and covered with hand-shoes, as the Dutch call gloves; I doubt not, I say, but such a custom would make taking wet in his hands as dangerous to him, as now taking wet in their feet is to a great many others. The way to prevent this, is to have his shoes made so as to leak water, and his feet washed constantly every day in cold water. It is recommendable for its cleanliness: but that which I aim at in it, is health; and therefore I limit it not precisely to any time of the day. I have known it used every night with very good success, and that all the winter, without the omitting it so much as one night in extreme cold weather; when thick ice covered the water, the child bathed his legs and feet in it, though he was of an age not big enough to rub and wipe them himself; and when he began this custom was puling and very tender. But the great end being to harden those parts, by a frequent and familiar use of cold water, and thereby to prevent the mischiefs that usually attend accidental taking wet in the feet in those who are bred otherwise, I think it may be left to the prudence and convenience of the parents, to chuse either night or morning. The time I deem indifferent, so the thing be effectually done. The health and hardiness procured by it, would be a good purchase at a much dearer rate. To which, if I add, the preventing of corns, that to some men would be a very valuable consideration. But begin first in the spring with luke-warm, and so colder and colder every time, till in a few days you come to perfectly cold water, and then continue it so winter and summer. For it is to be observed in this, as in all other alterations from our ordinary way of living, the changes must be made by gentle and insensible degrees; and so we may bring our bodies to any thing, without pain and without danger.

How fond mothers are like to receive this doctrine, is not hard to foresee. What can it be less, than to murder their tender babes, to use them thus? What! put their feet in cold water in frost and snow, when all one can do is little enough to keep them warm? A little to remove their fears by examples, without which the plainest reason is seldom hearkened to: Seneca[1] tells us of himself, Ep. 53, 83, that he used to bathe himself in cold spring-water in the midst of winter. This, if he had not thought it not only tolerable, but healthy too, he would scarce have done, in an exorbitant fortune, that could well have born the expence of a warm bath, and in an age (for he was then old) that would have excused greater indulgence. If we think his stoical principles led him to this severity, let it be so, that this sect reconciled cold water to his sufferance. What made it agreeable to his health? For that was not impaired by this hard usage. But what shall we say to Horace[2], who warmed not himself with the reputation of any sect, and least of all affected stoical austerities? Yet he assures us, he was wont in the winter season to bathe himself in cold water. But, perhaps, Italy will be thought much warmer than England, and the chillness of their waters not to come near ours in winter. If the rivers of Italy are warmer, those of Germany and Poland are much colder, than any in this our country; and yet in these, the Jews, both men and women, bathe all over, at all seasons of the year, without any prejudice to their health. And every one is not apt to believe it is miracle, or any peculiar virtue of St. Winifred's Well[3], that makes the cold waters of that famous spring do no harm to the tender bodies that bathe in it. Every one is now full of the miracles done by cold baths on decayed and weak constitutions, for the recovery of health and strength; and therefore they cannot be impracticable or intolerable for the improving and hardening the bodies of those who are in better circumstances.

If these examples of grown men be not thought yet to reach the case of children, but that they may be judged still to be too tender, and unable to bear such usage, let them examine what the Germans of old, and the Irish now, do to them, and they will find, that infants too, as tender as they are thought, may without any danger, endure bathing, not only of their feet, but of their whole bodies, in cold water. And there are, at this day, Ladies in the Highlands of Scotland who use this discipline to their children in the midst of winter, and find that cold water does them no harm, even when there is ice in it.

Section 8

I shall not need here to mention swimming, when he is of an age able to learn, and has any one to teach him. 'Tis that saves many a man's life; and the Romans thought it so necessary that they ranked it with letters; and it was the common phrase to mark one ill-educated, and good for nothing, That he had neither learnt to read nor to swim: "Nec literas didicit nec natare." But besides the gaining a skill which may serve him at need, the advantages to health by often bathing in cold water, during the heat of summer, are so many, that I think nothing need be said

---

1 塞涅卡 (Lucius Annaeus Seneca, 约前 4-65), 古罗马政治家、悲剧作家、雄辩家、斯多葛派哲学家。
2 贺拉斯, 古罗马 "黄金时代" 文学代表人物之一, 与维吉尔、奥维德并称古罗马三大诗人。
3 圣温妮费德水井位于英国威尔士弗林特郡, 是迄今保存最完好的一座中世纪圣井。传说圣贝诺的侄女在寻求庇护时逃难至此, 被人砍头, 当其头颅滚落山谷之处时, 奇迹般地出现了泉水, 而圣贝诺为其侄女温妮弗雷德重新接上头, 使她重生, 她日后成为一名女修道院院长, 并成为圣徒。据说井下花园的石头上覆盖了一层红色苔藓, 每年都会奇迹般更新, 因此, 自中世纪以来, 此圣井就成为上至王公贵胄、下至平民百姓的朝圣之地。

to encourage it; provided this one caution be used, that he never go into the water when exercise has at all warmed him, or left any emotion in his blood or pulse.

Section 9

Another thing that is of great advantage to every one's health, but especially children's, is to be much in the open air, and as little as may be by the fire, even in winter. By this he will accustom himself also to heat and cold, shine and rain; all which if a man's body will not endure, it will serve him to very little purpose in this world; and when he is grown up, it is too late to begin to use him to it. It must be got early, and by degrees. Thus the body may be brought to bear almost any thing. If I should advise him to play in the wind and the sun without a hat, I doubt whether it could be borne. There would a thousand objections be made against it, which at last would amount to no more, in truth, than being sun-burnt. And if my young master be to be kept always in the shade, and never exposed to the sun and wind, for fear of his complexion, it may be a good way to make him a beau, but not a man of business. And altho' greater regard be to be had to beauty in the daughters; yet I will take the liberty to say, that the more they are in the air, without prejudice to their faces, the stronger and healthier they will be; and the nearer they come to the hardships of their brothers in their education, the greater advantage will they receive from it all the remaining part of their lives.

Section 10

Playing in the open air has but this one danger in it, that I know; and that is, that when he is hot with running up and down, he should sit or ly down on the cold or moist earth. This I grant; and drinking cold drink, when they are hot with labor or exercise, brings more people to the grave, or to the brink of it, by fevers, and other diseases, than anything I know. These mischiefs are easily enough prevented whilst he is little, being then seldom out of sight. And if, during his childhood, he be constantly and rigorously kept from sitting on the ground, or drinking any cold liquor whilst he is hot, the custom of forbearing, grown into habit, will help much to preserve him, when he is no longer under his maid's or tutor's eye. This is all I think can be done in the case: For, as years increase, liberty must come with them; and in a great many things he must be trusted to his own conduct, since there cannot always be a guard upon him, except what you have put into his own mind by good principles, and established habits, which is the best and surest, and therefore most to be taken care of. For, from repeated cautions and rules, never so often inculcated, you are not to expect any thing either in this, or any other case, farther than practice has established them into habits.

Section 11

One thing the mention of the girls brings into my mind, which must not be forgot; and that is, that your son's clothes be never made strait, especially about the breast. Let nature have scope to fashion the body as she thinks best. She works of herself a great deal better and exacter than we can direct her. And if women were themselves to frame the bodies of their children in their wombs, as they often endeavour to mend their shapes, when they are out, we should as certainly have no perfect children born, as we have few well-shaped that are strait-laced, or much tampered with. This consideration should, methinks, keep busy people (I will not say ignorant nurses and bodice-makers) from meddling in a matter they understand not; and they should be afraid to put nature out of her way in fashioning the parts, when they know not how the least and meanest is made. And yet I have seen so many instances of children receiving great harm from strait-lacing, that I cannot but conclude there are other creatures as well as monkeys, who, little wiser, than they, destroy their young ones by senseless fondness, and too much embracing.

选自 John Locke, *Some Thoughts Concerning Education*, London: J. and R. Tonson in the Strand, 1779, pp. 1-13.

Of the Abuse of Words

1. Woeful abuse of words. Besides the imperfection that is naturally in language, and the obscurity and confusion that is so hard to be avoided in the use of words, there are several wilful faults and neglects which men are guilty of in this way of communication, whereby they render these signs less clear and distinct in their signification than naturally they need to be.

2. Words are often employed without any, or without clear ideas. First, in this kind the first and most palpable abuse is, the using of words without clear and distinct ideas; or, which is worse, signs without anything signified. Of these there are two sorts:

I. Some words introduced without clear ideas annexed to them, even in their first original. One may observe, in all languages, certain words that, if they be examined, will be found in their first original, and their appropriated use, not to stand for any clear and distinct ideas. These, for the most part, the several sects of philosophy and religion have introduced. For their authors or promoters, either affecting something singular, and out of the way of common apprehensions, or to support some strange opinions, or cover some weakness of their hypothesis, seldom fail to coin new words, and such as, when they come to be examined, may justly be called insignificant terms. For, having either had no determinate collection of ideas annexed to them when they were first invented; or at least such as, if well examined, will be found inconsistent, it is no wonder, if, afterwards, in the vulgar use of the same party, they remain empty sounds, with little or no signification, amongst those who think it enough to have them often in their mouths, as the distinguishing characters of their Church or School, without much troubling their heads to examine what are the precise ideas they stand for. I shall not need here to heap up instances; every man's reading and conversation will sufficiently furnish him. Or if he wants to be better stored, the great mint masters of this kind of terms, I mean the Schoolmen and Metaphysicians (under which I think the disputing natural and moral philosophers of these latter ages may be comprehended) have wherewithal abundantly to content him.

3. II. Other words, to which ideas were annexed at first, used afterwards without distinct meanings. Others there be who extend this abuse yet further, who take so little care to lay by

words, which, in their primary notation have scarce any clear and distinct ideas which they are annexed to, that, by an unpardonable negligence, they familiarly use words which the propriety of language has affixed to very important ideas, without any distinct meaning at all. Wisdom, glory, grace, &c., are words frequent enough in every man's mouth; but if a great many of those who use them should be asked what they mean by them, they would be at a stand, and not know what to answer: a plain proof, that, though they have learned those sounds, and have them ready at their tongues ends, yet there are no determined ideas laid up in their minds, which are to be expressed to others by them.

4. This occasioned by men learning names before they have the ideas the names belong to. Men having been accustomed from their cradles to learn words which are easily got and retained, before they knew or had framed the complex ideas to which they were annexed, or which were to be found in the things they were thought to stand for, they usually continue to do so all their lives; and without taking the pains necessary to settle in their minds determined ideas, they use their words for such unsteady and confused notions as they have, contenting themselves with the same words other people use; as if their very sound necessarily carried with it constantly the same meaning. This, though men make a shift with in the ordinary occurrences of life, where they find it necessary to be understood, and therefore they make signs till they are so; yet this insignificancy in their words, when they come to reason concerning either their tenets or interest, manifestly fills their discourse with abundance of empty unintelligible noise and jargon, especially in moral matters, where the words forthe most part standing for arbitrary and numerous collections of ideas, not regularly and permanently united in nature, their bare sounds are often only thought on, or at least very obscure and uncertain notions annexed to them. Men take the words they find in use amongst their neighbors; and that they may not seem ignorant what they stand for, use them confidently, without much troubling their heads about a certain fixed meaning; whereby, besides the ease of it, they obtain this advantage, that, as in such discourses they seldom are in the right, so they are as seldom to be convinced that they are in the wrong; it being all one to go about to draw those men out of their mistakes who have no settled notions, as to dispossess a vagrant of his habitation who has no settled abode. This I guess to be so; and every one may observe in himself and others whether it be so or not.

5. Unsteady application of them. Secondly, another great abuse of words is inconstancy in the use of them. It is hard to find a discourse written on any subject, especially of controversy, wherein one shall not observe, if he read with attention, the same words (and those commonly the most material in the discourse, and upon which the argument turns) used sometimes for one collection of simple ideas, and sometimes for another; which is a perfect abuse of language. Words being intended for signs of my ideas, to make them known to others, not by any natural signification, but by a voluntary imposition, it is plain cheat and abuse, when I make them stand sometimes for one thing and sometimes for another; the wilful doing whereof can be imputed to nothing but great folly, or greater dishonesty. And a man, in his accounts with another may, with

as much fairness make the characters of numbers stand sometimes for one and sometimes for another collection of units: e. g. this character 3, stand sometimes for three, sometimes for four, and sometimes for eight, as in his discourse or reasoning make the same words stand for different collections of simple ideas. If men should do so in their reckonings, I wonder who would have to do with them? One who would speak thus in the affairs and business of the world, and call 8 sometimes seven, and sometimes nine, as best served his advantage, would presently have clapped upon him, one of the two names men are commonly disgusted with. And yet in arguings and learned contests, the same sort of proceedings passes commonly for wit and learning; but to me it appears a greater dishonesty than the misplacing of counters in the casting up a debt; and the cheat the greater, by how much truth is of greater concernment and value than money.

6. III. Affected obscurity, as in the Peripatetick and other sects of philosophy. Thirdly, another abuse of language is an affected obscurity; by either applying old words to new and unusual significations; or introducing new and ambiguous terms, without defining either; or else putting them so together, as may confound their ordinary meaning. Though the Peripatetick philosophy has been most eminent in this way, yet other sects have not been wholly clear of it. There are scarce any of them that are not cumbered with some difficulties (such is the imperfection of human knowledge), which they have been fain to cover with obscurity of terms, and to confound the signification of words, which, like a mist before people's eyes, might hinder their weak parts from being discovered. That body and extension in common use, stand for two distinct ideas, is plain to any one that will but reflect a little. For were their signification precisely the same, it would be as proper, and as intelligible to say, "the body of an extension," as the "extension of a body"; and yet there are those who find it necessary to confound their signification. To this abuse, and the mischiefs of confounding the signification of words, logic, and the liberal sciences as they have been handled in the schools, have given reputation; and the admired Art of Disputing hath added much to the natural imperfection of languages, whilst it has been made use of and fitted to perplex the signification of words, more than to discover the knowledge and truth of things: and he that will look into that sort of learned writings, will find the words there much more obscure, uncertain, and undetermined in their meaning, than they are in ordinary conversation.

7. Logic and dispute have much contributed to this. This is unavoidably to be so, where men's parts and learning are estimated by their skill in disputing. And if reputation and reward shall attend these conquests, which depend mostly on the fineness and niceties of words, it is no wonder if the wit of man so employed, should perplex, involve, and subtilize the signification of sounds, so as never to want something to say in opposing or defending any question; the victory being adjudged not to him who had truth on his side, but the last word in the dispute.

8. Calling it "subtlety." This, though a very useless skin, and that which I think the direct opposite to the ways of knowledge, hath yet passed hitherto under the laudable and esteemed names of subtlety and acuteness, and has had the applause of the schools, and encouragement of

one part of the learned men of the world. And no wonder, since the philosophers of old (the disputing and wrangling philosophers I mean, such as Lucian wittily and with reason taxes), and the Schoolmen since, aiming at glory and esteem, for their great and universal knowledge, easier a great deal to be pretended to than really acquired, found this a good expedient to cover their ignorance, with a curious and inexplicable web of perplexed words, and procure to themselves the admiration of others, by unintelligible terms, the apter to produce wonder because they could not be understood: whilst it appears in all history, that these profound doctors were no wiser nor more useful than their neighbours, and brought but small advantage to human life or the societies wherein they lived: unless the coining of new words, where they produced no new things to apply them to, or the perplexing or obscuring the signification of old ones, and so bringing all things into question and dispute, were a thing profitable to the life of man, or worthy commendation and reward.

9. This learning very little benefits society. For, notwithstanding these learned disputants, these all-knowing doctors, it was to the unscholastic statesman that the governments of the world owed their peace, defence, and liberties; and from the illiterate and contemned mechanic (a name of disgrace) that they received the improvements of useful arts. Nevertheless, this artificial ignorance, and learned gibberish, prevailed mightily in these last ages, by the interest and artifice of those who found no easier way to that pitch of authority and dominion they have attained, than by amusing the men of business, and ignorant, with hard words, or employing the ingenious and idle in intricate disputes about unintelligible terms, and holding them perpetually entangled in that endless labyrinth. Besides, there is no such way to gain admittance, or give defence to strange and absurd doctrines, as to guard them round about with legions of obscure, doubtful, and undefined words. Which yet make these retreats more like the dens of robbers, or holes of foxes, than the fortresses of fair warriors: which, if it be hard to get them out of, it is not for the strength that is in them, but the briars and thorns, and the obscurity of the thickets they are beset with. For untruth being unacceptable to the mind of man, there is no other defence left for absurdity but obscurity.

10. But destroys the instruments of knowledge and communication. Thus learned ignorance, and this art of keeping even inquisitive men from true knowledge, hath been propagated in the world, and hath much perplexed, whilst it pretended to inform the understanding. For we see that other well-meaning and wise men, whose education and parts had not acquired that acuteness, could intelligibly express themselves to one another; and in its plain use make a benefit of language. But though unlearned men well enough understood the words white and black, &c., and had constant notions of the ideas signified by those words; yet there were philosophers found who had learning and subtlety enough to prove that snow was black; i. e. to prove that white was black. Whereby they had the advantage to destroy the instruments and means of discourse, conversation, instruction, and society; whilst, with great art and subtlety, they did no more but perplex and confound the signification of words, and thereby

render language less useful than the real defects of it had made it; a gift which the illiterate had not attained to.

选自 John Locke, *An Essay Concerning Human Understanding*, State College: Pennsylvania State University, 1999, pp. 479-498.

二、医疗史专题：《约翰二世·科穆宁皇帝为君士坦丁堡救世主基督修道院所立的规章》节选

导读

《约翰二世·科穆宁皇帝为君士坦丁堡救世主基督修道院所立的规章》选自拜占庭重要的原始文献集《拜占庭修道院奠基文献》(*Byzantine Monastic Foundation Documents*)，《拜占庭修道院奠基文献》对现存于世的约61个拜占庭修道院奠基文献进行了完整的翻译、介绍和注释，是我们了解拜占庭修道院及其附属机构（包括医院和养老院等），修道院中修士、修女以及与之发生关系的世俗之人的第一手材料。这些文献中有7世纪阿帕·亚伯拉罕（Apa Abraham）的遗书，也有来自阿索斯圣山各修道院的珍贵文献。这61个文献相互之间既有范式上的共性，又因各修道院的不同特点而颇具个性，这些共性与个性反映了多个世纪以来拜占庭修道院的变化。因此，这一历史文献集具有极高的史料和史学价值。

《约翰二世·科穆宁皇帝为君士坦丁堡救世主基督修道院所立的规章》由拜占庭帝国科穆宁王朝皇帝约翰二世（1087—1143）颁布。下面节选了其中与医疗救治相关的条文。拜占庭医学对人类医学最重要的贡献在于其在公共卫生领域的创新，具体表现为医学史上第一所医院，以及随着公共卫生水平的提高和军事斗争的需要而发展起来的军事医学和医疗制度的建立。以君士坦丁堡的救世主基督医院为例，1112年拜占庭皇帝约翰二世建立救世主基督修道院时，同时兴建了附属的救世主基督医院，另含一所老人之家和一所麻风病医院。拜占庭的医院制度是多种现代医院制度的鼻祖，例如门诊—住院制度、医院分区制度、医生的轮值制度和护理制度等，这些读者均可从节选的条文中阅读到。

需要注意的一是"typika"一词，多译为"奠基文献"，一般用在为特定修道院撰写和颁布的文书中，它为特定修道院的合法性和有限的自治权提供法律上的依据；二是极少部分文献中出现了错别，因其是被拜占庭帝国的皇帝颁布，故保持原貌不予更改。

外国史学要籍选读

Pantokrator: Typikon of Emperor John II Komnenos for the Monastery of Christ Pantokrator in Constantinople

Date: October 1136 　　　　　　　　　　　　　　Translator: Robert Jordan

Edition employed: Paul Gautier, "Le typikon du Christ Sauveur Pantocrator," REB 32 (1974), 1-145, with text at 27-131.

Manuscripts: Parisinus graecus 389, fols. 1-61 (before 1740); Codex 85, nunc 79, Theological School, Halki, now in the Patriarchal Library, Istanbul, fols. 69-122v (1749).

　　Typikon (奠基文献) of the Imperial Monastery of the Pantokrator (救世主基督)
　　... it raised me above all treachery and plotting and at the right time painlessly set me at the position of absolute power in the ancestral empire of the Ausones [Romans], agreeing, as one might say, with the final command and wish of my late father's divine soul. Then after that extraordinary elevation it also destroyed the cunning plots of my visible and invisible enemies and rescued me from every trap subjecting all my enemies under my feet. How will I recount in full the wonders that God's right arm achieved for me against Persians, Scythians (斯基泰人), Dalmatians (达尔马提亚人), Dacians (达西亚人), and Paeonians (培奥尼亚人), the many unspeakable victories that it often wondrously wrought with me on them all, making me stronger than all the invaders, dispersing and scattering the ambushes of those within and those without, destroying and binding hand and foot those of my friends and relations who stood against me and wickedly distanced themselves from brotherly concord?

　　So, what might I offer to the All-Merciful One for such great favors? What could I give thee, Master who lovest goodness, for such great debts except that I turn to thee completely and submit whole-heartedly to thy will? Under its guidance I built a new church dedicated to thine almighty wisdom and portrayed in front of the church and in the sanctuary the Indescribable One and I offer thee that which is thine own, for through thy help I found someone to share its planning, construction, and completion, my partner and helper in life, though before the complete establishment of the task she left this world by thy mysterious decision and by her departure cut me apart and left me torn in two.

　　Yet though I am not able to fathom the depths of thine incomprehensible wisdom which beneficially manages our lives, I give thanks for thy patience and at last according to my capabilities I unveil my enterprise bringing thee a band of ascetics, a precious gathering of monks, whose duty it is to devote themselves to the monastery and propitiate thy goodness for our sins. To these I add another holy group, a chosen band, a precious portion, a very fine company of dedicated men—priests, deacons, and as large a number as is necessary for the church and the sanctuary. For I am building another sacred dwelling also for the most-pure Virgin, thy virgin mother, and I am maintaining its offering of praise in a fitting manner through a holy assembly of clergy. Along with these I bring thee, the Lover of goodness, some fellow-servants, whom thou in thy compassion called brothers (Matt. 25:40), worn out by old age and toil, oppressed by poverty and suffering from diseases of many kinds. Those whose bodies are ravaged by leprosy are all receiving the appropriate care, others are being relieved of their burdens, revived from weakness, and are receiving complete healing of their wounds, and others are being freed from want, finding consolation in a sufficient supply of food and clothing. We bring thee these people as ambassadors to intercede for our sins; by them we attract thy favor and through them we plead for thy compassion. For we have taken due thought for the protection, care, and managing of these animate and inanimate temples, and now we prescribe in detail what will be done in their regard.

So then we wish the sequence of divine praises in this most-holy monastery to proceed according to the ecclesiastical rule set up by us.

[1. Ceremonial of the Office]...

[2. Incenses]...

[3. Chants and Prayers in Honor of the Emperors]...

[4. Order of Precedence]...

[5. Other Instructions]...

[6. Illumination of the Main Church on Ordinary Days]...

[7. Illumination of the Main Church on Feast Days]...

[8. Liturgical Offerings and Commemorations]...

[9. Regulations for Dinner]...

[10. Care of Sick Monks]

If anyone is so sick that he is bed-ridden and cannot walk, the appropriate care should be provided in his cell. Also the superior should with sincerity take care of all those who are ill, securing a doctor to visit the monastery and provide soothing plasters and oils so that they can be stored up in the sick room; and he himself should call, often visiting those who need care, ministering to all their needs with white bread, the best wine, and other things that can comfort those who are ill.

The sanatorium should have six made-up beds for those who wish to lie down and another for the doctor who will stay here too to care for the sick whenever necessity demands. Useful articles for washing oneself should be placed in it in sufficient quantity—I mean basins, ewers, and soap dishes, towels, hair wipers, hand towels, etc.—and enough for six to wash at the same time; and not only will those who are ill use these things but also in fact all the monks. Care must especially be taken that those who look after them should show their care for them in every action and in their concern, believing Christ who said "As you did it to one of the least of these my brothers, you did it for me". This is what concerns the sick.

[11. Regulations for Supper]...

[12. Dietary Regulations]...

[13. Claustration and Abstention from Bathing during Lent]...

[14. Honor and Respect Due the Superior]. . .

[15. Bathing Permitted]. . .

[16. Reception of Postulants]. . .

[17. Entrance Gifts Not Required]. . .

[18. Entry Forbidden to Women]. . .

[19. Number and Responsibilities of the Monks]. . .

[20. Confession to the Superior]. . .

[21. No Overnight Absences]. . .

[22. Communal Provision of Clothing]. . .

[23. Superior's Discretionary Authority]. . .

[24. Election of the Superior]. . .

[25. Installation of the Superior]. . .

[26. Privileges of the Superior]. . .

[27. Revenues of the Dependent Monasteries]. . .

[28. Constitutions of the Dependent Monasteries]. . .

[29. Church of the Mother of God Eleousa and Its Lighting]. . .

[30. Clergy Stationed in the Church of the Eleousa]. . .

[31. Duties of the Clergy of the Eleousa]. . .

[32. Remunerations of the Clergy of Eleousa]. . .

[33. Liturgical Ritual of the Church of Eleousa]. . .

[34. The Church of St. Michael and Its Lighting]. . .

[35. Liturgical Ritual of the Church of St. Michael]. . .

[36. Establishment of a Hospital]

Since my majesty also prescribed a hospital which should shelter fifty bedridden sick people, I wish and decree that there should be that number of beds for the comfort of these sick people. Of these fifty beds, ten will be for those suffering from wounds or those with fractures, eight others for those afflicted with ophthalmia and those with sickness of the stomach and any other very acute and painful illnesses; twelve beds will be set aside for sick women and the remainder will be left for those who are moderately ill. But if from time to time there is a lack of people ill either from wounds or from ophthalmia and other very acute illnesses, the number will be made up from other sick people afflicted with simply any disease whatever. Each bed should have a mat, a mattress with a pillow and a coverlet, and in the winter also two blankets made of goat's hair. So since these fifty beds have been divided into five wards, there will be an extra bed also in each ward in which will be placed any patient whose condition of emergency requires that he lie down but who because the beds are full cannot find an appointed place to lie down. Apart from these beds, six more extra beds will be set aside with mattresses pierced through the middle for those who cannot move at all, either because of the severity of their illnesses or their utter weakness or sometimes even the pain of the wounds they may suffer.

[37. Bedding and Clothes for the Sick]

They must maintain a continuous supply of as many as fifteen or even twenty shirts and cloaks for the poorer invalids or those suffering from more acute illnesses so that whenever they go to bed they can change into these and their own clothes can be washed and kept for them to put on whenever they had got rid of their illness and are about to leave. Each year they should change any of these bedclothes and other clothes that are completely unserviceable, unsew the mattresses and pillows and pull apart the wool, and change the torn linen or sew it up again for the comfort of those in the beds. However any of the old clothes and bedclothes that have been changed and are of use for the invalids will be kept by the infirmarian, but the rest will be distributed to the poor.

[38. Medical Personnel]

When these fifty beds have been divided up into five wards, each ward will be served by two doctors, three certified assistants, two auxiliary assistants, and two orderlies. However, each evening four male and one female assistant from the assistants will remain with the patients, that is one to each ward, and they are called watchers. There will be two doctors for the women's ward, and they will be accompanied by one female doctor, four certified female assistants, two auxiliary female assistants, and two female orderlies. Of these doctors appointed to the wards the two chief ones will be called protomenitai, and there will be two in addition to the doctors on the wards called primikerioi, one teacher to teach medical skill, and two attendants. For the sick who visit from outside there will be four extra doctors of whom two will be physicians and two surgeons. These two surgeons will serve the women's ward also whenever any of the women has an illness caused by an open wound. These four doctors who have been assigned to the sick who visit from outside will be accompanied by four certified assistants and four other auxiliary ones, two of whom will also serve the monastery for a month alternately.

[39. The Doctors]

Then all these doctors will be divided into two groups and half of them will minister for one month, the other half the next month. The same will apply to the two primikerioi. They will visit the hospital each day without fail. But from the beginning of May to the feast of the Exaltation of the Cross they will also visit in the late afternoon and after the customary singing of a psalm they will examine the sick carefully and scrutinize each person's illness in accurate detail, treating each person with appropriate remedies, making suitable arrangements for all, and showing great devotion and a careful concern for all as they are going to render an account of these actions to the Pantokrator.

[40. Primikerioi]

So also, each of the primikerioi will go round all the beds independently each day for a month alternately and will ask each of the patients how he is being treated and whether he is being tended by those appointed to this task with proper care and attention, and he will actively correct what is not right, reprove the negligent, and firmly put an end to anything being done improperly. He will also supervise the bread that is given to the patients and anything else laid down to be given to them on a daily basis. He will watch over everything with care and will properly attend to and straighten out each matter. For this reason he should not be in charge of a ward, since supervision only has been laid upon him and no other task. If any of the sick who visit the hospital from outside is found to be seriously ill, the doctor assigned to them will explain to the primikerios about them and on his instruction another doctor, the most experienced of the rest, will go and examine the invalid and take appropriate measures to bring him healing.

[41. The Infirmarian and the Superintendent]

Besides the doctors described above, there will also be an infirmarian and a superintendent who will receive all that is necessary in sufficient quantities and will supply it plentifully not only for those lying in bed inside but also for the sick coming from outside, as has been stated. These men will pay no heed to the expense of these things in maintaining an unfailing supply of everything.

[42. Exhortation to the Hospital Staff]

We give this instruction jointly to all, to the doctors, the supervisors, assistants, and the rest, that they all turn their gaze on him, the Pantokrator, and not neglect their careful examination of the sick, knowing what a great reward this work has when it is properly carried out and again what danger it brings when it is neglected and falls short of what is fitting. For Our Master accepts as his own what is done for each of the least of our brother sand measures out rewards in proportion to our good deeds. So then with regard to these our brothers we will all behave as people unable to escape the unsleeping eye of God and view with apprehension and great fear the time when we shall fall into his hands.

[43. Service Personnel]

To the aforementioned group of doctors, assistants, and others these also will be added— one chief pharmacist, three certified druggists, and two auxiliaries, one doorkeeper, five washerwomen, one man to heat water, two cooks, one groom who is going to work with the horses at the mill and will also receive and keep an eye on the horses of the doctors during the time that they are treating the patients, a gatekeeper, another to act as a caterer, two priests for the churches, two readers—one of the priests, however, will also have episcopal sphragis to hear the confessions of very sick patients, lest they should die a spiritual and ruinous death should they depart from this life without making their confession—two bakers, four undertakers, one priest for funerals, one cleaner of drains, and one miller.

[44. Commemorations]

On the occasions of the commemorations of the sovereign and father of my majesty of blessed memory, and of the lady of blessed memory, my very dear wife, and furthermore when commemorating my own majesty and my very dear son the basileus Lord Alexios (if he also wishes to be buried in the same tomb with me, as has often been mentioned), all these people will gather in the church of the most immaculate Lady and Mother of God with those of the sick who are able to move, carrying out a procession and singing "Remember, Lord, thy servants since thou art good," and "Rest with the saints," and "Ardent intercession." Then they should make an ektenes (广泛的), say Kyrie eleison (上帝怜悯我) forty times and "God will bless the founders," and they should partake in a collation and depart. Four maritime modioi of eucharistic bread will be provided for the collation and four similar measures of wine.

On returning, the doctors along with the other servants of the hospital should receive four hyperpyra nomismata and the fifty sick people one trachy nomisma each, that is for each procession in these commemorations. Also, sixteen large torches should be provided for the processions of the whole year so that the primikerioi can have them to light at the time of the processions.

In addition to this we decree that seventy-two monastic modioi of wheat, that is six modioi each month, should be given for the offerings of bread and kollyba that take place on the first day of each month and are distributed to the doctors, assistants, and other servants of the hospital. Similarly, for the offerings of bread and kollyba that are going to take place on the Saturdays of Meatfare, Cheesefare, and Pentecost in memory of the brothers who die in this same hospital, fifteen similar modioi of wheat should be given and forty follies for the decoration of each of these baskets, and the doctors and other servants should receive two hundred and fifty follies on each of these three Saturdays.

[45. Allotments for the Sick and for Service Personnel]

We decree that the fifty patients along with the four assistants—those also called watchers—the four orderlies, the one female assistant, the female orderly, and the man to heat water should receive each day one white loaf weighing one-fifteenth of a maritime modios and as food they should all be provided together with a similar modios of beans and another modios of another kind of legumes—but if peas are being provided, instead of a modios a half modios will be provided—and in addition to these two foods a hundred onion heads. But sometimes, instead of one of the legumes, fresh vegetables will be supplied, and sufficient oil will be provided by the superintendent for the preparation of these two courses. For wine and all other refreshment the fifty will receive one trachy nomisma each or it will be quite in order to distribute to the fifty each day the preferred gold nomisma (诺米斯马币) of the day in tetartera (四分之一) or noummia, and each of them will receive three follies for their soap each Sunday. There will also be a bakery in which bread will be made for our brothers in Christ—the residents of both the hospital and the old age home—and it should have two milling establishments and three horses.

[46. Bathing of the Sick]

Since those who are ill need to bathe, as many as the doctors prescribe this for will bathe twice a week in the hospital's bath in the company of sufficient assistants and orderlies. But if someone because of his condition needs more frequently the therapy that comes from bathing, the doctor who is attending this sick person will be able to take him into the bathhouse without anyone hindering him.

[47. Washing and Cooking Utensils]...

[48. Doctors Assigned to the Monastery]

We decree that there should be a further two extra doctors to serve the monastery month by month and tend in every way to those in it who are sick, receiving from the hospital the appropriate remedies for the invalids, both medicines, plasters, and other necessary articles. The people who should be assigned to the monastery should be from among the more established of the hospital's auxiliaries, since they are going to receive advancement from there to the hospital. First they will take the place of those who are missing in the women's ward, then also with promotion in the other wards in succession, as has been mentioned. In place of the auxiliaries who are promoted and gain appointed status, we decree that of necessity other auxiliaries should be brought in who should carry out their service to the hospital and the monastery, as has been stated previously.

[49. Allotment of Supplies for the Infirmarian]

So that the infirmarian may not have any excuse for providing the monastery with what it needs in a niggardly fashion, he also will be receiving annually twenty hyperpyra nomismata for the things which should be provided for the monastery besides what has been prescribed for the hospital. Since four orderlies and one female orderly were included in the distribution of the daily bread and food of the patients in the hospital, and since there are two orderlies for each ward, the orderlies will receive this daily allocation, half of them on one day and half on the next. The same applies to the female orderlies so that they will carry out their task eagerly.

Sixty-six maritime measures of olive oil will be supplied to the infirmarian for the preparation of all the ointments and for the making up of plasters, and furthermore for the two lamps that burn continuously in the churches of the hospital, for eight other lamps that must burn in the churches during matins, the liturgy, and vespers, for the five lamps in the wards of the patients that will burn together with the one lamp in the portico, for the two lamps in the lavatories, for the triple lamp which should burn at the doctors' office, and for every other outlay of olive oil that he will make. Of this oil two measures will be of old oil and two others of unripe oil.

Similarly fifty maritime measures of honey will be supplied to the infirmarian for medicines, rose-water, oxymel, the liquid of Diospolis (迪奥斯波利斯), sour grape juice with honey, and for every other outlay of honey made by him, including the juices that will be distributed at the feast of the Savior and at the feast of the Holy Anargyroi (阿纳格罗伊) celebrated on the first of November. He will also be supplied with forty measures of vinegar for all the different outlays made by him, as has been described, and twenty peisai of firewood for the cooking of the medications and the cooking of the juices and the kollyba offering. He will also receive a hundred litrai (升) of pure wax weighed out on the steelyard and two hyperpyra nomismata for incense for the churches along with what is distributed for the mulled wine, and for the candles in the churches along with what is also distributed, three theotokia for vine-oil, ten trachea nomismata for the purchase of cups and plates, two theotokia for cold cauterizers, and one theotokion for the purchase of lamps.

Each month he will receive five monastic modioi of fine wheat flour, one hundred weighed litrai of sugar for the whole year, three barrels of grapes, two barrels of pomegranates, four barrels of wild grapejuice for must, four maritime modioi of barley for juice for each of the two feasts, and one loaf each day for poultice and leavened bread. He will receive two hyperpyra nomismata for the purchase of candles for the patients, the doctors, the assistants, the orderlies, etc. during the festival of Palms and Holy Week, and two hyperpyroi litrai at the beginning of spring for the purchase of medical supplies, medicines, plasters, and the other preparations for the hospital excluding the antidote theriac and the Mithridate. Similarly he will also receive ten maritime modioi of wheat and ten similar measures of wine yearly for the two churches of the hospital, that of the men and that of the women, for the offerings of bread and wine.

[50. Allotment of Supplies for the Superintendent]...

[51. Miscellaneous Dispositions for the Hospital]

There will be one large brazier in the hospital, one small one in the surgery, and another similar one in the women's ward, and they will be supplied yearly with twenty wagons of coal. Each week four liturgies will be celebrated in the hospital, on Wednesday, Friday, Saturday, and Sunday for the glorification of Our Lord and in our memory, excluding the feasts of Our Lord and other significant ones which occur during the week. For on those days also the divine mystery will be specially celebrated. Commemorations of the sick who die should take place three times a year, as has been stated above, that is during [the Saturdays of] Meatfare, Cheesefare, and at Pentecost. Two aspra trachea nomismata, or a twenty-fourth part of the preferred gold nomisma of the day, will be given to the priest taking funerals for incense and candles for each of the sick who die. The washing of the feet of the sick by the superior will take place on Holy Thursday and the fifty sick will receive one trikephalon nomisma each; for the purchase of candles on that same day for the washing of the feet, three hyperpyra nomismata will be provided to be distributed to the whole medical establishment. No assistant or servant of the monastery or of any of those carrying out any task in the monastery or of those acting under its authority will occupy a bed in the hospital. For the fifty beds will be kept free for our brothers in Christ, and the care of the sick of the monastery will take place in the monastery, as has been made clear above. Those who drink a purgative will also lie down with those with ophthalmia and those suffering from a bowel disease so that they may not interrupt the sleep and rest of the other sick people by their continual getting up and the pains which come on them from this.

[52. Salaries of the Hospital Staff]

We prescribe that all staff in the hospital who have been appointed to look after the sick are to receive the following:

The two primikerioi as their allowance should receive seven and a half golden nomismata each of the most preferred type of the day, for their food half a similar nomisma each, and for their grain allowance forty-five annonikoi modioi of grain each.

The two chief doctors, those whom we have decreed should be called protomenitai, should receive seven similar nomismata each, for their food half a nomisma each, and for their grain allowance thirty-eight modioi of grain each.

The two chief surgeons should receive precisely the same.

The other four after them should receive six and a half similar nomismata each, for their food a third of a nomisma each, and thirty-six modioi of grain each.

The two doctors of the monastery should receive four similar nomismata each, for their food a quarter of a similar nomisma each, and thirty modioi of grain each.

The two physicians for the sick who come from outside and the two surgeons appointed as assistants should receive four similar nomismata each, for their food a quarter of a nomisma each, and thirty modioi of grain each.

The infirmarian should receive eight similar nomismata, for his food two-thirds of a similar nomisma, fifty modioi of grain, sixty modioi of barley, and a thousand bundles of hay.

The female doctor should receive three similar nomismata including her food allowance, and twenty-six modioi of grain.

The two attendants should receive three similar nomismata each, for their food a sixth of a nomisma each, and twenty-eight modioi of grain each.

The superintendent who is also going to carry out the job of the cellarer should receive four similar nomismata, for his food a third of a nomisma, and thirty-six modioi of grain.

The chief pharmacist should receive three and a sixth similar nomismata, for his food a third of a similar nomisma, for the wine and food of the druggists when they make their preparations twenty-five trachea nomismata, forty-two annonikoi modioi of grain, for sieves one theotokion nomisma, and in the month of May for the gathering of herbs six old hyperpyra nomismata, and nine similar modioi of grain.

The sixteen certified assistants and the four female assistants should each receive two and a half of the new preferred nomismata of the day, for their food a sixth of a nomisma each, and twenty-four modioi of grain each.

The eight auxiliary assistants and female assistants should receive two similar nomismata each, for their food a twelfth of a nomisma each, and twenty modioi of grain each.

The three certified druggists should receive three and a third similar nomismata each, for their food a sixth of a nomisma each, and twenty-four modioi of grain each.

The two auxiliary druggists should receive two and a half similar nomismata each, for their food a twelfth of a nomisma each, and twenty modioi of grain each.

The four auxiliary assistants who have been allocated to those from outside and to the monastery should also receive the same.

The eight orderlies together with the three female orderlies should receive four similar nomismata each, for their food a quarter of a nomisma each, thirty modioi of grain each, and for their monthly allowance each of them should receive four similar trachea nomismata every month.

The two readers should receive including their food allowance three similar new hyperpyra nomismata each, twelve maritime modioi of grain each, nine measures of wine each, and for their monthly allowance four nomismata each every month.

The doorkeeper should receive as his allowance including that for his food three similar new nomismata, twenty-four annonikoi modioi of grain, and for his monthly allowance four trachea nomismata every month.

The man who heats the water should receive as his allowance three similar nomismata, for his food a quarter of a nomisma, thirty similar modioi of grain, and a monthly allowance of four trachea nomismata every month.

The two cooks along with the caterer should receive including their food allowance three similar nomismata each, thirty similar modioi of grain each, and four trachea nomismata each every month.

The five washerwomen should receive one and a half similar nomismata each, twelve similar modioi of grain each, for their monthly allowance four nomismata each every month, and each Sunday twelve follies each for soap to wash the clothes of the sick who are confined to bed.

The priest to take funerals should receive including his food allowance three new nomismata, twenty modioi of grain, and four trachea nomismata every month.

The four undertakers should receive two similar nomismata each, and twelve modioi of grain each.

The gatekeeper should receive two and a third new hyperpyra nomismata, for his food a sixth of a nomisma, and fifteen annonikoi modioi of grain.

The two bakers should receive as an allowance four similar hyperpyra nomismata each, for their food one similar nomisma each, and for their grain allowance thirty similar modioi of grain each.

The groom who is going to work with the horses of the mill and must keep the horses of the doctors during the time that they are on duty should receive four similar hyperpyra nomismata, and twenty-four similar modioi of grain; for the upkeep of these three milling horses five hundred and forty-seven annonikoi modioi of barley will be provided, three thousand bundles of hay, and sufficient straw; for baking the bread for the sick in the hospital and the brothers in the old age homes one hundred and eighty maritime peisai of firewood each year, for sieves for the bakery two theotokia nomismata each year, and for kneading troughs and linen covers and all the rest that goes with them three more theotokia nomismata.

There will also be a miller who must receive, if there are two milling establishments, two hyperpyra nomismata and sixteen annonikoi modioi of grain, but if there is one, half of this, and a drain cleaner who will receive two new hyperpyra nomismata as his allowance, for his food a sixth of a similar nomisma, and fifteen monastic modioi of grain.

In addition to these there will be a sharpener who must clean up the medical instruments which are going to be kept in the hospital and used to bleed the sick. For in the hospital itself there will be stored at all times lancets, cauterizing irons, a catheter, forceps for drawing teeth, instruments for the stomach and head—simply whatever is necessary for them all. There will also always be copper washbasins and ewers, one for each ward, for the doctors to wash after they have finished tending the sick with whatever is beneficial for the curing of each one, and the sharpener will receive one and a half new hyperpyra nomismata, and twelve annonikoi modioi of grain.

The hospital will also be sure to have the services of a hernia surgeon who will also receive as his allowance three and a third similar new hyperpyra nomismata, for his food a third of a nomisma, and for his grain allowance thirty similar modioi of grain.

The coppersmith who must also be the cooper will receive two similar hyperpyra nomismata, and twenty modioi of grain.

As a monthly allowance the doctors and the assistants will receive five trikephala nomismata each month, in the same way the protomenites will receive one similar trikephalon nomisma for distribution to the sick who come from outside, and the watchers will be given as their monthly allowance thirty-six trachea nomismata each month.

[53. Allocation of Other Sums]...

[54. Doctors Not to Undertake Outside Work]

However the doctors will not be allowed to go out of the city to tend any of the ruling class, even if they are very important and related to the emperor. In general we forbid any of the doctors to carry out additional work. So we forbid even more these doctors to perform unpaid service by imperial command on occasional secular excursions, and furthermore we forbid the taking of any medical articles from the hospital for these excursions, making this present document of ours a request to those who will be emperors after us.

[55. Teacher of Medicine]

We also prescribe that there should be a teacher to teach the principles of medical knowledge, who will also receive exactly the same allowances as the infirmarian. The aforementioned food allowances have been prescribed for him for this reason, that he may attend to the task of teaching and teach the student doctors of the hospital the knowledge of medicine in a consistent and zealous manner. For the teaching post is not being set up by us as an office so that the man thought fit for this responsibility receives his food allowance but neglects his teaching, since the man who is discovered not to be performing this service will be deprived of the receipt of his food allowance and someone else will be appointed instead who will carry out in full the teaching of medical knowledge according to our instructions.

[56. Cemetery of Medikariou]...

[57. Standards of Measurement]...

第七章　跨学科与新范式

[58. Establishment of an Old Age Home]...

[59. Allowances of Old Age Home Residents]...

[60. Transfer of the Sick to the Hospital]

If any of the old men in this old age home are afflicted with any other sickness besides the one for which they were thought fit to enter the old age home, the priest of the old age home will notify the infirmarian of the hospital and information will be supplied to the medical team and they will command one of the doctors or assistants to take care of the sick man, as has been stated, so that he finds relief from this disease. But if the illness is judged to be too serious he will be put to bed in the hospital and will be entitled to the necessary care and medical attention, and when he has regained his strength once more, he will return to the old age home. Each of the old men in the old age home will be washed twice a month in the bath of the hospital.

[61. Appointment of an Infirmarian]...

[62. Allowances for the Orderlies]...

[63. Establishment of a Lepers' Sanatorium]...

[64. Responsibilities of the Stewards]...

[65. Inventory of Properties]...

[66. Rights to Unlisted Properties]...

[67. Typikon Subject to Emendation by the Founder]...

[68. Secret Testament of the Founder]...

[69. Independent Status of the Monastery]...

[70. Defender of the Monastery]...

[71. Supplication to the Pantokrator]...

[72. Final Exhortation to the Monks]

What about you, my fathers and brothers? For now I shall address a few words to you also. You yourselves remember your own undertakings entered into in the presence of God and the angels, reckon up the promises made to God, shudder at the penalty laid down for their denial, bear in mind the rewards that are stored up for your labor, and taking to heart the mortification of human life that each one of you promised, desire to be rid of every earthly passion, setting aside all shouting, blaspheming, strife, and jealousy and acquiring the fruit of the Spirit, joy, love, peace, patience, obedience, accepting as your master himself the one who receives from him your leadership and, like sheep their shepherd, following the leader of your souls to the life-giving pastures of salvation, being eager to obtain the inheritance of the chosen ones.

Remember also our wretchedness and, as you are able, beseech God for us. Pray also for the rulers now dead, for the parents of my majesty, for my very dear son the basileus Lord Alexios, for the most fortunate sebastokratores, for the rest of my very dear children, and the whole world. May you keep the small flock of the Savior safe for me and may we all be kept safe by the gracious will of the Pantokrator.

The present rule of my own monastery of Christ Pantokrator was signed by my majesty in the month of October, of the fifteenth indiction, and of the six thousand six hundred and forty fifth year [= 1136 A. D.].

John Komnenos in Christ our God a faithful emperor Born-in-the-Purple, and Emperor of the Romans.

选自: John Thomas, A. C. Hero (eds.), *Byzantine Monastic Foundation Documents: A Complete Translation of the Surviving Founders' Typika and Testaments*, Washington, D. C. : Dumbarton Oaks Research Library and Collection, 2000.

推荐阅读

1. T. S. Miller, *The Birth of the Hospital in the Byzantine Empire*, Baltimore: Johns Hopkins University Press, 1997.

2. Byzantine Emperor Maurice, *Maurice's Strategikon: Handbook of Byzantine Military Strategy*, translated by George T. Dennis, Philadelphia: University of Pennsylvania Press, 1984.

3. A. Kazhdan, "The Image of the Medical Doctor in Byzantine Literature of the Tenth to Twelfth Centuries", *Dumbarton Oaks Papers*, Vol. 38, No. 1, 1984.

三、环境史专题：约翰·缪尔笔下的美国国家公园

导读

约翰·缪尔（John Muir，1838—1914）是美国乃至世界范围内著名的环境学家、冰川学家、早期的生态理论家。他也是美国环境保护运动最早的倡议者之一，美国国家公园体系的奠基者之一。当代美国著名环境史家唐纳德·沃斯特（Donald Worster）曾为缪尔作传，认为后者对于20世纪美国人关于自身与环境之间关系的思考有深远影响。缪尔一生曾游历过很多地方，进行科学考察，留下了大量专著、散文集和书信，其优美的文笔吸引了数以百万计的读者。他最重要的考察要数对在加州的内华达山脉，尤其是中心地带约塞米蒂地区的考察。该地长期与世隔绝，是世界上罕见的原始冰川地形遗址，亚热带的气候令其植被丰茂，著名的加州红杉林便生长于此。缪尔不仅在考察此地期间留下了大量科考论文、游记散文，还推动成立了"约塞米蒂国家公园""加州红杉林国家公园"。下面选择的这一篇文章，便出自他1901年出版的游记散文集《我国的国家公园》。

阅读这篇文献，当然可以欣赏作者优美的文笔，欣赏他在描绘大自然时丰富而精准的用词。但除此之外，如果将其当成一篇环境史的文献来读，又能有哪些发现呢？可以选择的一个阅读角度是通过作者的叙述，去揣摩19世纪末20世纪初的美国人是如何理解他们与自然的关系的。在阅读过程中可以思考

这样一些问题：缪尔对自然环境或自然景观的价值是如何认识的？他如何理解自然景观与宗教、神圣领域的关系？缪尔对于国家公园的意义和价值是如何理解的？为什么要成立国家公园？国家与自然景观之间的关系又是什么？为什么说自然景观是一种需要保护的资源？缪尔关于保护这样一种资源又提出了哪些建议？最后，缪尔的环境思想除了对美国产生了一些具体的制度性影响外，还塑造了怎样的环境文化？

环境史是最近二三十年兴起的一种新的史学范式，这种新范式处理历史有其独特的切入点，以之分析和解读史料的方式与其他范式也有所区别。初次接触这类史料，还应对这一新范式有所认识。

The Yosemite Nationai Park

Of all the mountain ranges I have climbed, I like the Sierra Nevada the best. Though extremely rugged, with its main features on the grandest scale in height and depth, it is nevertheless easy of access and hospitable; and its marvelous beauty, displayed in striking and alluring forms, wooes the admiring wanderer on and on, higher and higher, charmed and enchanted. Benevolent, solemn, fateful, pervaded with divine light, every landscape glows like a countenance hallowed in eternal repose; and every one of its living creatures, clad in flesh and leaves, and every crystal of its rocks, whether on the surface shining in the sun or buried miles deep in what we call darkness, is throbbing and pulsing with the heartbeats of God. All the world lies warm in one heart, yet the Sierra seems to get more light than other mountains. The weather is mostly sunshine embellished with magnificent storms, and nearly everything shines from base to summit, —the rocks, streams, lakes, glaciers, irised falls, and the forests of silver fir and silver pine. And how bright is the shining after summer showers and dewy nights, and after frosty nights in spring and autumn, when the morning sunbeams are pouring through the crystals on the bushes and grass, and in winter through the snow-laden trees!

The average cloudiness for the whole year is perhaps less than ten hundredths. Scarcely a day of all the summer is dark, though there is no lack of magnificent thundering cumuli. They rise in the warm midday hours, mostly over the middle region, in June and July, like new mountain ranges, higher Sierras, mightily augmenting the grandeur of the scenery while giving rain to the forests and gardens and bringing forth their fragrance. The wonderful weather and beauty inspire everybody to be up and doing. Every summer day is a workday to be confidently counted on, the short dashes of rain forming, not interruptions, but rests. The big blessed storm days of winter, when the whole range stands white, are not a whit less inspiring and kind. Well may the Sierra be called the Range of Light, not the Snowy Range; for only inwinter is it white, while all the year it is bright.

Of this glorious range the Yosemite National Park is a central section, thirty-six miles in length and forty-eight miles in breadth. The famous Yosemite Valley lies in the heart of it, and it includes the head waters of the Tuolumne and Merced rivers, two of the most songful streams in the world; innumerable lakes and waterfalls and smooth silky lawns; the noblest forests, the loftiest granite domes, the deepest ice-sculptured cañons, the brightest crystalline pavements, and snowy mountains soaring into the sky twelve and thirteen thousand feet, arrayed in open ranks and spiry pinnacled groups partially separated by tremendous cañons and amphitheatres; gardens on their sunny brows, avalanches thundering down their long white slopes, cataracts roaring gray and foaming in the crooked rugged gorges, and glaciers in their shadowy recesses working in silence, slowly completing their sculpture; new-born lakes at their feet, blue and green, free or encumbered with drifting icebergs like miniature Arctic Oceans, shining, sparkling, calm as stars.

Nowhere will you see the majestic operations of nature more clearly revealed beside the frailest, most gentle and peaceful things. Nearly all the park is a profound solitude. Yet it is full of charming company, full of God's thoughts, a place of peace and safety amid the most exalted grandeur and eager enthusiastic action, a new song, a place of beginnings abounding in first lessons on life, mountain-building, eternal, invincible, unbreakable order; with sermons in stones, storms, trees, flowers, and animals brimful of humanity. During the last glacial period, just past, the former features of the range were rubbed off as a chalk sketch from a blackboard, anda new beginning was made. Hence the wonderful clearness and freshness of the rocky pages.

But to get all this into words is a hopeless task. The leanest sketch of each feature would need a whole chapter. Nor would any amount of space, however industriously scribbled, be of much avail. To defrauded town toilers, parks in magazine articles are like pictures of bread to the hungry. I can write only hints to incite good wanderers to come to the feast.

While this glorious park embraces big, generous samples of the very best of the Sierra treasures, it is, fortunately, at the same time, the most accessible portion. It lies opposite San Francisco, at a distance of about one hundred and forty miles. Railroads connected with all the continent reach into the foothills, and three good carriage roads, from Big Oak Flat, Coulterville, and Raymond, run into Yosemite Valley. Another, called the Tioga road, runs from Crocker's Station on the Yosemite Big Oak Flat road near the Tuolumne Big Tree Grove, right across the park to the summit of the range by way of Lake Tenaya, the Big Tuolumne Meadows, and Mount Dana. These roads, with many trails that radiate from Yosemite Valley, bring most of the park within reach of everybody, well or half well.

The three main natural divisions of the park, the lower, middle, and alpine regions, are fairly well defined in altitude, topographical features, and vegetation. The lower, with an average elevation of about five thousand feet, is the region of the great forests, made up of sugar pine, the largest and most beautiful of all the pines in the world; the silvery yellow pine, the next in rank; Douglas spruce, Iibocedrus[1], the white and red silver firs, and the Sequoia gigantea, or "big

---

1 　原产于新西兰、新喀里多尼亚等地的一种松树。

tree," the king of conifers, the noblest of a noble race. On warm slopes next the foothills there are a few Sabine nut pines; oaks make beautiful groves in the cañon valleys; and poplar, alder, maple, laurel, and Nuttall's flowering dogwood shade the banks of the streams. Many of the pines are more than two hundred feet high, but they are not crowded together. The sunbeams streaming through their feathery arches brighten the ground, and you walk beneath the radiant ceiling in devout subdued mood, as if you were in a grand cathedral with mellow light sifting through colored windows, while the flowery pillared aisles open enchanting vistas in every direction. Scarcely apeak or ridge in the whole region rises bare above the forests, though they are thinly planted in some places where the soil is shallow. From the cool breezy heights you look abroad over a boundless waving sea of evergreens, covering hill and ridge and smooth-flowing slope as far as the eye can reach, and filling every hollow and down-plunging ravine in glorious triumphant exuberance.

Perhaps the best general view of the pine forests of the park, and one of the best in the range, is obtained from the top of the Merced and Tuolumne divide near Hazel Green. On the long, smooth, finely folded slopes of the main ridge, at a height of five to six thousand feet above the sea, they reach most perfect development and are marshaled to view in magnificent towering ranks, their colossal spires and domes and broad palm like crowns, deep in the kind sky, rising above one another, —a multitude of giants in perfect health and beauty, —sun-fed mountaineers rejoicing in their strength, chanting with the winds, in accord with the falling waters. The ground is mostly open and inviting to walkers. The fragrant chamaebatia [1] is outspread in rich carpets miles in extent; the manzanita, in orchard-like groves, covered with pink bell-shaped flowers in the spring, grows in openings facing the sun, hazel and buckthorn in the dells; warm brows are purple with mint, yellow with sunflowers and violets; and tall lilies ring their bells around the borders of meadows and along the ferny, mossy banks of the streams. Never was mountain forest more lavishly furnished.

Hazel Green is a good place quietly to camp and study, to get acquainted with the trees and birds, to drink the reviving water and weather, and to watch the changing lights of the big charmed days. The rose light of the dawn, creeping higher among the stars, changes to daffodil yellow; then come the level enthusiastic sunbeams pouring across the feathery ridges, touching pine after pine, spruce and fir, libocedrus and lordly sequoia, searching every recess, until all are awakened and warmed. In the white noon they shine in silvery splendor, every needle and cell in bole and branch thrilling and tingling with ardent life; and the whole landscape glows with consciousness, like the face of a god. The hours go by uncounted. The evening flames with purple and gold. The breeze that has been blowing from the lowlands dies away, and far and near the mighty host of trees baptized in the purple flood stand hushed and thoughtful, awaiting the sun's blessing and farewell, —as impressive a ceremony as if it were never to rise again.

---

1 生长于美国加利福尼亚州的一种草本植物，有较浓的花香味。

When the daylight fades, the night breeze from the snowy summits begins to blow, and the trees, waving and rustling beneath the stars, breathe free again.

It is hard to leave such camps and woods; nevertheless, to the large majority of travelers the middle region of the park is still more interesting, for it has the most striking features of all the Sierra scenery,—the deepest sections of the famous cañons, of which the Yosemite Valley, Hetch-Hetchy Valley, and many smaller ones are wider portions, with level parklike floors and walls of immense height and grandeur of sculpture. This middle region holds also the greater number of the beautiful glacier lakes and glacier meadows, the great granite domes, and the most brilliant and most extensive of the glacier pavements. And though in large part it is severely rocky and bare, it is still rich in trees. The magnificent silver fir (Abies magnifica), which ranks with the giants, forms a continuous belt across the park above the pines at an elevation of from seven to nine thousand feet, and north and south of the park boundaries to the extremities of the range, only slightly interrupted by the main cañons. The two-leaved or tamarack pine makes another less regular belt along the upper margin of the region, while between these two belts, and mingling with them, in groves or scattered, are the mountain hemlock, the most graceful of evergreens; the noble mountain pine; the Jeffrey form of the yellow pine, with big cones and long needles; and the brown, burly, sturdy Western juniper. All these, except the juniper, which grows on bald rocks, have plenty of flowery brush about them, and gardens in open spaces.

Here, too, lies the broad, shining, heavily sculptured region of primeval granite, which best tells the story of the glacial period on the Pacific side of the continent. No other mountain chain on the globe, as far as I know, is so rich as the Sierra in bold, striking, well-preserved glacial monuments, easily understood by anybody capable of patient observation. Every feature is more or less glacial, and this park portion of the range is the brightest and clearest of all. Not a peak, ridge, dome, cañon, lake basin, garden, forest, or stream but in some way explains the past existence and modes of action of flowing, grinding, sculpturing, soil-making, scenery-making ice. For, notwithstanding the post-glacial agents—air, rain, frost, rivers, earthquakes, avalanches—have been at work upon the greater part of the range for tens of thousands of stormy years, engraving their own characters over those of the ice, the latter are so heavily emphasized and enduring they still rise in sublime relief, clear and legible through every after inscription. The streams have traced only shallow wrinkles as yet, and avalanche, wind, rain, and melting snow have made blurs and scars, but the change effected on the face of the landscape is not greater than is made on the face of a mountaineer by a single year of weathering.

Of all the glacial phenomena presented here, the most striking and attractive to travelers are the polished pavements, because they are so beautiful, and their beauty is of so rare a kind,—unlike any part of the loose earthy lowlands where people dwell and earn their bread. They are simply flat or gently undulating areas of solid resisting granite, the unchanged surface over which the ancient glaciers flowed. They are found in the most perfect condition at an elevation of from eight to nine thousand feet above sea level. Some are miles in extent, only slightly blurred or scarred by spots that have at last yielded to the weather; while the best preserved portions are brilliantly polished, and reflect the sunbeams as calm water or glass, shining as if rubbed and burnished every day, notwithstanding they have been exposed to plashing, corroding rains, dew, frost, and melting sloppy snows for thousands of years.

The attention of hunters and prospectors, who see so much in their wild journeys, is seldom attracted by moraines, however regular and artificial-looking; or rocks, however boldly sculptured; or cañons, however deep and sheer-walled. But when they come to these pavements, they go down on their knees and rub their hands admiringly on the glistening surface, and try hard to account for its mysterious smoothness and brightness. They may have seen the winter avalanches come down the mountains, through the woods, sweeping away the trees and scouring the ground; but they conclude that this cannot be the work of avalanches, because the striae show that the agent, whatever it was, flowed along and around and over the top of high ridges and domes, and also filled the deep cañons. Neither can they see how water could be the agent, for the strange polish is found thousands of feet above the reach of any conceivable flood. Only the winds seem capable of moving over the face of the country in the directions indicated by the lines and grooves.

The pavements are particularly fine around Lake Tenaya, and have suggested the Indian name Py-we-ack, the Lake of the Shining Rocks. Indians seldom trouble themselves with geological questions, but a Mono Indian once came tome and asked if I could tell him what made the rocks so smooth at Tenaya. Even dogs and horses, on their first journeys into this region, study geology to the extent of gazing wonderingly at the strange brightness of the ground, and pawing it and smelling it, as if afraid of falling or sinking.

In the production of this admirable hard finish, the glaciers in many places exerted a pressure of more than a hundred tons to the square foot, planing down granite, slate, and quartz alike, showing their structure, and making beautiful mosaics where large feldspar crystals form the greater part of the rock. On such pavements the sunshine is at times dazzling, as if the surface were of burnished silver.

Here, also, are the brightest of the Sierra landscapes in general. The regions lying at the same elevation to the north and south were perhaps subjected to as long and intense a glaciation; but because the rocks are less resisting, their polished surfaces have mostly given way to the weather, leaving here and there only small imperfect patches on the most enduring portions of cañon walls protected from the action of rain and snow, and on hard bosses kept comparatively dry by boulders. The short, steeply inclined cañons of the east flank of the range are in some places brightly polished, but they are far less magnificent than those of the broad west flank.

One of the best general views of the middle region of the park is to be had from the top of a majestic dome which long ago I named the Glacier Monument. It is situated a few miles to the north of Cathedral Peak, and rises to a height of about fifteen hundred feet above its base and ten thousand above the sea. At first sight it seems sternly inaccessible, but a good climber will find that it may be scaled on the south side. Approaching it from this side you pass through a dense bryanthus[1]-fringed grove of mountain hemlock, catching glimpses now and then of the colossal dome towering to an immense height above the dark evergreens; and when at last you have made your way across woods, wading through azalea and ledum[2] thickets, you step abruptly out of the tree shadows and mossy leafy softness upon a bare porphyry pavement, and behold the dome unveiled in all its grandeur. Fancy a nicely proportioned monument, eight or ten feet high, hewn from one stone, standing ina pleasure ground; magnify it to a height of fifteen hundred feet, retaining its simplicity of form and fineness, and cover its surface with crystals; then you may gain an idea of the sublimity and beauty of this ice-burnished dome, one of many adorning this wonderful park.

In making the ascent, one finds that the curve of the base rapidly steepens, until one is in danger of slipping; but feldspar crystals, two or three inches long, that have been weathered into relief, afford slight footholds. The summit isin part burnished, like the sides and base, the striae and scratches indicating that the mighty Tuolumne Glacier, two or three thousand feet deep, overwhelmed it while it stood firm like a boulder at the bottom of a river. The pressure it withstood must have been enormous. Had it been less solidly built, it would have been ground and crushed into moraine fragments, like the general mass of the mountain flank in which at first it lay imbedded; for it is only a hard residual knob or knot with a concentric structure of superior strength, brought into relief by the removal of the less resisting rock about it,—an illustration in stone of the survival of the strongest and most favorably situated.

Hardly less wonderful, when we contemplate the storms it has encountered since first it saw the light, is its present unwasted condition. The whole quantity of postglacial wear and tear it has suffered has not diminished its stature a single inch, as may be readily shown by measuring from the level of the unchanged polished portions of the surface. Indeed, the average postglacial denudation of the entire region, measured in the same way, is found to be less than two inches,—a mighty contrast to that of the ice; for the glacial denudation here has been not less than a mile; that is, in developing the present landscapes, an amount of rock a mile in average thickness has been silently carried away by flowing ice during the last glacial period.

A few erratic boulders nicely poised on the rounded summit of the monument tell an interesting story. They came from a mountain onthe crest of the range, about twelve miles to the eastward, floating like chips on the frozen sea, and were stranded here when the top of the monument emerged to the light of day, while the companions of these boulders, whose positions chanced to be over the slopes where they could not find rest, were carried farther on by the shallowing current.

---

1 一种杜鹃科装饰类植物。
2 杜香属植物,隶属于杜鹃科。

The general view from the summit consists of a sublime assemblage of iceborn mountains and rocks and long wavering ridges, lakes and streams and meadows, moraines in wide-sweeping belts, and beds covered and dotted with forestsand groves, —hundreds of square miles of them composed in wild harmony. The snowy mountains on the axis of the peaked and crested, rise in noble array along the sky to the eastward and northward; the gray-pillared Hoffman spur and the Yosemite domes anda countless number of others to the westward; Cathedral Peak with its many spires and companion peaks and domes to the southward; and a smooth billowy multitude of rocks, from fifty feet or less to a thousand feet high, which from their peculiar form seem to be rolling on westward, fill most of the middle ground. Immediately beneath you are the Big Tuolumne Meadows, with an ample swath of dark pinewoods on either side, enlivened by the young river, that is seen sparkling and shimmering a sit sways from side to side, tracing as best it can its broad glacial channel.

The ancient Tuolumne Glacier, lavishly flooded by many a noble affluent from the snow-laden flanks of Mounts Dana, Gibbs, Lyell, Maclure, and others nameless as yet, poured its majestic overflowing current, four or five miles wide, directly against the high outstanding mass of Mount Hoffman, which divided and deflected it right and left, just as a river is divided against an island that stands in the middle of its channel. Two distinct glaciers were thus formed, one of which flowed through the Big Tuolumne Cañon and Hetch-Hetchy Valley, while the other swept upward five hundred feet in a broad current across the divide between the basins of the Tuolumne and Merced into the Tenaya basin, and thence down through the Tenaya Canon and Yosemite Valley.

The map like distinctness and freshness of this glacial landscape cannot fail to excite the attention of every observer, no matter how little of its scientific significance he may at first recognize. These bald, glossy, westward-leaning rocks in the open middle ground, with their rounded backs and shoulders toward the glacier fountains of the summit mountains and their split angular fronts looking in the opposite direction, everyone of them displaying the form of greatest strength with reference to physical structure and glacial action, show the tremendous force with which through unnumbered centuries the ice flood swept over them, and also the direction of the flow; while the mountains, with their sharp summits and abraded sides, indicate the height to which the glacier rose; and the moraines, curving and swaying in beautiful lines, mark the boundaries of the main trunk and its tributaries as they existed toward the close of the glacial winter. None of the commercial highways of the sea or land, marked with buoys and lamps, fences and guide boards, is so unmistakably indicated as are these channels of the vanished Tuolumne glaciers.

The action of flowing ice, whether in the form of river-like glaciers or broad mantling folds, is but little understood as compared with that of other sculpturing agents. Rivers work openly where people dwell, and so do the rain, and the sea thundering on all the shores of the world; and the universal ocean of air, though unseen, speaks aloud in a thousand voices and explains its modes of working and its power. But glaciers, back in their cold solitudes, work apart from men, exerting their tremendous energies in silence and darkness. Coming in vapor from the sea, flying invisible on the wind, descending in snow, changing to ice, white, spirit like, they brood outspread over the predestined landscapes, working on unwearied through unmeasured ages, until in the fullness of time the mountains and valleys are brought forth, channels furrowed for the rivers, basins made for meadows and lakes, and soil beds spread for the forests and fields that manand beast may be fed. Then vanishing like clouds, they melt into streams and go singing back home to the sea.

To an observer upon this adamantine old monument in the midst of such scenery, getting glimpses of the thoughts of God, the day seems endless, the sun stands still. Much faithless fuss is made over the passage in the Bible telling of the standing still of the sun for Joshua. Here you may learn that the miracle occurs for every devout mountaineer, for everybody doing anything worth doing, seeing anything worth seeing. One day is as a thousand years, a thousand years as one day, and while yet in the flesh you enjoy immortality.

选自 John Muir, *Our National Parks*, Boston and New York: Houghton, Mifflin and Company, 1901, pp. 76 -93.

推荐阅读

1. Donald Worster, *A Passion for Nature: The Life of John Muir*, Oxford: Oxford University Press, 2008.

2. J. 唐纳德·休斯:《什么是环境史》,梅雪芹译,北京:北京大学出版社,2008年。